Virgins

Virgins

A NOVEL
BY CARYL RIVERS

ST. MARTIN'S / MAREK
New York

Library of Congress Cataloging in Publication Data

Rivers, Caryl.
  Virgins.

  I. Title.
PS3568.I8315V5   1984   813'.54   84-13341
ISBN 0-312-84951-6

First Edition
10 9 8 7 6 5 4 3 2 1

To Alan, Steven and Alyssa, with all my love.
And to Clare Crawford-Mason.

Girls, you have dreams, if you act, they will come true.
To turn your dreams to a fact it's up to you.

(School song, Academy of the Holy Names)

Virgins

ONE

Sean

"Let's neck," Sean said. I yawned and said, "Sure," and Sean pulled his father's car, the white Caddy with the fins that looked like they belonged to an albino shark, over to the side of the road in Sligo Creek Park. The Caddy had special blue plates in front that said "Year Of Our Lady" on them. They were two years old, a gift to Sean's father from the archbishop, so Sean's father wouldn't take them off. I thought they were tacky. Sean's father was an assistant professor of communication and speech dynamics at St. Anselm's Junior College, and he wouldn't be caught dead with a plastic Jesus on his dashboard like some Puerto Rican cabbie. But he drove around flashing these plates with a picture of the Blessed Mother on them, and she was wearing a startled expression like she'd just been goosed. I told Sean that flaunting the B.V.M. on your license was not exactly what J.C. would want for his mom. When he said, "Come, follow me," he didn't mean you should do it in a white Cadillac El Dorado.

Sean pulled me close and started kissing me with his mouth closed. He always started out that way and worked up to opening his mouth in about twenty minutes. I could feel the hard enamel of his teeth behind his lips. I'd done this number before, and it wasn't exactly thrilling. We were the only Catholic kids in the city who could neck for two hours and still stay in the state of grace.

Sean had it all figured. He even drew a diagram, like those charts they have in butcher shops that show what parts of meat come from which part of the cow. He had me sectioned off like top round, filet, and brisket. Only in this case the parts weren't stamped approved by the U.S.D.A., but by the Father, the Son, and the Holy Ghost.

Anything above the neck was O.K., although there was some question about open-mouthed kissing. Tongue-swabbing, Sean decided, was only a venial sin, but you had to work up to it, not dive right in, tongues atwirl. Toes to thighs, to within a half inch of you-know-where, also venial. Touching boobs on top of clothes (patting, no squeezing) was probably venial, but even more borderline than tongues, so must be reserved for special occasions, like the prom or graduation. Bare finger on bare tit was Mortal Sin City. Needless to say, genitalia, male or female, was untouchable, the big No No.

Sean was scrupulous about that. One touch of forbidden fruit, he was sure, would turn him into a raging animal and maybe blow his chances for the priesthood all to hell.

Necking with Sean was safe, if not all that exciting. He had that map imprinted on his brain cells, and I could just relax and let him keep on the lookout for Sin. I even sort of liked the non-sin stuff, especially kissing the hollow of his throat, that soft lovely spot just above where the dark hair on his chest started, and smelling the nice, musky male scent of him. My kissing him there really got to him, because sometimes he would squirm and moan a little, and even though I was absolutely forbidden to touch him below the waist, I knew things were happening Down There. I had a somewhat proprietary feeling about Sean's penis, anyhow. It was the first one I ever saw.

We were sitting, one hot August day, in Sean's back yard, in the pup tent Sean's father bought when he started the Catholic Cub Scout troop for Sean's older brother, Bill. (God forbid that Catholic kids should get their wolf badges

2

with Protestants. You started looking for red maple leaves or toasting hot dogs with non-Catholics, and you'd wind up blaspheming against the B.V.M.) We were both hot and bored, and Sean said, "Let's play doctor."

I said O.K. and he told me I had to pull my pants down and sit with my legs open while he examined me. He took a little stick and started to poke around in my privates. I thought it was wonderful and naughty, Sean poking and me sitting there all spread out. To this day the smell of damp, moldy canvas makes me sweat like a horny sailor.

Then Sean said it was my turn and he pulled his pants down, and lifted his lovely pink *thing* so I could look at it. Those were the days before parents taught their kids the correct anatomical names, so we were stuck with "wee-wee" and "weenie" and "thing."

Sean's *thing* was soft and pink and lovely; I thought it was beautiful, so round and perfect, with the little ridge and the cute little hole in the center. I had just gotten around to a few tentative pokes with the stick when there was the swooshing sound of fabric in motion—the tent flap being ripped asunder—and in swept Sean's father, the assistant professor from St. Anselm's, coming down upon us like a wolf on the fold.

"Oh my GOD!" he screamed, and grabbed both of us by the arms, dragging us both out of the tent while Sean struggled to pull up his underpants with one hand. He marched us both off to my mother—the McCaffreys lived next door—and told her what I had been doing to his son. He said I was a slut. My mother took offense.

"She is five years old!" my mother said. "And if my daughter is a slut then your son is a pervert. He was the one standing there with his pants down!"

They yelled at each other, and then Dr. McCaffrey dragged Sean home and gave him a beating, and the next day the pup tent was unceremoniously hauled down. But I always remembered the day as one of my very favorites, and if I had been asked to list the wonders of nature that I had seen with my very own eyes, I would have said the Luray Caverns of Virginia, the Great Falls of the Potomac, and Sean's penis, not necessarily in that order. From that day forward, though, Sean and I knew that grown-ups behaved in very peculiar ways and that to survive we had to form an alliance against them. We still felt that way, a lot.

"You better stop kissing me," Sean said, and I knew the lights on his Illuminated Map of Sin were flashing like the bulbs on the pinball machines in the Grotto Grill.

"O.K.," I said, and I knew what he was going to do next: stretch out on the seat with his head on my lap so I could run my fingers through his hair. Sean liked to be touched and held a lot. Even when we were kids, playing in the sandbox my father built for us, he would curl up next to me and I'd put my arms around him, and I'd put one of the little cars we played with on top of his head and let it run down his nose and leap out into space. Sean could play that game for an hour at a stretch. Maybe it was because his parents didn't touch him a lot. Sean's mother was a small, dowdy woman cowed almost into nonexistence by her brilliant husband. Dr. McCaffrey believed that sparing the rod spoiled the child, and sometimes I could hear the smacks of the leather belt clear up in my bedroom on the second floor when Sean or Bill were getting it. I wondered, when Sean was a priest, who would hold him, but I didn't think about that very much because it sent a sad feeling all through me, the way I used to feel when I heard the sounds of the belt from next door.

Sean must have been thinking the same thing—sometimes I thought we could read each other's mind, like space people—because he said, "Can you believe it? Senior year. I mean, we were just kids, and now we're adults."

"I don't feel like an adult," I said.

"Me neither. But we are, almost. It's like that song, you know, about childhood. Once you pass its portals you can never go back through. There's a door, Peggy, right behind us. And it's closing. We'll never be kids again."

Sean had a deep streak of melancholy; it was the Irish in him. Irish genes do that to people—maybe it's from eating too many cold potatoes or listening to all those songs about your mother dying and your father getting hung by the British for blowing up the post office, but every Irishman I've ever met has that deep, black moodiness tucked away inside. When it came on Sean I felt it too, because I had enough Irish genes myself. Suddenly I saw the door, closing slowly, inexorably, and when it slammed shut the sunlight and the laughter behind it would be gone forever. I wanted to cry out, "Not yet! Oh, not yet!"

"I wonder if we'll be like *them*, Peggy," he said.

"Your father?"

"All of them. Adults. They just seem—so tired, like they never have any fun."

"Not us," I said. "Come on, Sean, don't be morbid. You're going to be the youngest cardinal in history. You'll have your own T.V. show. You'll be hotter than Bishop Sheen. God will be green with envy over your Neilsens."

Suddenly he giggled and sat bolt upright. Keeping up with Sean sometimes was hard. One minute he'd be brooding like Heathcliff and the next he'd be cracking up.

"You know what I'd do if I were Bishop Sheen?" he said.

"No, what?"

"I'd get out there, in front of the cameras, with sixty million people watching me—even *Eisenhower* would be watching—and I'd twirl my cape around, you know, the way he does. And I'd look right into the camera and I'd say, 'THERE IS NO GOD!' And then I'd swirl around again, and I'd walk off. Jeez, can you *imagine* it! The president would be shitting; the *pope* would be shitting. Can you just picture it?"

I started to giggle, and that made us laugh harder, and

5

the two of us were cracking up, picturing Bishop Sheen announcing in that deep, rich actor's voice of his, "THERE IS NO GOD!" while twenty million members of the Sodality of Our Lady gagged on their miraculous medals and the entire senior officer corps of the Knights of Columbus impaled themselves on their swords. Sean had that kind of mind; it honed on absurdity like a heat-seeking missile. It was completely at odds with the side of him that wanted to be a priest—the moody, mystical side. What the other side wanted I didn't know. Maybe just to sit and laugh and neck with me and almost sin and never grow up.

"Cardinal McCaffrey," I said. "Will I have to call you Your Excellency?"

"Call me that right now if you want. Show a little respect."

I poked him in the ribs. He said, "A left jab by Miss Peggy Morrison of the *New York Herald Tribune.*"

"Peg," I said. "Peg Morrison. That's my new byline, I decided. Peggy sounds too childish."

"By Peg Morrison. Yeah, I like it."

The nice thing about Sean was that he took me seriously, and almost nobody else did. My heroine was Maggie Higgins, the first woman war correspondent for the *Herald Trib,* and I wanted to be her. I wanted to look adorable in my fatigues, write tough Hemingway prose, and win the Pulitzer Prize by the time I was twenty-five. Sometimes, when I was being morbidly romantic, like Sean, I imagined that lots of men would fall in love with me, but I'd spurn them all because I carried in my breast this undying love for a Jesuit priest—they called him the Hero Priest of the Amazon—who was out saving souls at his mission in the jungle. One day, war would break out, and of course I would be sent to cover it. I was somewhat vague on the geography of all this, because it was not my good subject. I guessed maybe the Amazon was in Brazil someplace, so America would be at war with Brazil. I would come in with the first wave of American troops, and people would say to me, "You can't go out there! You're a woman!" And I'd say, "It's my job. It's where I belong, out there!"

One day, the fighting would be raging right near Sean's mission, and as I was writing tough prose about our glorious victories on my portable Olivetti, a stray bullet would strike me and I would fall to the ground with a groan. The wound would be fatal, but not *messy* or anything. Just a neat little bloodstain on the front of my fatigues. I would look incredibly beautiful as I lay there, shot, and Sean, in his white robes, would come running out and hold me in his arms.

I would know I was dying, and with my last breath I would say to him, "I have always loved you!" and he would sob and call out my name and then my eyelids would flutter and I'd die in his arms. Later, they'd make a movie about my life and call it *The Peg Morrison Story*, and maybe Susan Hayward would star in it—except she'd be too old by then—and the last scene would be a gas. People all over the country would be sobbing into their handkerchiefs. The only problem was that I wouldn't get to see it, because I'd be dead.

"Hey, it's getting late," Sean said. "The Nemesis of Smut will be pissed if I don't get the Caddy back."

I had to laugh every time I heard Sean refer to his father that way. Dr. Liam McCaffrey had a set speech, which he gave to various sodalities and Knights of Columbus about five times a month, about how dirty movies and birth control were rotting America's moral fiber. He got the Catholic Layman of the Year award for his unending battle against tit on the silver screen and tubes of contraceptive jelly on the shelves at People's Drug Store. A writer for the *Catholic Herald*, carried away by the Muse, had dubbed Dr. McCaffrey "The Nemesis of Smut." Sean was delighted. He called himself "Son of Nemesis of Smut"—or, for short, "Son of Smut."

When we got back to Sean's house, his father was in the living room, reading the *Saturday Evening Post* and drinking his usual Scotch and water. He looked up at the two of us.

"Well, kids, how was the movie?"

"Pretty good," Sean said. "Jeff Chandler saved Susan Hayward from being raped by Cheyennes. At least I think that's what they had in mind. They danced around in their loincloths and panted a lot."

Dr. Liam McCaffrey frowned. He had caught the scent, however faint, of Smut.

"Was there cleavage in this movie?"

Cleavage, according to Dr. McCaffrey, was taking the nation back to paganism. He frothed at the mouth over Jane Russell. I think he believed that each tit took us at least 5,000 years back into prehistory.

"Well," Sean said, "in one scene Susan Hayward got her dress ripped, and there was pretty much cleavage. It got the Cheyennes stirred up a lot. They danced real fast and stared at the cleavage."

Sean's face, as he said this, was as innocent of guile as any third grader in a white Communion suit. I had to turn away to hide a grin. I could never figure out, if Dr. McCaffrey was supposed to be so brilliant, why he never knew it when Sean was jerking his chain. But he never did.

"I'll get my committee to look into it," he said. Thank you, Sean, for that information." He shook his head. "Eternal vigilance," he said with a sigh.

And then he looked at me, as if he had just realized I was there, and he said, "Well, Peggy."

He never quite knew what to say to me, after all these years. He didn't have any daughters, and he was uncomfortable around girls. He tried to be nice, but I had the feeling he had never really forgiven me for messing around with Sean with his pants down.

"Hi, Dr. McCaffrey."

"How's school, Peggy?"

"It's just fine."

"The basketball team going to take it this year?"

"We're going to try. I've been practicing my jump shot. We only got beat by Nativity by two points last year."

"Well, that's good." He looked at me, and then he looked again.

"Well, Peggy, you've really grown up. You're quite a young lady."

And he was staring right at my boobs as he said it. Really staring. I shifted my weight uncomfortably, and then I guess he realized what he was doing and flicked his eyes away from my chest.

I couldn't really blame him for being fascinated with my boobs. I certainly was. They came late, sort of a hormonal afterthought. It was as if my body thought it had done all its work at puberty, and it rested for a while, leaving me certain I was going to go through life with a chest as flat as a picket fence. Then it said, oops, forgot something, and a pair of boobs just popped out, in my junior year, surprising everybody, me most of all.

I wanted to say, "Where the hell *were* you?" every time I looked at them, but they added a whole new dimension to my movie star fantasies, which I thought I'd outgrown. I'd wrap a scarf around them and lean into the bathroom sink and gaze into the mirror. I'd let my lips open and my eyelids droop, the way Marilyn Monroe always did, but I wasn't sure if I looked sexy or like I was coming down with mono. If I hunched my shoulders a lot, I could come up with enough cleavage to give the Nemesis of Smut a heart seizure. From the front I looked like Marilyn—sort of—and from the side like the Hunchback of Notre Dame.

"Oh, Sean," Dr. McCaffrey said, "a letter came from the seminary today. The class begins June 24th. And you're in, it's definite."

"Oh," Sean said.

Then Dr. McCaffrey put his arm around Sean's shoulder, but in a way that didn't seem natural; it was sort of a fake "hearty" pose, like he was getting his picture taken with the student who's just won the essay contest on "How Catholic Youth Can Fight Dirty Movies."

"We're very proud of Sean, Peggy," he said. "It was always a dream that Sean's mother and I had to give one of our sons to God."

The way he said it made it sound as if he were wrapping Sean up with a bow and sending him parcel post to God the way you sent Christmas presents to an aunt in Chicago. It seemed to me it was Sean who was doing the giving, not his father.

"Well, that's wonderful, sir," I said.

Dr. McCaffrey gave Sean's shoulder a fatherly squeeze, and as they stood together that way, I tried to see the resemblance, but I couldn't. Everybody remarked on how handsome Sean's father was; distinguished, they said, probably because of the gray hair around his temples. But I thought he had a pig-like face, because his eyes were small and beady, and his skin always seemed to have a reddish tinge to it; that might have had something to do with the Scotch and water that always seemed riveted to his hand. He seemed huge next to Sean—he wasn't fat, but he had large shoulders and a massive chest, while Sean was tall and rangy, and as slim as an arrow. I could never imagine Sean being fat. Sean's eyes, the ones that could look so innocent, were cool and green and they looked out from beneath eyelashes that were long and silky. I'd have killed to have Sean's eyelashes. I had nice eyes, but the lashes were short and sparse, and when I tried to put mascara on them to make them longer it always ran—even when the label swore in blood that you could only get the stuff off with a substance used in chemical warfare—and it made me look like a raccoon. It wasn't fair, it seemed to me, that Sean got the eyelashes. What was a priest going to do with lashes like those?

"He's going to make a fine priest," Dr, McCaffrey said, beaming. "A Jesuit. Maybe even teach at Georgetown someday, right, Sean?"

That was where Sean's father wanted to teach, Georgetown, where even the freshmen drove Jags and wore English tweed. At St. Anselm's, to which flocked the sons and daughters of cab drivers and G.S. fives, Dr. McCaffrey thought he was casting his Speech Dynamics as pearls before swine.

"I want to go to the missions," Sean said.

"Oh, of course, a few years in the missions is good training for any young priest. But Sean, you have too fine a mind to spend your life saving the souls of—" he paused— "colored people."

"There's a quota on that, Pop," Sean said. "Only 200 colored souls per priest. You save too many of 'em and heaven starts to look like Seventh and U, full of jungle bunnies."

"Sean!" his father said. "I don't like to hear you use language like that. Not in this house!"

"Yes, sir," Sean said. His face was blank as a billiard ball. I had to turn away again. Dr. McCaffrey had recently discovered his black brethren—when he got an award and 500 bucks from a black parish to speak at a fund-raising dinner. He regaled the black Catholics with dire warnings about Jane Russell, which must have puzzled them somewhat. Black people had a few other things to worry about in those days beside large white mammary glands. But before Dr. McCaffrey discovered Brotherhood, "jungle bunny" was one of the more complimentary phrases he used about black folks.

"Pop, I'm going to walk Peggy home," Sean said, and we walked out the back door and up the well-worn path to my house. I thought that if I had a dollar for every time I'd come this way, I'd be rich as Rockefeller. Sean was quiet, and as usual, I knew what he was thinking.

"He is proud of you, Sean," I said. "I mean, he's an asshole, but he's proud of you."

Sean shrugged. "No, it's not me. Its the future Father McCaffrey he's proud of—some guy in a black suit. But I'm not *him* yet."

"You will be."

"Yeah, that'll really give the Nemesis of Smut an orgasm."

I laughed. Sean had learned that one from me, but he had a pretty foul mouth on his own.

"God, Sean, you're going to have to learn to talk all over again in the seminary. Everything you say is either obscene or blasphemous."

He grinned. "*Ego te absolvo*, Mr. Smith. And stay the fuck away from mortal sin."

He took my hand as we walked to my back door. I reached for the door handle but he put his hands on my shoulders and pulled me close to him. That was a surprise; we usually got ourselves necked out in the Caddy. He opened his mouth right away and he held me hard against him, as if he were afraid I might just float away. The way he was kissing me wasn't safe or relaxing. I thought, suddenly, that he was kissing me like a man, not like a boy, and I started to feel exactly the way I did when I read page 128 of *Savage Warrior*, when Soldred the Viking starts to unlace the smock of the maiden Ingrid so his lips can taste the nectar of her honeyed breasts.

Sean just kept kissing me, hard, and I felt the Natural Wonder getting very stiff and pressing against my thighs. I was sure the lights on the Illuminated Map of Sin were flashing, but Sean didn't even seem to notice. He just kept on kissing and kissing and my knees were getting weak and I was starting to get all tingly and I wondered about the theology of that. I decided tingly was only venial, but I was a little worried about Sean. He was kissing away like there was no tomorrow and if this kept up, he'd never get the Natural Wonder back to where it belonged.

12

"I got algebra," I said.

"What?" he said, his eyes sort of glazed.

"Algebra."

"Right. Oh yeah, algebra," he said. "Me too." And off he ran.

I went into the house, and my dad was in the kitchen, having a glass of milk and a ham sandwich, his favorite nighttime snack.

"Out with Sean again, Peg?" He smiled at me, his brownish-gray eyes lighting up a little, as they always did when he teased me. "You two are getting to be an item."

"Oh, Dad!"

"Sean still saying he's going to be a priest?"

"Yeah, he is."

He sighed, and put down his glass of milk. I looked at his hands, long and tapered, strong but graceful. I had the same hands—the hands of a pianist—or a basketball player, he said when he looked at them. He had dark, wavy hair, and he was as lean and hard as he must have been in the days when he played semi-pro basketball, not all paunchy in the chest like Sean's father.

"Liam's putting that nonsense into his head," he said. "There's such a thing as too much religion."

I chuckled. "Sister Justinian would croak if she heard you say that."

"Sister Justinian is not God," he said to me sternly. "Just because you're a Catholic, Peg, that doesn't mean you can't think for yourself."

"Dad, what if the Church said one thing and you think, deep in your heart, that it's wrong?"

"The Church is just people, Peg," he said. "People can be wrong. The Church said Galileo was wrong because he said the earth revolved around the sun."

My father was one of the few people I'd ever met who talked like that. Most kid's parents said the nuns and the priests were right, and that was that. My dad wasn't even a college graduate, like Dr. McCaffrey. He dropped out of school to start his electrical business. He read all the time, though—hard books, like philosophy, not just novels like *The Robe*.

"Hey," he said, "have you been practicing the jump shot?"

In response, I grabbed his napkin, crumpled it up, went up off my left foot and dropped it neatly in the wastebasket across the room.

"That's good. Remember, you've got to get the ball off the backboard and take it back up. You can't wait for the ball to come to you."

"Life is like basketball," I said, mimicking him perfectly. "Go after the ball."

He laughed. "Don't be fresh, young lady. Who do you play this week?"

"Nativity. We'll mash their faces in."

He laughed. "That's the spirit. None of that ladylike stuff." He gave me the elbow. I hipped him neatly in return.

"Good. Very good. Say, Peg, is Sean going out for the team at Sacred Heart this year?"

"No. He doesn't think he'd make it."

Dad had tried to teach Sean a jump shot, but Sean never quite got the hang of getting the ball off at exactly the right second, at the top of the jump. I would say to him, "Sean, you can *feel* when it's right," and he'd scowl and say, "You can, but *I* can't." We used to play horse together a lot at my backyard hoop, but lately Sean was getting pissed because I beat him all the time. Sean had a well-muscled, finely proportioned body. To look at him, you'd think he was well coordinated, but he wasn't somehow.

"If I could just have a few months with that kid!" my father said. "He's tall, he's strong. I *know* I could make a player out of him."

"Sean hasn't got the killer instinct," I said.

"Neither did you, little Miss Goody Two-Shoes." He

laughed and elbowed me again. "Now look at you. A tiger!"

I growled, and hipped him good and shoved him right into the refrigerator. He made an elaborate show of falling and being hurt, real hammy.

"I can't *believe* the refs would fall for that!"

"All the time," he said with an elfish grin. In semi-pro, he was so good at faking injuries and drawing fouls that they called him "Fall Down Morrison."

He took his glass and put it in the sink and said, "Have you finished your homework?"

"Just got my algebra."

"Well, get to it. You know, Peg—"

I knew exactly what was coming. Lecture Number Seventeen. I raised my finger in a cautionary gesture.

"Just because you're an athlete, Peg," I said, "you can't neglect your studies. Brain, not brawn, is what gets you ahead in this world. Basketball is not life!"

He picked up a dishtowel and threw it at me. "Get out of here," he said.

I grinned and ran up stairs to do my algebra, propped up in bed with my papers on my knees. I did three problems and started daydreaming, looking at the picture of Bob Cousy I had pasted on my door. He was the centerpiece of my collection of pictures of Great Catholic Athletes. I used to want to be him, play for the Celts, be a star. Lately, though, I'd reconsidered—especially since I got the boobs. I really wouldn't want to have a flat, hairy chest, even if I could score thirty-five points a game. If I was Bob Cousy, I probably wouldn't want to kiss Sean, and he certainly wouldn't want to kiss me.

I slipped right into onc of my "What if?" daydreams. I had them a lot, and the scenario was always the same. Some higher power, probably God, was offering me an awful choice—you know, like would you rather freeze to death or be burned at the stake. I thought, What If I had to choose between Sean's lips and my jump shot? There was a toughie. It was one of the best feelings in the world, letting go of the ball, feeling in the tips of your fingers that it was good, hearing the clean swoosh of the ropes. On the other hand, Sean's lips were warm and sweet—honeyed nectar, just like Ingrid's breasts.

Fortunately, I thought, as I went back to my math, God's attention was focused elsewhere. He was too busy being God to dream up Terrible Choices for Peggy Morrison, girl jock and kisser *extraordinaire*. God was in his heaven, all was well with the world, and I could go on dunking and kissing to my heart's content.

Senior year was going to be absolutely swell.

TWO

Con

"*I*'m going to be a comet, blazing across the sky!" said Con (short for Constance Marie Wepplener) taking a bite of a Mars bar. "And then I'll disappear. I'll probably die young."

"Oh Con, don't say that!" I said.

"Who wants to live to be old, all wrinkled and ugly? Ugh. I'll probably die at thirty-five."

"Oh, I thought you meant *young*."

Con smiled.

> I burn the candle at both ends
> It will not last the night.
> But Oh my friends and Oh my foes
> It gives such lovely light.

"Did you make that up, Con?"

"Peggy, you nerd, that's Edna St. Vincent Millay."

"A *saint* wrote that?"

"God, Peggy, she's not a saint. She's a famous poet." She rolled her eyes upward in dismay. I had failed her again.

I thought Con was the most sophisticated girl I had ever met, and I was proud that she was my best friend. She had moved to Crystal Springs, Maryland, from Long Island, and maybe that was why she knew all those things.

She actually knew Condé Nast was a person and she had read four books on the Index; she could quote Omar Khayyám verbatim, and she knew a lot of real neat stuff about sex. She's the one who taught me to say, "Oh, don't have an *orgasm*!" When I met Con, freshman year, I thought an orgasm was some kind of big monkey.

But Con had really shocked me the day she announced, "I'm going to have *lovers*." I thought that was the most sophisticated thing I had ever heard anybody say, anywhere.

"Wow!" I said. "Real *lovers*?" The very word tingled inside my mouth, like an illegal substance. Just saying it was probably some kind of sin.

"Of course. Aren't you?"

"Well, sure," I said. I tried to picture a lover. He was a guy in a black suit with his hair parted in the middle and slicked down with Vitalis and he wore patent leather shoes and had a cigarette holder sticking out of his mouth. I imagined Con with her lover. She'd be wearing her uniform dress—navy-blue serge with a white collar and cuffs and a little red tie—and brown oxford shoes, and her lover would be pressing her to his breast as they did the tango. But I guessed Con wouldn't be wearing her uniform by the time she got her lover. She said she certainly wasn't going to have some drippy high school kid as a lover, some ick whose idea of romance was buying you a Mighty Mo and a chocolate shake at the Hot Shoppes and then trying to stick his tongue in your ear in the back seat of a Chevy.

"Love is an *art*, Peggy," Con said. "It's like a beautiful painting. It has to be done just right."

Con kept changing the candidate for her first lover. The current one was Aly Khan, who ought to be good at love because he was an international playboy, had been married to Rita Hayworth, and had pots of money.

"Yeah, I guess Aly Khan wouldn't stick his tongue in your ear," I said.

"He might," Con said thoughtfully. "But first he'd pour in champagne, and then he'd sip it out very, very slowly."

"But what if you hadn't cleaned your ears, Con? Poor Aly'd get a mouthful of ear wax."

Con looked at me as if I were a stupid child. "Aly Khan would never, never make love to anyone with ear wax," she said.

That let me out. I mean, I cleaned my ears a lot, but my ears were just big waxers, I guess. I went through tons of Q-tips. But how would Aly know, I wondered. Did he just go up to people and say, "Hi, I'm Aly Khan, and I want to make passionate love to you on my yacht. But first, one question: Do you now have, or have you ever had, ear wax?"

But maybe some people, you just looked at them and you knew. Rita Hayworth, for example, didn't have ear wax or dandruff or lint in her navel. You couldn't, and be a Love Goddess. Aly Khan probably poured champagne in her navel. I was beginning to have my doubts about sophisticated lovers. I mean, maybe high school kids were sort of clumsy, but at least you didn't have to worry about being so goddamn *clean*. You knew they weren't going to try to lick their chocolate malteds out of your belly button. With Aly Khan, you'd have to spend your whole *life* in the shower.

But I could see Con and Aly together. Con, I thought, could do anything. She was the first freshman in history to get appointed a page editor on the school paper, the *Marian Messenger*, at Immaculate Heart High School. Immaculate Heart was the girls' high in Crystal Springs, and Sacred Heart, the boys' school that Sean went to, was half a block away. Con and I first started being friends when I wrote a story for the paper about the junior varsity basketball team, modestly taking note of my own efforts in its behalf. Con read my story and gave a little whoop of pleasure.

"A writer, we have a real writer, at last!" Then she said to me, "Look, kid, you're not Dorothy Parker but you've got a style. I can really make something out of you." And so my career in journalism was launched.

Con got me started reading F. Scott Fitzgerald and Hemingway and Virginia Woolf, and, of course, her own personal heroine, Dorothy Parker. I thought Con's philosophy of life was thrilling. I, too, wanted to be Beautiful and Damned. I wanted to fall in love in Paris with a beautiful young man who had a tragic war wound. I wanted to make love in a sleeping bag in the middle of a war. I thought of Sean and me in a sleeping bag. The only problem was that he'd have his damned Map along, and Hemingway never wrote about that:

Maria pressed her lips against the lips of Robert.

"No Maria," Robert said, "it is a Near Occasion of Sin."

"Roberto, my love, I must have you!" she cried, as the bullets ricocheted off the rocks above their head, rocks that were turning red in the blazing light of dawn.

"You may kiss me," Roberto said, as the cries of the advancing fascist soldiers rang in their ears, "but no tongue kissing for twenty minutes, no touching below the waist, and no squeezing, only patting."

"But Roberto, we may die before the sun is high in the sky. They may drill us before we even *get* to tongue kissing."

"Yeah, but just think, Maria, we'll go in the State of Grace."

Con and I hung out, every minute that we weren't in class, in the newspaper office, the *Messenger* room. She was the editor-in-chief and I was the managing editor. It was our sanctuary, our personal haven, our escape from the perennial wimphood that was decreed to be the proper mental state for nice Catholic young ladies.

"You and I, Peg," Con decreed, "have minds like *men*. We're different from most women. We're not going to be like them. We're not going to be people nothing ever happens to."

That was the worst thing of all, I thought, a life where nothing ever happened. I looked around me and saw women ironing dresses and hanging out clothes and shopping for food and playing mah-jongg on hot summer afternoons, and I knew I couldn't bear to spend my life that way, day after drab day, with nothing ever happening. The world of women seemed to me like a huge, airless prison where things didn't change. Inside it, I thought, I'd turn gray and small and shrivel up to nothing.

"We are the intellectual elite," Con said. "Most people are sheep. We have brains, and that's why we were born to lead."

And I ached to be a leader, to be the intellectual elite, to be bold and reckless and daring. But only part of me was like that, a small, throbbing mass of rebellion and independence inside me, surrounded by huge globs of niceness, hundreds of thousands of timid, conforming little cells desperately crying out for approval. I wanted to smash them, ruthlessly. I wanted to break all the rules—refuse to polish my oxfords, chew gum in class, wear sleeveless dresses (forbidden by the nuns), and let the masses thrill at the sight of my bare white arms; I wanted *not* to go to church on a Holy Day of Obligation and *to* eat meat on Friday. I wanted to live! And Con knew how to do it better than anyone else in the world.

Con had short, curly black hair, a perfect heart-shaped face, and beautiful skin; but she was what we called, in those days, "pleasingly plump" and it was the despair of her life. She cut out a picture of what she wanted to look like from *Vogue*—a photograph of a reed-thin, hard-faced blonde wearing the expression of a hanging judge. "A real ball-buster," as Con put it. She talked dirty better than anyone else I knew. She was writing a novel, and she said it had oral sex in it.

"You mean they talk about sex a lot?"

Con rolled her eyes upward. "Oh God, you don't know *anything*! You don't know what oral sex is?"

"Not exactly."

"A blow job."

"Oh, *that*!" I said, but I blushed a deep tomato red.

"Peggy," she said, "you don't know enough about sex."

"Sure I do," I said, and I told her about *Savage Warrior*. "Ingrid and Soldred do lots of stuff," I said. I told her about how Soldred and Ingrid lay naked in the big ship with the dragon on it and sated their lips with the sweet juices of passion, and let their fingers turn into little stallions wandering in an enchanted garden. (When Soldred was off whacking heads, Ingrid galloped her own little stallion through her enchanted garden, a revelation that got me to confession a lot more than ever before.)

"Kid stuff," Con said.

I was shocked. Soldred and Ingrid, kid stuff? I thought they were dreadfully avant-garde.

"Just wait," she said. The next day she smuggled into school a book she had swiped from her uncle's house—he was a Navy commander—that he had bought in Paris. It had drawings of Oriental-looking people doing the most interesting things to each other. I never knew there were so many items that could be placed in so many orifices of the human body.

"Con, look at this. Those people, they're doing it like, like—Cocker Spaniels!"

"Yeah," she said, perfectly blasé. "So they are."

"Con, you don't think—that Aly and Rita do that?"

"Why not?" she said. "Peg, you know it does get *boring* doing it the same old way all the time."

I certainly was learning a lot. I mean, I'd gotten pretty darn sophisticated, but to think of Aly and Rita doing it like Lassie and Spot—that was a bit much. Con told me that the pictures came from temple drawings.

22

"Temples? Like churches?"

"In the Orient, love is sacred," Con said.

"Somehow, I can't see Father Ryan ordering a stained-glass window for St. Malachy's with pictures of people screwing," I said.

"Wouldn't be so any people asleep at nine o'clock Mass," Con said.

Not only did Con furthur my sex education, but she enlisted me in what she called a Sacred Crusade in journalism. "We owe it to ourselves, and to History, to be *magnificent!*" she said, throwing up her arms to the sky. Con did get pretty dramatic at times. "We are going to be the *Messenger* staff that will be remembered as long as a single brick of Immaculate Heart High School is left standing under the sun. We must do it! Then she recited:

> One moment in annihilation's waste
> One moment of the well of life to taste
> The sun is setting and the caravan
> Starts for the dawn of nothing—Oh make haste!

"I'm not sure I get that," I said.

"Don't you see? We have only the moment. If we blow it, it's gone forever. We have one chance to be brilliant, to be *immortal!* One moment of the well of life to taste, Peggy!"

Rules, Con said, were made to be broken, and we were going to break them—gloriously, stylishly, immediately. And so the Miracle Caper was hatched.

Con, myself, and our comrade-in-rebellion, Mollie, the page one editor, hatched it at the conference table under the portrait of our patron saint, St. Theresa, the Little Flower.

In the portrait, St. Theresa had her arms folded and she was looking heavenward, enveloped in a yellow ray of light, an expression on her face as if she had just swallowed a sour ball. That was the side of the picture we kept facing out when the nuns were around. But when we locked the

23

door, we flipped the picture. There was St. Theresa's face, still wearing the sour-ball look, pasted onto a body wearing a white brassiere and girdle. Underneath we had written the caption: *I DREAMED I WAS CANONIZED IN MY MAIDENFORM BRA.*

But it wasn't St. Theresa who was our concern at the moment; it was Mother Marie Claire. Mother Marie just happened to be the foundress of the Sisters of Claire, the order that taught at Immaculate Heart. The order was staging a big campaign to get Mother Marie declared a saint, but Con said that somebody who started schools in Tallahassee, Florida, Crystal Springs, Maryland, and Scranton, Pennsylvania, probably didn't deserve to be canonized.

"God does not even know where Scranton *is*," Con said. "He may see every sparrow that falls, but ask Him about Tallahassee and He draws a blank."

Nonetheless, we decided that in our capacity as the staff of the *Marian Messenger*, it was our duty to give Mother Marie a leg up on sainthood. Mother Marie was somewhat deficient in the miracle department—you had to have at least one first-class miracle to get to be a saint—and we were going to try to provide one.

Con and Mollie and I gathered one September afternoon in the far corner of the athletic field, behind the equipment shed, out of the sight of prying clerical eyes. Sean hopped the fence to join us. He wasn't supposed to be there, of course. Fraternization between Sacred Hearters and Immaculate Hearters during school hours was an instant thirty demerits. But he couldn't resist the chance to witness a bona fide miracle.

"You can be an official witness," Con told him. "So when the Vatican needs a person to sign papers, you'll be it."

"Me? I'm not even supposed to be here," Sean said. "I'll get a shitload of demerits if I get caught."

"Would you let a few demerits stand in the way of sainthood for Mother Marie Claire?" I asked him.

24

Sean looked thoughtful. Mollie said, "Look at it this way. Wouldn't you want a saint in your corner when you hit the Pearly Gates?"

"You have a point," Sean said.

"I wouldn't count on Mother Marie Claire," Con said. "Even if she gets to be a saint, she'd still be out in the left field bleachers. From where she sits, God looks like a flea."

"Come on, Con," I said, "she may be a two-bit saint, but at least she's ours."

"Yeah," Sean said, "who else you got that has a shot at it?"

"Sister Justinian might make it," Mollie said.

"What did she do?"

"Single-handedly wiped out the soul kiss at Immaculate Heart."

"That's not what *I* hear," Sean said.

"For a while, anyhow," Mollie said. "She says that God punishes people who soul kiss by giving them cancer of the tongue."

"What!" Sean said.

"Stick out your tongue," Con ordered. Sean complied. "Oh yeah, little green things. Definitely cancer."

"She didn't really say that," Sean said.

"Oh yeah," I told him. "She told this story about a kid who soul kissed all the time. When he got cancer, he repented, and the last words he said before they cut his tongue out were *Jesus, Mary, and Joseph.*"

"Oh God, that's sick!" Sean said.

"Yeah," Con said, "I would have asked for Scotch on the rocks. Stupid kid."

"Enough talk," Mollie ordered. "I got to be in geometry in twenty minutes." She looked at me. "You got 'em?"

I nodded. I took out a stack of 200 Mother Marie Claire bookmarks. They showed a stern-faced woman in a nun's wimple and veil, and the expression on her face made St. Theresa's sour-ball stare seem positively orgasmic.

Sean picked one up and looked at it. "Did they take this picture after she died? She looks awful."

Con looked at the bookmark. "That's her on a *good* day. Irene Dunne she is not."

"Come on, hurry it up," said Mollie. "Get the fire started."

If Mother Marie had any miracle talents, stopping fires seemed to be the major one. The nuns claimed that it was her forte, and they were hopeful that her talents in that department were going to improve. That's where we came in. If we could get a good fire going, and then throw in a stack of Mother Marie bookmarks, she'd have a chance to put it out cold. Mollie had the *Messenger* camera, and we'd get the miracle on "Candid Camera."

Sean, who used to be a Boy Scout, was given the job of getting the fire going. He arranged the twigs and paper in a pyramid shape and lit them with a match (twenty demerits for possession). "That ought to do it," he said.

When the fire was going good, I tossed in a bookmark.

"Mama, do your stuff," Con chanted.

"That's blasphemous," I cautioned.

"Sorry."

We watched the bookmark as the flames lapped at it, and slowly, Mother Marie's unsmiling face curled, melted, and turned to flame.

"More," Con ordered.

I tossed in more bookmarks. The fire licked at them, curled them, and turned them to flame.

"She's not doing so hot," Sean said.

"And it's just a little fire, too," I said. I was really disappointed. Somewhere deep down in my heart, I really had believed that Mother Marie Claire could pull it off. It was sort of like Santa Claus; with your rational mind you knew there wasn't any fat guy with reindeers who stumbled down your chimney, but if he showed up one Christmas Eve, you wouldn't really be surprised.

I threw in more bookmarks and we all stood and watched them burn. Just then, an unexpected puff of wind caught one of the flaming Mother Maries, picked it up and wafted it into the air. It landed about fifty feet away, in a patch of dry brown grass. There hadn't been any rain in a week, and this part of the field had been untouched by the mower. The minute the flaming fragment touched down, the dry grass blazed up.

"Oh shit," Con said.

We all ran to the burning grass and tried to stamp out the flames with the soles of our feet. But the wind had carried even more embers aloft, and we couldn't stamp fast enough to keep up with the new tongues of flame licking at the grass all around us.

"Quick, the rest of the bookmarks," Mollie shouted. This was Mother Marie's big chance. I scattered more bookmarks among the flames. They curled and vanished.

"Shit, we got to get the fire department," Sean called out. "We're going to burn the whole fucking school down."

We gazed in dismay at the spreading flames. Con looked up at the sky. "You really blew it, Mother Marie!" she said.

"Yeah, I guess sainthood just isn't in the cards," Mollie said.

"Will you kids move your butts! We really got to get out of here!" Sean yelled.

We all took off at a dead run for the fence, about fifty yards away. Sean and I, old hands at fence climbing, went over easily. Mollie followed suit. But Con was only halfway over the fence when her underpants snagged on the wire notches on top of the fence. She was stuck there, with only one leg over on the safe side of the fence. She lifted her uniform skirt and tugged at the pants, but they wouldn't pull free.

"Peg, help!" she screamed. I ran back and pulled and tugged at the panties, but to no avail.

27

"Hurry up, for God's sakes!" Sean yelled.

"No good. I may have to rip them," I said.

"Do it! Just hurry!" There was a twinge of panic in Con's voice. "Sean, turn around!"

Sean obligingly turned away.

I pulled with all my might. Con's panties ripped down the middle and she pulled free, leaving the panties still caught on the fence, waving like a banner in the wind.

We sprinted into the woods that separated Immaculate Heart from Sacred Heart, and then we heard the wail of a siren. Fortunately for us, someone had seen the fire and called the fire department.

We walked along the path that led through the woods.

"We've got to get back into the building without being spotted," I said. That was going to be difficult. We couldn't go back across the athletic field, and if we circled and came in through the front door or the side door, someone would see us and know we'd been out of the building when the fire started. For Sean it was easy. He could just slip back through the woods.

"We could hide here until they put the fire out," Mollie suggested.

"No good," I said. "We're all supposed to be in class in a few minutes. If we're all missing, they'll smell a rat for sure."

"We are in deep shit," Mollie said.

Then I had an inspiration. "Hey, the big tree by the *Messenger* room. We can go right up it and crawl across the limb to the window. The chem lab's got the only windows you can see out of, and nobody's in there now."

"That's on the second floor!" Con said. I knew about her problems with heights. Getting up on a kitchen stool made her dizzy.

"It's either that or get arrested for arson," I said.

Caught between a rock and a hard place, Con reluctantly agreed. We all made our way to the base of the tree, a large old oak with a great many branches close to the ground, perfect for climbing. I scrambled up first, crawled out on the wide limb and crawled across it, opened the window, and dropped inside the room.

"Come on, it's easy," I called down.

Mollie climbed up next, and swung herself into the room. Con was still standing by the tree, next to Sean.

"I can't do it," she said. "I'm sick. I'm nauseous."

"You haven't even left the ground," Sean said. "How can you be dizzy?"

"Just thinking about it makes me want to throw up."

"Come on, Con, you've got to. I'll help you."

"O.K.," she said. Then she remembered. "I haven't got any *pants* on."

"O.K., I'll go," Sean said.

Con grabbed his arm. "No! You can't! You have to help me!"

"Con!" I yelled. "Your tie! Use your tie!"

The red tie that we wore with our uniform dress was tied just above the breastbone in a square knot. It was the size of a large diaper, made of red nylon.

Con ripped off the tie. "Turn around!" she commanded Sean.

"I seem to be doing this a lot," he said.

With a considerable bit of struggling, Con managed to wrap the tie, dydee-style, around her privates, and secured it with a knot. "I'm ready," she said.

Sean helped her to get to the first branch. Then he climbed up on it too and helped boost her to a second branch, and then a third. Con was breathing hard and beads of moisture stood out on her forehead. Finally, with Sean keeping a tight hold on her, she made it to the level of the limb near the window.

"Now just crawl across," Sean said.

"Oh God!" Con breathed. Her whole face was bathed in sweat now. "I'm going to be sick!"

"Don't look down," I said. "Just crawl across, fast. Come on, Con. You've got to do it, or we'll all go to jail!"

"Jesus, Mary, and Joseph!" Con prayed.

"GO!" Sean ordered.

Con crawled out on the limb, and she got halfway across, and that's when she made her mistake. She looked down. A wave of nausea engulfed her, and she closed her eyes and froze, smack in the middle of the limb, on her hands and knees.

"I can't!" she wailed. "I can't!"

"Come on, Con, you can do it," I said. She just stayed there, frozen. Suddenly, the breeze stirred up again, and it lifted her skirt like the sail on a frigate, leaving her white cheeks, bisected by a ribbon of red nylon, exposed to nature and to Sean.

"Oh GOD!" she breathed, but she was too terrified to move, or even to grab her skirt.

"Con, hurry up!" I yelled.

"Con, for God's sakes, you can't just kneel up there bare-assed in a tree," Sean said.

"Jesus, Mary, and Joseph!"

"Con, the whole sophomore gym class is right beyond those trees," Sean called. "You got ten seconds, and then I'm bringing them all over to look at your tail."

That did it. Con scrambled over and we grabbed her arms and hauled her in the window. Sean flashed the Churchill V for Victory sign and disappeared into the woods. Con collapsed, panting, into a chair.

"I'm *mortified*!" she said. "Oh God, I'm *mortified*!"

"I should have got a picture," Mollie said.

"My God, there I was in that tree with my *ass* hanging out!" Con said.

"I'll make Sean take a vow of silence," I said. "He won't tell."

"I must have looked like a *cow* up there. A huge *cow*!"

"You did look pretty funny," Mollie said.

"Nobody breathes a word of this. Not a *word*!"

"Our lips are sealed."

"They'd better be," Con said, with a glance at us that said she'd strangle us with piano wire if we opened our mouths.

The next morning, the whole school was called to a special assembly. Everybody knew something was up, because we didn't even say the pledge of allegiance or sing "Mother Dear, Oh Pray For Me." Sister Robert Mary walked up to the stage, her mouth set in a grim line, followed by Sister Justinian. Sister Robert Mary waved what was left of Con's panties in the air.

"Some Catholic girl, some girl in *this* school, set the fire," she said. "I cannot believe that any girl could be so *sick* as to want to do this horrible thing. I want the girl responsible to step forward right now."

A pall of silence settled on the room. I looked at Con out of the corner of my eye. She was nonchalantly peeling the nail polish off her thumb. Her lip was firm; her hands did not tremble. We sat in silence for a while, and then Sister Justinian said, "We have asked the Holy Ghost to intervene in this matter. The Holy Ghost will lead us to the culprit. We will not let this matter rest until we have hunted her down like a dog!" Sister Justinian had a way with words.

Later that day we heard that girls were being called into the principal's office, one by one. When it was my turn, Sister Robert Mary held up Con's tattered pants and said, "Peggy, do you recognize these?"

"They're not mine, Sister."

"Have you seen any girl wearing panties like these?"

I peered at them. They were the standard white nylon panties, elastic at the waist and legs.

"Well, I guess half the kids in school wear pants like those."

"Hmmm," said Sister Robert Mary.

31

"Maybe," I said, "it wasn't any of the kids from here. Maybe it was kids from Hoover High."

"That's possible, of course."

"Those public school kids, they drink and they smoke." Suddenly, I had an inspiration. "Maybe it was an anti-Catholic act. There are a lot of people who hate Catholics at Hoover High."

"Have you found that to be so?" the principal said.

"Oh yes, Sister. When I walk home from school, sometimes, wearing my uniform, the Protestant kids taunt me for being a Catholic."

I was warming to my tale. I never knew what a good liar I could be. My pulse was steady, my palms only slightly moist.

"What did they say to you, dear?"

"Oh." I hadn't thought she was going to ask me that. Nobody really ever taunted me. Sometimes they'd make fun of my uniform—these girls in their cute little sweaters and skirts, they'd giggle and yell, "Hey, the Navy just hit port," and I'd clench my jaw and walk right by them, while I prayed to God to send a plague of flies to eat their faces.

"Well," I said, "they, uh . . ."

"I know this is difficult for you, dear, but you should tell me about these things when they happen."

"Well, they said . . ." My mind was a total blank. It was the Holy Ghost punishing me for lying by burning out my brain cells. I pictured a miniature dove, inside my head, kicking the crap out of my neurons with its little clawed feet.

"They said, 'Death to Catholics!'" I blurted out.

"They said *that*?"

"Oh yes. And they said the pope ate babies. They said there was an underwater tunnel from the Vatican and one day the pope and his army were going to invade America and murder all the Protestants."

"I'm going to call the principal of Hoover High and we'll put a stop to this, right away," she said, firmly.

"Oh no, Sister, don't do that!"

"Why not?"

"Well, it's just a few kids. Most of them don't taunt Catholics."

"It just takes a few rotten apples to spoil the barrel, dear. Thank you very much, Peggy, for telling me about this. You've been a big help. You may go back to your class now."

"Thank you, Sister."

I walked out into the hall and leaned against the wall. My legs were shaking. Not only did I lie like a rug, but I may have started a civil war between Immaculate Heart and Hoover High. In two days, I had turned from a nice, polite Catholic girl into an arsonist, a warmonger, and a liar.

My head hurt. I figured the Holy Ghost was still in there, stomping around.

"I'm sorry," I said to the Holy Ghost, "but I would have got my friends expelled. Their lives would be *ruined*."

And I knew that if I had to do it all over again, I'd do the same thing—only I'd have toned down my act with Sister Robert Mary. So my apologies to the Holy Ghost weren't valid. I had no remorse. If it had been just me, I'd have confessed and taken my punishment. But it seemed that Con and Sean and Mollie meant more to me than the Holy Ghost, and that meant more than *God*, and if that wasn't a sin, what was? It was wrong, but it *felt* right. It was very confusing.

I grubbed in my purse and found a couple of Midol. I went over to the water fountain and gulped them down. I didn't have much hope. They worked O.K. for cramps, but nowhere on the label did it say they were any good against the Third Person of the Holy Trinity of God.

THREE

The Modesty Crusaders

On the second Saturday in October, the phone rang and Sean's voice said, "Peggy, would you come over? I think my father is going to do something really dumb."

"So what else is new?" I said.

"You better come over."

I caught the edge of panic in Sean's voice, so I high-tailed it out the back door and over to Sean's house. In the driveway, I saw a blue-and-white van, and it said MARY-LIKE in big white letters on the side, and underneath it, in smaller letters, were the words, "Fashions the Blessed Mother Approves."

Oh *shit*," I thought to myself, and when I went in the back door Sean was waiting for me in the hall.

"Is that—" I said, and Sean nodded, putting his finger to his lips.

"They're actually here?" I said.

"A bunch of *fruitcakes*!" he whispered. "My father thinks it's practically the Second Coming."

I walked to the front foyer and peered into the living room. There they were, the famous Modesty Crusaders from New Jersey, led by Father Clement Kliblicki of Paramus. Sean's father had been singing their praises ever since he saw an article about them in *Time* magazine.

"A true Catholic hero! A St. George taking arms against the dragon of immodesty!" he declared. He bored Sean and me to death; we didn't think that modesty was such a big deal in a world that also contained the A-bomb.

"Did your father bring them here?" I asked Sean.

"I think so. I heard Pop talking to them on the phone last week, but who'd have thought they'd actually come?"

But here was Father Clement Kliblicki, in the flesh, sitting in Sean's living room. He was a tall, pasty-faced man with skin the shade of milk and vivid eyes, a sort of intense Ichabod Crane. Only a year ago he had been an obscure pastor in Paramus, spending most of his time—when he wasn't running beano games or saying Mass—worrying about tits. Which made the bond between Father Clement and Dr. McCaffrey obvious right away. But while Dr. McCaffrey's specialty was celebrity tit, Father Clement was concerned with the garden variety of mammary gland—specifically, the sort possessed by your average high school kid. It was his thesis that American clothing manufacturers were doing the devil's handiwork by making dresses that displayed too much pubescent flesh, exposing the innocent eyes of Catholic young men to acres and acres of female bosom. Such a sight, he reasoned, would turn even the most pious Holy Communicant into a lust-crazed satyr, itching to get hands that should have been folded in prayer down the front of some girl's prom dress.

So Father Clement adopted the old Populist technique of direct action. He formed the Modesty Crusade, and sallied forth to do battle with Seventh Avenue. The Sodality League of New Jersey chipped in for the van and a supply of 500,000 labels, on which were stamped the words, "This is a Marylike dress!" and underneath the line, "Approved by the Virgin Mary."

Father Clement and his band swept like Mongol hordes

35

into the retail stores of New Jersey, looking for dresses that could get the stamp of approval of the B.V.M. The idea was that Catholic parents would buy for their daughters only those frocks that carried the Marylike tag, avoiding the others like the wages of sin. Sales of immodest dresses would plummet, the giants of Seventh Avenue would be brought cowering to their knees, and Modesty would reign.

"Do you believe they have a van, a fucking *van*!" Sean whispered.

"Why not? The Apostles would have used one. They could have kept the loaves and fishes in the back with the spare."

Sean groaned and motioned toward the living room. "Would you look at them? Pathetic. Pathetic!"

Sitting beside Father Clement on the couch was his aide-de-camp, Brother Jonas, a monk set free from some abbey. He had switched jobs, from stamping grapes to stamping out plunging necklines. He wore a brown robe, and his feet, in open sandals, were really grubby. Brother Jonas looked as if he had collected dirt from half the retail outlets in Jersey on his tootsies.

Then there were Mrs. Sullivan and her daughter, Deirdre. Mrs. Sullivan, a woman of about fifty-five, had the hard, flinty eye of an I.R.A. executioner, and Deirdre was a pale, washed-out blonde who sat quietly and said little, her eyes shifting about the room. Completing the little band of modesty warriors was Mr. Hardy, who weighed 300 pounds if he weighed an ounce, and who laughed at everything anybody said, whether it was funny or not.

"If my father gets mixed up with these people, he's really going to make an ass of himself," Sean said.

"Sean, I hate to say it—"

"I know, but this is the worst. Really the pits. Peggy, that man is crazy. I mean *really* crazy. You should hear him."

I walked into the living room and Dr. McCaffrey introduced me to the Crusaders. Father Clement shook my hand and stared at my chest, and Brother Jonas, who had taken a vow of silence, merely nodded. Mrs. Sullivan and Deirdre both shook my hand, and Mr. Hardy laughed.

Then Father Clement took out sketches of his latest project, a new manufacturing firm that was to be called Marylike, Inc., and which would make the kind of fashion suitable for Catholic girls. Dr. McCaffrey examined the sketches and handed them to me. I looked them over. If the B.V.M. really liked this stuff, I thought, her taste was in her mouth—and she was usually quite chic, judging by her pictures. She always dressed in your basic white tunic, blue mantle, no glitzy accessories or heavy makeup. If she'd been around today, I thought, she'd go for Chanel or Main-Bocher; she wouldn't be caught dead in one of the outfits Father Clement dreamed up, which were, in a word, icky.

First of all, they looked as if they were designed for eleven-year-olds, with puffed sleeves and high necks and little mother-of-pearl buttons. No self-respecting high school kid in America would put one of those on her back.

But as I watched Dr. McCaffrey listening to Father Clement; I knew right away what caused the panic in Sean's voice. The Nemesis of Smut had a transcendent look about him, a joy born of the hope of a new crusade stirring in his breast. His eyes were ravenous, as if he were starved for every word that fell from the pallid lips of Father Clement. Dr. McCaffrey sometimes had that same look about him—an air of demented luminosity—when he stood in front of the congregation every year to lead the Legion of Decency pledge. But that was fairly harmless. Everybody was against dirty movies—even the people who were first in line when *The Outlaw* came to town. But Father Clement Kliblicki and his merry band were clearly of a different order. They were dedicated, totally committed to action, and arguably loony. They would stop at naught in their guerilla action against the apex of the evils of modern society: the strapless prom dress.

Dr. McCaffrey turned to me and asked me what I thought of the sketches. That presented an obvious moral dilemma. If I told the truth ("The stuff is swill.") Dr. McCaffrey would be rotten to Sean for at least a month. I thought that now was the time for "mental reservation"—which meant that you held back part of the truth for good and sufficient moral reasons. It was a good way to lie, but not sin, one of those neat Catholic tricks for getting around the rules. There were a lot of those, I discovered.

So I said, "They're very interesting," but Dr. McCaffrey was so flushed with enthusiasm that he didn't recognize a mental reservation when he heard one, and I was off the hook. Father Clement then began to outline the next phase of his campaign against immodesty, a bold and daring step.

"It is not enough simply to identify unMarylike dresses," he said. "We must openly express our disapproval. Christ threw the money lenders out of the temple. We must follow his example!"

I saw Sean go pale. He was right, I thought; his father really was going to do something dumb. Dr. McCaffrey was still looking raptly at Father Clement. Mrs. Sullivan's eyes lighted up—she looked as if she'd just been ordered to firebomb the British Embassy. Deirdre just looked vacant. If it hadn't been a time when drugs were used only by saxophone players and ghetto blacks, I'd have said Deirdre was off in some chemical fairyland all her own. She looked more stoned than any druggie I've ever seen.

"Direct Action!" thundered Father Clement. "We must *act* against immodesty, against the immoral garments leading to sin and putrefaction!"

Father Clement was the only person I ever met who talked like the editorials in the *Catholic Herald*.

"Grind them into dust!" Mrs. Sullivan chortled. Mr. Hardy laughed cheerfully.

38

"Uh, Father, what exactly do you have in mind?" Sean asked, nervously.

"An exorcism."

"Exorcism?"

"To pray the devil of immodesty out of our presence, to command him to leave our fair community, to return to the fires and brimstone of hell, never to return to Crystal Springs!"

"Oh," Sean said. "You mean you're going to do it here, in our house?"

"No," Dr. McCaffrey said happily. "The Hecht Company."

Sean went from pale to dead white. I knew at the moment he was wishing for the good fortune to have been born a Unitarian. The Hecht Company was the largest department store in Crystal Springs, the place where we all shopped.

"The Hecht Company? Don't you think that's sort of— public?" Sean said.

"Did Christ hide behind the safe walls of his dwelling in Nazareth? Did he not go into the streets, amid the teeming masses and the squalor of life?" roared Father Clement.

"That sounds like the Hecht Company," I said. "Especially on Saturday."

Sean flashed me a dirty look. He did not think this was funny at all. "Uh, Pop, couldn't you do it somewhere else?"

"The Hecht Company is perfect. Perfect. The money changers in the temple!"

I knew what *that* meant. The Hecht Company made a ton of money, and it was owned by Jews, which pissed off a lot of Catholics and Protestants. Dr. McCaffrey was one of those anti-Semites who never really said what he meant, but managed to get the point across.

"Well," Dr. McCaffrey said, "shall we be off!" as if we were going for a Sunday drive and not to an exorcism of the devil.

"I wouldn't miss it!" I said, and I grabbed Sean by the hand and dragged him out the door. He had turned from white to pale green. I thought he was going to throw up.

"This is all a dream, a bad dream!" he said. "In a minute I will wake up and all these crazy people will be gone."

"I bet the Hecht Company never had an exorcism before, especially not in the junior miss department," I said.

"Oh Peggy, he's going to make such a fool of himself. In public!"

"Remember the time he got his picture in the *Post* for burning the Jane Russell poster at the Catholics for Decency rally at Griffith Stadium? That was pretty public."

"But this one is really going to take the cake!" he moaned.

We climbed into the van, and we all rode in silence to the parking lot of the Hecht Company. My heart was beating rapidly; I felt like the commandos who hit the beach at Normandy ahead of the invasion force. Sean looked as if he were about to be led off to a hanging—his own.

We all trooped into the store together, drawing stares, and marched in a group onto the elevator. Father Clement pushed the button marked *Three: Junior Miss, Promtime Departments*.

Not surprisingly, the salesladies all gaped at us as we marched out of the elevator; it wasn't every day that somebody who looks like St. Francis of Assisi strolls into Promtime.

One of the salesladies approached Brother Jonas, tentatively.

"Can I help you, sir?"

Brother Jonas just stared straight ahead.

"He's taken a vow of silence," I explained.

"Oh," said the saleslady, backing away.

Father Clement lost no time; he walked directly up to a rack of formal dresses and began rifling through them.

"Filth!" he thundered about a little pink number with

blue bows on it. Next he came to a green taffeta. It had puffed sleeves, but the neckline was just a tad too low to get the approval of the B.V.M. "Temptation to the Morals of Youth!" cried Father Clement.

Finally, he came to one dress with a high collar and mother-of-pearl buttons. He smiled. He nodded to Mrs. Sullivan, who rushed over and pinned a "Marylike" tag on the dress. By now, a small crowd was beginning to gather.

Dr. McCaffrey was also looking through the dresses hanging in one of the alcoves, and he pulled out a dress with a mandarin collar and long sleeves.

"This is Marylike, don't you think?"

"Absolutely," I said, and added under my breath, "if the Blessed Mother is big on the Dragon Lady look."

Dr. McCaffrey kept going through the dresses. "Here's another!" he announced gleefully, holding it up. A saleslady walked over to him.

"Sir, what are you doing? And who is that—person over there?"

"We are Catholic Crusaders for Modesty," Dr. McCaffrey said. "We are examining your frocks to see which ones the Blessed Mother would approve. I'm Dr. Liam McCaffrey, assistant professor of communication and speech dynamics at St. Anselm's Junior College."

"Pop," Sean said through clenched teeth, "you don't have to give your name!"

In the alcove across the room, where Father Clement was advancing through the dress rack like Sherman through Georgia, a saleslady approached him and said firmly, "Sir, you can't pin things onto our merchandise!"

"Render unto Caesar the things that are Caesar's and to God the things that are God's!" Father Clement declaimed in his best reach-to-the-last-pew voice. Mrs. Sullivan chimed in, "Amen!"

"We are acting in the name of the Virgin Mary!" called out Dr. McCaffrey, pinning on another Marylike label.

"Did he say something about a *virgin*?" one saleslady said to another. "Estelle, I think they're a bunch of sex perverts. Call Mr. Bernstein! Quick!"

Father Clement was still tugging and hauling at dresses, when suddenly he stopped dead still, as if he had been flash-frozen on the spot. His ice-white face grew even colder with anger, and his eyes narrowed. Then suddenly he ripped a dress from a hanger and held it up. It was a black strapless sheath, with a deep V in front, cut tight around the hips. It was a dress I'd have given my eyeteeth to wear, but I figured you had to be at least twenty to carry off a look that sophisticated.

Father Clement elevated the dress above his head, almost as if he were raising the Host at Mass, then he waved it wildly above his head and threw it on the floor with a flourish. "Spawn of Satan!" he cried.

Sean edged up to his father. "Pop, can we go home now?"

But Dr. McCaffrey was looking at Father Clement Kliblicki with total fascination; he was watching a Catholic hero, a veritable St. George, in action.

Another saleslady, bolder than the others, walked right up to Father Clement and said, "Sir, we simply cannot allow you to throw merchandise on the floor."

"Merchandise!" Father Clement sneered. "Merchandise! Satan's evil handiwork!" and he leaned over and spat on the black dress.

"Oh *God*!" Sean said.

The saleslady screamed, "You can't do that!" She reached down to retrieve the dress, but Father Clement advanced on her and barked, "Woman, do not soil your hands with the work of Lucifer! The spirit of Beelzebub, prince of devils, is in this dress. I shall cast him out!"

The saleslady backed off. "Mister, you are a nutcake!" she said.

Father Clement stood over the dress, which now lay in

a crumpled heap on the floor. He drew himself to his full height, and raised his hands like Charlton Heston asking the Red Sea to part.

"I abjure thee, Satan," he said. "Begone! Begone, prince of darkness. I renounce thee and all thy works! Begone!"

Father Clement pointed his finger in righteous wrath at the dress, his eyes flashed with anger, and his voice carried all the way to Small Appliances. He was a spellbinder, all right. I half expected the black dress to start twisting and snarling and sending up little puffs of brimstone. But the dress just lay there. If Beelzebub *was* inside, Father Clement was going to have to juice up the exorcism to get him out.

Just then a large, beefy man in a dark suit hurried into the Junior Miss department. He took one look at the bizarre scene and said, "What the hell is going on here?"

"Begone, Satan!" Father Clement cried.

The store manager—that's who the large man turned out to be—turned to one of the salesladies and said, "Estelle, who is that *lunatic*?"

Dr. McCaffrey stepped forward. "Sir, that is Father Clement Kliblicki, Catholic Crusader for Modesty. Perhaps you read about him in *Time* magazine."

The manager, Mr. Bernstein, stared at Sean's father.

"That fruitcake was in *Time*? What the hell does he think he's doing?"

"I am driving the spirit of Satan from our presence!" called out Father Clement. "His handiwork is all about us here in this temple of filth!"

"Are you calling the Hecht Company a temple of filth?" demanded Mr. Bernstein.

"You shall know the truth, and the truth shall set you free!" said Father Clement, his forefinger still waving at Beelzebub, who was lying low.

"Listen, buddy, this is class merchandise we got in

Promtime. You want sleazy stuff you can throw on the floor, go over to Sears Roebuck."

"Cesspool! Father Clement yelled. "Palace of Putrefaction!" He spat on the black dress again.

"You goddamned screwball, give me that dress!" yelled Mr. Bernstein.

Mrs. Sullivan stepped in front of the store manager, handbag raised like a bludgeon. "Lay one hand on the holy hairs of his head and I'll mash your face in!" she shrieked.

"Estelle, call the cops! Quick," the manager said. Estelle ran to the phone.

Sean grabbed my hand. "Oh God," he said; "we're going to get arrested!"

"Not *we*, Sean. *Them!*"

There was a high noon standoff for a minute, with Mrs. Sullivan facing down the manager, as Father Clement proceeded with the exorcism. Then Mr. Bernstein darted around her and snatched the dress from the floor.

"Don't touch that!" screamed Father Clement, grabbing the bottom half of the dress. Now the manager had one end of the black dress and Father Clement had the other. They both began tugging at it.

"Give me the goddamn dress, you lunatic!" the manager yelled.

"Spawn of Satan!" screamed Father Clement.

They kept pulling and pulling and then there was a horrible ripping sound and the dress tore right down the middle, sending the Modesty Crusader sprawling into the dress rack and the store manager bouncing off a cash register. The priest got to his feet. He moved toward the manager, raising his hand to exhort Satan once again to begone—at least from the half of the dress he still held—but Mr. Bernstein thought the priest was preparing to strike a blow. Dr. McCaffrey, who now was standing next to Father Clement, saw what was happening and tried to step in between the two men. He did so, however, just as Mr.

Bernstein, who had been a Golden Glover before he went into retailing, cranked up a roundhouse right. It caught Dr. McCaffrey square in the jaw, and he went down as if he'd been poleaxed.

"Oh no! Pop!" Sean yelled, and ran to bend over his father. He started slapping Dr. McCaffrey on the face, saying, "Talk to me, Pop! Say something!"

Just at that moment the police arrived, and the first one they grabbed was Mrs. Sullivan, who had climbed on the store manager's back and was pummeling him with her fists.

"Arrest them! Arrest them!" They're all crazy!" hollered the store manager, and one of the officers tried to sort things out, which wasn't easy, as you can imagine.

The manager, the salesladies, Father Clement, and Mrs. Sullivan were all talking at once. Brother Jonas didn't say a word. Deirdre still looked stoned and Mr. Hardy was chuckling.

Dr. McCaffrey finally came to and Sean helped him to his feet. One of the policeman said to Sean, "Son, who is this man?"

"He's Dr. McCaffrey from St. Anselm's," Sean said. "He's my father."

"What was he doing on the floor?"

"Well, it's sort of a long story."

The policeman looked at Dr. McCaffrey, who was shaking his head, trying to clear it.

"The saleslady says you were putting tags on merchandise. Is that right?"

"Yes," said Sean's father, "You see, Father Clement Kliblicki, Catholic Crusader for Modesty—"

"Sir, I'm afraid I'll have to ask you to come with me."

The police led Sean's father and the Modesty Crusaders away, and Mr. Hardy tossed the keys to the van to Sean.

"Call Tom Harrigan," Dr. McCaffrey called out. "He's the archbishop's lawyer!"

Sean and I walked out to the van together. He was still very pale.

"I can't believe it; my father's in the slammer," he said.

"They'll probably just make him pay a fine. I mean he didn't try to kill anyone or anything."

We climbed in the van and Sean switched on the ignition. "Peggy," he said, "there lots of sane, rational people in the church. Smart people. Scholars. Scientists. Not crazy at all. How does my father get mixed up with Father Clement Kliblicki and his Modesty Crusaders?"

"Just lucky, I guess."

As it turned out, I was right about the Modesty Crusaders getting off with a fine. Father Clement and his merry band climbed back into their van and drove off to New Jersey. A month later we heard that Father Clement had been picked up by the police again, this time for trying to exorcise the spirit of Beelzebub out of a Port Authority bus going from Paramus to Teaneck. His bishop shipped him off for psychiatric observation.

Sean's worst fears didn't materialize. Dr. McCaffrey wasn't a laughingstock after all. He was one of those people who could get dropped in a pile of cow shit and come up smelling like Chanel No. 5. When the story got out that he had been arrested trying to defend modesty, he became an instant martyr. He had a telegram from the Chicago archdiocese asking him to come out and make a speech, and he got promoted to associate professor. He even got invited to appear on a national Catholic T.V. program, "Catholic View." Of course, the way Dr. McCaffrey told the story was a lot different from the way it really happened. He left out the parts about Father Clement trying to exorcise the devil, and about himself getting decked with a right to the jaw.

Sean and I sat watching "Catholic View," marveling at the way a lunatic brawl could be transformed, with a few well-chosen words, into a dignified crusade for God. Dr. McCaffrey was in his glory. He actually did look distinguished as he told his story, showing off his big vocabulary and his Speech Dynamics.

Sean looked at the image of his father on the screen and shook his head. "He's really something, isn't he? I mean, he's coming off like a hero, a fucking hero!"

Sean shook his head again and laughed, and I suddenly realized how much he loved his father. He didn't have any illusions about him; he knew the Nemesis of Smut was vain and pompous and a bloody fool most of the time, but he loved him anyhow. And I felt sad, because I knew, deep down, that Sean would never please his father, not really. The things that Dr. McCaffrey liked about being a Catholic were the things the Church gave him—the license plates from the archbishop, the pictures in the *Catholic Herald*, the little brass plaque that said "Layman of the Year." For him, the Church was God's Rotary Club.

Dr. McCaffrey was a taker. But Sean was a giver. The part of the church that drew Sean like a magnet was the hard part, the dirty part—his heroes were men who worked in filth and disease, who cared for people no one else cared about, who went where the rest of us refused to go. Damien the Leper was Sean's kind of Catholic, romanticized, of course—all heroes are. But somehow, I couldn't imagine Damien the Leper on the platform with Dr. McCaffrey at the Legion of Decency rally.

Sean wouldn't collect all the little bibelots and trinkets of the church that were so important to Dr. McCaffrey— and so, in his father's eyes, he would always be a failure. Was that another of those unpleasant surprises you got from growing up? They seemed to be coming along pretty regularly these days. Was it true that the things you wanted most were the things you never could get? Was that something I'd have to learn, too?

I wondered.

FOUR

All the King's Men

I was struggling with the Punic Wars in Latin II when the P.A. system squawked on. "Will Miss Peggy Morrison please report to the principal's office?"

I walked down the hall, wondering what I'd done now. Had Sister Robert Mary finally identified Con's panties? But Con was in my class and they'd have called her too. Maybe I'd won the *Catholic Herald* writing contest. I did a great essay on "How Catholic Youth Can Help America." A finky topic, but I'd really jazzed it up, quoted Thomas Jefferson. O.K., Tom was a Prod, but he had a way with words.

I walked into the office and Sister Robert Mary was standing there. She looked at me—strangely, I thought. She wasn't mad. She looked sort of, I don't know, serious.

"Peg, I'm afraid I have some very bad news."

Bad news? Was I being expelled? Did I lose the contest? What could be bad news?

"Peggy, your father had a heart attack."

I blinked and looked at her. My father had a heart attack? Sissy Ryan's father had one. He was in the hospital for a month.

"Is he in the hospital, Sister?"

"No, Peggy, he isn't. Peggy dear"—She put her arm around me, which was really weird. She'd never done that before.

"Peggy, your father died this morning. An hour ago."

"Died?" I stood looking at her. The word didn't make sense.

"I'm so very sorry, Peggy. Your mother's on the way here from the hospital. She said I should tell you, not make you wait."

I looked at her. Died. The word twisted out of meaning. I tried to make it mean something, but it didn't.

"He had a heart attack at work, Peggy. He never regained consciousness. He didn't suffer. God took him quickly."

God took my father? Nonsense. I'd go home tonight and he'd be there, eating a ham sandwich and giving me lectures. I'd give him the hip and he'd fake a fall and I'd do my homework. That was life—how it was, how it always would be. It couldn't be any different.

"Peggy, are you all right?"

"Yes, Sister."

Right now, my father was at work. I saw him, at his desk, in his shirtsleeves, over his desk, the calendar I sold to him for the Mission drive, the one with the bright green and red and purple pictures of saints getting martyred. Why didn't Sister Robert Mary just let me go back to class and finish the Punic Wars?

"Peggy, do you want to sit here?"

"Could I go back to Latin?"

"Peggy, didn't you hear me say your mother's coming?"

"Oh."

I sat down. Probably it was a mistake. Probably they'd called the wrong kid. Maybe it was Peggy Milano, and they just got the Peggy's mixed up and Sister Robert Mary would say, "Sorry about that, Peg," and it was Mr. Milano who was dead. I pictured him, lying on the floor, white as a sheet, everybody standing around and saying, "Too bad, but that's the way it goes." Mr. Milano was an old guy, bald. It was probably him.

I just sat there, feeling sorry for poor dead Mr. Milano, but then my mother came in the office and she had a stunned look on her face and she hugged me and said, "We've got each other, Peggy! Oh, Peggy!" and I wanted to explain to her about the mistake. But I didn't.

We went home, and my aunt was there, and neighbors and friends started coming in and everybody hugged me and said how sorry they were.

People were coming and going all day. About seven o'clock Sean came in with his mother and father. People were sitting around the living room, talking about my father and my mother was laughing and crying as they talked, and I just sat and listened. I had a strange, detatched feeling, like I was watching all of this on T.V. I knew I was acting really weird. I wanted my emotions to work but they didn't; it was like trying to get your mouth to work after you'd had novacaine.

I went into the kitchen to get a drink of water and Sean followed me.

"Peggy, are you O.K?"

Why was everybody asking me that?

"I'm O.K."

"You just seem kind of—strange."

"Strange?"

"Yeah. You act like nothing has happened."

"Something has happened. My father died." *Died*. Still no meaning. Gibberish. Like I said my father zlotched. Zlotched. A funny sound. I laughed.

Sean looked at me, horrified. "Peggy, it isn't *funny*!"

"Zlotched sounds funny."

"What?"

"Oh, nothing."

"Jeez, Peg, I don't know what's with you."

"I don't either."

I don't remember anything at all about the next day. Lots of people were around; my mother hugged me a lot. I know I went around trying not to act weird but not feeling anything. I guessed I was a terrible person, not feeling anything, and that's why God took my father.

The following day was the wake. My mother was riding to the funeral home with my aunt and uncle. She looked at me, a worried look, and said I should go with Sean in the Caddy. We drove, in silence, Sean giving me the same worried look as my mother, to the Warner E. Pumphrey Funeral Home in Crystal Springs, a block away from the Hecht Company.

"I wonder how old Clement Kliblicki is doing," I said and laughed, and I thought I saw Sean wince. I looked at Pumphrey's, a large brick building, and thought that its lawn and flowers were manicured as carefully as the fingernails of the dead people on view inside. The nuns made us go there in seventh grade when Jimmy Ryan died of blood poisoning and say the Rosary around his coffin. I thought it was barbaric to make people lie out in public after they were dead and didn't have any say in the matter. If I died, they'd probably lay me out in that icky blue dress my mother thought was so cute but I thought was vomitous. I was really pissed at my mother for a minute, laying me out in that blue dress.

Sean took my hand as we walked to the door. I stopped in front of it.

"I don't want to do this," I said.

"Peg, you've *got* to!" Sean said, and he literally dragged me through the door. The scent of carnations hit me like a pail of water thrown in my face. I stopped again.

"The goddamn flowers are going to make me throw up."

"You'll get used to them." He looked at me, exasperated. "Peg, it makes people feel b̶ ̶̶er. I mean, if they didn't have *anything*, if your father just—disappeared—it would be worse. People want to say goodbye."

"No they don't. They just want to go in and gawk at a dead person."

"Peggy, for God's sakes!"

He looked at me, real mad, and the flowers were choking me and I suddenly just felt sick and confused, and like I wanted to cry. I bit down on my lip. I wasn't going to cry. I hadn't cried since I was eight years old and got my first Wonder Woman comic book and found my true persona: beautiful, strong, brave, stoic. I invented stories about myself, the Brave Child. The Nazis tortured me, but I didn't give them the invasion plans. The Godless Atheistic Communists pulled out my fingernails to get me to renounce my faith, but they didn't get a whimper.

But the dampness was seeping into my eyes, so I bit down harder on the inside of my lip until I felt the warm blood come. Dammit, I wasn't going to cry, not in front of these people, these—strangers. I didn't cry the day Puddy Kelly tried to pound my face to jelly when I wouldn't give him my arithmetic homework. I didn't cry the day Sean and I were duck-walking through the storm sewers and I stepped on a nail and it went right through my Keds and into my foot. I let Sean carry me home piggy back, but I didn't make a sound. I didn't even cry when the doctor pulled the nail right out of my foot, and it really hurt, bad. There were tears in Sean's eyes as he watched the nail come out; he winced as if he could feel it as much as I did.

I looked at Sean now; his green eyes were dark with concern, the anger had flared and gone. He was so different from me. I kept everything inside, tucked away like a hermit crab deep inside a borrowed shell. I could lie with the face of an angel. Sean was as transparent as cellophane. He had tried to lie to me a couple of times, but it never worked, like the time Arlene Hobbs asked him to the junior prom at Georgetown Visitation. Arlene lived up the street, but her parents were snooty, so they didn't send her to Immaculate Heart, but to Visy where Arlene could hobnob with the daughters of ophthalmologists and periodontists. After the dance, Arlene told me, in that stuck-up psuedo-Wasp accent of hers, that Sean had a "passionate nature."

I got pissed at that and confronted Sean.

"Passionate nature? I bet you didn't give old Arlene the twenty-minute soul kiss rule," I said accusingly.

"I did too!" he declared, but his face froze into a mask so stricken and guilty that he looked like a mass murderer caught with blood on his hands, digging a grave under the carport for one of his victims. All he'd done was stick his tongue into old Arlene's mouth five minutes early, and you'd have thought he was Jack the Ripper. Boys, of course, weren't supposed to cry, but Sean did. He didn't know I knew it. In the movies, when John Wayne or Robert Ryan would get it on Iwo, and the violins would swell like crazy, Sean would just keep stuffing popcorn in his mouth, and I could see the tears in his eyes in the glow of the technicolor. Then he'd stage a fake coughing fit so he could blow his nose. He had coughing fits in *Flying Leathernecks*, *Return of Lassie*, and *East of Eden*. I bet he would have had one in *Bambi* if we went to see it again, when Bambi's mother got herself whacked out by man.

"Peggy, we can't just stand here. We have to go in," he said. He squeezed my hand. I nodded, and we walked into the room together. My mother and my aunt were standing by the coffin; all I could see of it was the bottom part, the dull gleam of the bronze. Father Ryan was there, and he walked over to me and kissed me on the cheek. His breath smelled like Chiclets. That struck me as really weird. Priests shouldn't smell like Chiclets; it was tacky. I couldn't picture Christ, preaching to the multitudes, sloshing his Chiclet from one side of his mouth to the other while he said, "Blessed are the poor in spirit."

"Peggy, I'm praying for your father. He's with God now. Nothing can hurt him, ever again."

"Thank you, Father," I said.

"Do you want to say a prayer?"

I saw that there was a kneeler set up right beside the coffin.

"Yes, Father," I said. I didn't want to cry anymore. I was just numb again. My mother walked over to me and said, "Peggy, are you O.K.?" That again. I nodded.

"He was very proud of you, Peggy," she said.

I walked with Sean to the coffin, and we knelt down. Inside the coffin was something very odd. It *looked* like my father; like somebody made a big doll of him out of rubber, and put it there, with a Rosary in its hands. It was very still, and smaller than he was, I thought. Not a lot, but a little. So still.

"It's not him," I whispered to Sean. He just looked at me.

I looked at the rubber doll that resembled my father. "I know it's not you," I said inside my head. You're someplace else, but I can't see you. You're invisible." I looked over to the side of the room and I saw him there, smiling that small smile he always wore when something struck him as faintly ridiculous. I *saw* him, as clear as the chair, the rug, the flowers. I still wonder, years later, whether I was hallucinating, or whether some warp, some tiny blister, formed between the dimensions of life and death and let me peer through. But he was there.

"Say something to me," I pleaded with him inside my head. "I'm the only one who can hear you."

But he didn't, or couldn't, and he started to fade away, like the Cheshire cat in *Alice in Wonderland*. I tried, through sheer force of will, to keep him there, and I suddenly understood that I would never again see that smile, never hear that voice with the soft edges of a southern accent telling me that basketball was—or wasn't—life.

54

The pain shot through me like a bolt of electricity. It was so terrible that I nearly doubled up with it. I must have made some sort of involuntary sound because Sean grabbed my arm and held it, and I just knelt there, wondering if the pain was going to kill me or if it was going to recede. It did, and I said to Sean, "I'm O.K.," and I reached out to touch my father's forehead. I recoiled; it was cold and hard, like marble.

I got up, then, and stood with my mother and my aunt in a receiving line as the people came in. Sean stood beside me. Nobody thought that was odd. Sean had been in and out of my house all of his life. The old ladies came through first, smelling of lavendar and patting my hand. The girls from school who came by had tears in their eyes; the boys shifted uncomfortably from one foot to the other and said, "Real sorry, Peg." The nuns came, even Sister Justinian. I saw her approaching, and couldn't imagine what she was going to say. The only emotions I had ever seen Sister Justinian display were contempt, steely calm, and an occasional burst of outright loathing. She smiled, occasionally, when girls broke down and wept because she said they were unfit to wear the uniform, a disgrace to their parents, and despised in the eyes of God. And *that* was for combing their hair too close to the sink.

She advanced on me, not so much taking my hand as commanding its presence.

"The Lord giveth, the Lord taketh away," she said.

"Yes, Sister."

"You're excused from homework." And she marched off.

And then there weren't any more people, and Father Ryan left, and my mother said to me, "Peg, a few people are coming back to the house. Do you want to go with us or with Sean?

"With Sean," I said. He and I were the last ones out of the room, and as I walked into the hallway, I paused to look back for a minute, and I wished I hadn't. Two men were closing the casket, and they were putting some *thing*, some sort of a stiff cover—over my father's face, and then they started to close the cover.

"He can't breathe!" I thought and I said, "No, No!" and Sean grabbed my hand and literally pulled me through the door. He hustled me out the front door and out to the parking lot. We just sat in silence for a minute—no other cars were left in the lot, and I said, "We have to get back," and he said, "In a minute."

I was deep in my own thoughts, the image of the lid closing over my father's face running like a continuous film behind my eyes; again and again, the lid came down. I thought it had made a thunderous clang. In my mind, it did. I knew, without a trace of doubt, that my childhood had ended this night, and with it had gone the illusion of safety I had carried with me through the years. Like Humpty-Dumpty, my safe little universe had tottered, fallen, scrambled into an insoluble mess on the sidewalk. All the king's horses and all the king's men couldn't put it together again. But was my father Humpty-Dumpty, or was I?

The fear was a cold, hard knot inside of me. I was alone. Everybody was alone. People died. Life ended. I began to tremble.

Sean put his arm around me. I kept sitting, rigid, trying to will the fear away. I could *make* it go away if I tried.

"You never cry, Peggy," Sean said.

"I never do."

The fear and the pain were knotted inside me, coiled together, with edges like barbed wire. I was afraid to breathe because even the air would hurt me inside, rub me raw. I never knew something could hurt so much.

Then I heard Sean say, "I loved him too, Peggy."

I looked at him and saw that the tears were spilling out of his eyes, running down his cheeks, and he wasn't even coughing to try to hide them. I reached up to touch his cheek to wipe the tears away, and the feel of the warm dampness of his skin opened something inside of me. I made a sound in my throat, a wailing, keening sound, and Sean pulled me against him and just held me tight. I started to cry, desperately, with my whole body, like a child cries. I just kept sobbing and couldn't stop, and Sean held me and stroked my back and just said, over and over, "It's all right. It's all right."

I was getting Sean's shirt all wet with my tears, but the cold knot inside me was dissolving, and Sean was holding me the way my father used to when I was a child and something frightened me, and I just wanted to burrow into his arms and not ever have to come up. Lots of times I felt older and wiser than Sean, but now I felt small and afraid, and his arms seemed to have grown larger. We used to be the same size, but his chest and shoulders had filled out and broadened, and his body was more a man's than a boy's now.

I cried and cried until there wasn't a drop of water inside me; I couldn't have peed just then, or spit. I felt limp and exhausted, but the fear was gone. It would come back, I knew. I'd learn to live with it. That was what growing up was all about. Sean kept holding me, and I thought about how I'd acted and what I'd felt, and I wasn't very proud of myself.

"It's me I'm crying for," I said. "I'm so selfish. It's *me* I'm thinking about."

"I know," he said. "But it's not selfish."

"He thought I was really special. He made me believe I could do anything."

"Some fathers do that," he said, and his voice held a twist of bitterness. But I was too absorbed with my own pain to notice his.

"I'm not really special. I'm just ordinary."

"No you aren't, Peggy."

"He made me do things when I was afraid to do them. He made me go after the ball, take it off the backboard. When he was there, I knew I could do it. Now there won't be anybody who thinks I'm special."

"I do," he said.

I sat up and looked at him.

"I mean—really special. I mean, I want to do the things I dream about. I want to be a journalist. But I won't be. I'll just dream about it. It's different for boys. Boys *have* to do something. Girls don't."

"Peg, you always do what you say you're going to do. Why should you stop?"

"I do?"

"Yeah. Remember when you said it would be neat to hike through the storm sewers and I said we'd drown and there were snakes in there?"

"Yeah."

"We did it, right?"

"And I stepped on the nail."

"And I had to carry you home. And what about the time you said we were going to build a tree house and I said we were just little kids and we couldn't do it. We built one, right?"

I giggled. "And you were inside it when it fell out of the tree."

"Thank God we were short and it was only three feet off the ground."

I'd been coming back to the tree house—Sean was on guard—with two Twinkies when I saw the tree house start to tip and plunge out of the tree. Sean gave an ear-shattering howl. He thought he was dead, but he only got the wind knocked out of him and sprained his wrist. He was pretty pissed at me, even when I let him eat both the Twinkies.

"Peggy, I figure, unless they *tie* you down, nobody is going to stop you from doing what you want."

I looked up at him; his cellophane face was clear, his

eyes reflecting no guile. He wasn't lying. He saw the brave, self-reliant girl I wanted to be, not the nice, docile little Catholic lady that I suspected lived at the heart of me. I looked at myself through his eyes. Of course I would do it. Why shouldn't I?

"You're my best friend, Sean," I said.

"And you're mine."

"We'll always tell each other how great we are. You are, you know. Great."

He shook his head. "No I'm not. I don't do anything great. The only thing I do really good is—be mediocre. I'm *really* good at that." He sighed. "They'll probably put it under my picture in the yearbook. 'Sean McCaffrey, 1956. Most mediocre.'"

He said it in that way he had sometimes, of fending off something that hurt by being funny about it.

"Sean, you're not mediocre. You're really smart and you care about things and you're not a real jerk like so many boys are."

"I'm terrible at sports."

"You're not terrible. You're just—"

"Mediocre."

"Oh, who cares that you're not a dumb jock?"

"Me."

"Sean, why do you always tear yourself down? My dad always says"—I paused—"my dad always *said* that you were the cream of the crop. Those were his exact words." (I didn't mention that he always added, "God knows how he turned out to be such a sweet kid with that pompous jackass for a father.")

"He said that? About me?"

"Um hmm. And Sean, all the kids at school are really jealous when I take you to dances."

"They are?"

"Yes, they say to me, 'Peggy, Sean is such a *hunk*.'"

His lips curved up into a little smile; he looked a trifle smug.

"No, they don't say that."

"Yes they do."

"Oh Peggy," he said, and then he was kissing me and I was kissing him back and my mouth opened under his and I was pressing my body against his with a fierce sort of urgency that I had never felt before. Later, when I knew a lot more about life, I understood that I wanted his mouth and his body so much that night because they were warm and alive, and they could blot out the cold feel of my father's skin against my hand. I'd always loved kissing Sean, but for the first time that night I felt real adult passion, a flame, all through me, and I understood how a woman could want a man inside her, right inside her body, which had always seemed just a little bit revolting.

The Natural Wonder was pressing against me now, all hard and insistent, and he was moving his hips against me and I was moving right back and I must have given a moan or something, because all of a sudden we both sat bolt upright and realized what we were doing. Fifty feet away my father was lying dead inside that *place* and we were necking away. In the parking lot at the Warner E. Pumphrey Funeral Home! It was a triumph of hormones over good taste, to say the least.

"Oh Peggy, I'm sorry," Sean said, the stricken look on his face.

"Sean, it's O.K."

"I'm such a *pig*. Oh, how could I?"

"Sean—"

He looked out the window of the car. It was right under the rear window at Pumphrey's. The work room, I guessed.

"Peg, we were necking, right under the place where they, right where—"

"Start the car, Sean."

He turned on the engine, awash in guilt. He kept groveling as he drove, as if he *personally* had killed my father.

"Peg, I swear, I didn't mean to do that. Honest."

I reached over and brushed a lock of hair off his forehead, tenderly. I couldn't put into words why we had done what we had done, but I knew it was all right. My father wouldn't have minded. But I knew I couldn't make Sean understand that. He'd write it down on his list of sins and he'd confess it to Father Ryan Friday night.

"Bless me, Father, I have sinned; I—ah—Father, I got a hard-on in Pumphrey's parking lot, right under the embalming room."

And Father Ryan would yawn and give him ten Hail Marys for a penance. Sean would say fifty Hail Marys, because he'd be sure that the geographic location of this particular hard-on couldn't be washed out with ten lousy Hail Marys.

We buried my father the next day, in a spot that was green and cool and beautiful. Sean stood by my side, holding my hand, as a bugler played Taps—my father had been in the Navy during the war. I liked that. It had a mournful dignity that was just right. Before I turned to go, I put my hand on the coffin and said to him, "I hope you're flying, up there, somewhere above the clouds. I hope it's wonderful, up there, and free. I love you. I'll always love you. Thank you for being my father."

My mother told me that night she was going to take over running the business. "I can do it, Peg. I know how to keep the books. I always thought I'd be a good businesswoman."

I looked at her, surprised. There were more little lines under her eyes now, but she was as pretty as ever. She was always my happy, pretty mother. Where did this strength come from?

"You can help, Peg. We're going to be O.K., you and I. We're going to make it."

And I knew she was right. For a lot of days afterward, I waited for something to happen—for the earth to split open, the sky to darken. *Something* should happen because my father died. But it didn't. The world just went on, the way it always did. Sometimes, I'd find myself laughing, and I'd feel guilty—what right did I have to laugh, if my father was dead? But life went on. It just rolled on; people died and it didn't stop. I went on, too.

I had to.

Five

The Big Sex Talk

*B*y late October, the campaign to be immortal was lagging, Con declared. We had begun in a blaze of glory, in the truest sense of that phrase, by nearly burning the school down and proving Mother Marie Claire's total lack of fitness for sainthood. But time was flying by, and we couldn't rest on our laurels.

"The moving finger writes, and having writ moves on," Con intoned, darkly. Mollie and I swore to come up with new ideas.

But my heart wasn't in it, really. That week the father–daughter basketball game was scheduled to be played, and I was dreading the whole thing. It would be the first time my father wouldn't be there.

It had been his idea in the first place. He got the inspiration for the game freshman year, and rounded up a bunch of other fathers for it. The game wasn't really serious. The fathers knew they couldn't beat us, not with their cigarette coughs and the leg muscles atrophied from desk jobs. Nobody was into fitness then; middle-aged men were expected to be paunchy. Nobody jogged either. It would have been mortifying for any of us to have our fathers running up and down the street in little pants with stripes on them. A beer belly was a badge of maturity. So the fathers didn't try to outplay us; they just devised the most outrageous ways to cheat. The whole affair had turned into a Harlem Globetrotters performance. Last year, the fathers even brought in a live mule to stand on so they could climb up on his back and drop the ball in the basket. Everybody roared when the mule went to the bathroom, right on the gym floor. The game had become a tradition, and all the kids in the school came out for it.

Last year my father pulled a stunt that broke everybody up. He pretended to have a fit and collapse on the court, and three other fathers, dressed in hospital whites, ran in and carried him out on a stretcher. I just laughed and laughed at the time.

The night of the game finally came around, and I pulled on my gym suit and my sneakers and went over to the gym. I played, but the whole thing didn't seem real; I felt as if I was watching myself and everyone else and I was in two places at once. I had a smile frozen on my lips. After a while I lost all the feeling in my face and I thought that if I got hit in the face by a stray pass, my face would just shatter like a vase and fall in little hard pieces on the floor. Everybody was real nice to me, especially the fathers, and that just made it worse. The game just went on and on and I wished it would stop. Finally it did.

Afterward, I got in the Caddy with Sean and he said, "Let's go park," and I said I didn't feel like necking.

"We don't have to neck. I just want to be with you."

We parked, and I sat quietly for a while and Sean put his arms around me. Finally I said, "I hate God."

"You don't mean that," he said.

"Yes I do. How can I pray to somebody who took my father away? Who lets killers and rapists and communists live and kills my father."

"I don't think God did it."

"Then who did it? President Eisenhower?"

"No," he said.

"If I was God, I wouldn't be so rotten as to take my

64

father away. How can I believe in a God who isn't as kind as I am. It doesn't make sense."

"I thought about that a lot when your dad died," Sean said. Sean was a thinker; he liked to sit, for hours sometimes, just turning an idea over and over in his mind, looking at it all different ways, until finally, things fell into place. "And I think maybe God doesn't *do* a lot. I think he set up the rules, and once He did that, even He can't break them."

"He can do everything."

"No he can't. God can't make a stone so big He can't lift it. That's impossible. Even God can't exist and not exist at the same time. He made the rules of nature, and can't break them."

"So He just—watches?"

"Maybe. He doesn't want bad things to happen, but He knows they have to. Maybe the universe can't exist without bad things to balance the good things. So He has to let them both happen."

"Sean, that means you don't believe in—miracles and things. The Blessed Mother appearing to St. Bernadette and to the children at Fatima." (It always seemed to me that the B.V.M. got to make all the appearances, as if she were God's emcee.)

"No," he said, "I don't believe it."

"Holy shit, and you're going to be a priest!"

He nodded.

"What's the point of praying, then, to some God who doesn't do anything?"

"Maybe just to get the strength so we can do things. Maybe just to touch him, to know he's there, that life isn't just—meaningless."

It's strange, but after that night I felt a lot better about God. Maybe He was just as sorry as I was that my father died.

I sat quietly beside Sean, and he just held me and

stroked my hair, and while I didn't feel safe the way I used to before my father died—I'd never feel that way again—I felt peaceful. I'll always be grateful to Sean for giving God back to me. It wasn't the old God, the child's God who hovered above my bed at night like a silver fog, keeping me safe from demons, but one I could accept when I came to understand that life is a complicated affair, full of twists and turns, and unfathomable mysteries.

With my anger at God muted, I could get my mind back to the business of being brilliant and daring. But it was Con, of course, who came up with the idea of our next leap for glory. Not surprisingly, it had to do with another saint.

We lived in a world that was just choc-a-bloc with saints. We had Holy Cards with their pictures on them, read books about their lives, saw movies (albeit rotten ones) about them. If you went to a Catholic school, you got the idea that saints proliferated like jackrabbits. I wouldn't have been surprised to run into one of them shopping at the Hecht Company, or riding the bus, or just crossing the street. I'd know him or her by the little golden halo floating an inch or so over the top of the sainted head, and by the expression. It would be either the sour-ball swallow like St. Theresa, or sort of a goofy Mona Lisa grin. Martyrs had that one a lot. Probably because they knew they were just moments away from heaven, just as soon as somebody stopped flogging or stabbing or burning them—more precisely, as soon as they expired from said activities—ZAP!—they'd be saints.

Con decided that she was thoroughly sick of saints. They were boring, she said, especially the big favorite of the moment, Maria Goretti. She was an Italian teenager who was raped and murdered by a handyman but forgave her murderer with her dying breath.

"People get raped every day, and they don't make them saints," Con reasoned. "Somebody should have taught that kid a few judo holds."

She was right, of course. It was only years later that I realized that the saints who were in vogue then were perfectly suited to the docile, subservient image of woman peculiar to the era. The feistier saints—scholars, rebels, warriors—took a back seat to St. Theresa, who stayed in a convent and prayed for fifty years, and St. Maria Goretti, who got raped.

The male saints were a little bit more interesting, but even their lives paled because of repetition. How many times can you listen with fascination to the yarn about St. Christopher, who was about to cross a stream when he saw a young child standing by the edge of the stream, hitching a ride.

St. Christopher lifted the tiny child on his back and started across the deep stream. But the child kept getting heavier and heavier, until Chris was staggering to his knees.

How can such a small child be so heavy? he wondered, and the Christ Child said, "It is because I carry the sins of the world on my shoulders."

Con wanted to do St. Christopher in the regular "Saints Corner" we ran in the *Messenger*, but with a zippier ending. She wanted to have Chris staggering and staggering, and finally, getting fed up with the whole thing, tossing the Christ Child in the drink and yelling, "Backstroke!"

We knew we'd never get away with that one, of course. But we had to do something about Saints Corner. It was a point of honor. We'd try to dump it, because it was terminally boring and nobody read it, but Sister Robert decreed that no issue of the *Messenger* would roll off the presses saintless.

Con came into the *Messenger* room the first week of November with a Saints Corner she'd written herself. That was unusual, because we usually fobbed off the sainthood beat on some lowly freshman.

"Who is it?" I asked.

"St. Leon of Skorytt."

"Who's he?"

Con told his story. He lived in a small Slavic province in the fourteenth century. A feudal landlord had stolen all the land that belonged to the peasants and he had even forbidden them to pray in their little village church. St. Leon, a man of humble birth himself, rallied his people with a fiery speech: "The more openly this despotism proclaims gain to be its aim and end, the more hateful and the more embittering it is," he cried. "But the landlord has forged the weapons that will bring death to himself; he has called into being the men who are to wield those weapons. Men of Skorytt, attack! You have naught to lose but the fetters that bind you!"

St. Leon led the people in revolt, and when they had won, his property was divided equally, according to the teachings of Christ. This being done, they lived in peace for a while, but then the people began to squabble among themselves. St. Leon tried to make peace, but was killed by one of his former allies, who smacked him in the head with an ax.

"That's pretty interesting," I said. "Where did you dig him up?"

"I didn't dig him up," Con said. "I made him up."

"Holy shit! You *invented* a saint. Fantastic!"

Con smiled. "That is not the half of it," she said. "Look at the name of the village. Familiar?"

"Sure," I said, "Everybody knows Skorytt. There's 'April in Skorytt.' Or how about 'The Last Time I Saw Skorytt'—"

"Look hard. The letters. Try rearranging the letters."

I tried, but I drew a blank. Con wrote it out for me.

"Oh my God!" I said.

She grinned triumphantly.

"Leon Trotsky. You made a saint out of Leon Trotsky!"

"The commie saint," she said. "Recognize the speech?"

I read it over. "Con, you didn't!"

"*The Communist Manifesto*. Practically word for word."

"Oh Con, you're right; we're going to be fucking *immortal!*"

The Sunday after the *Messenger* with St. Leon in it came out, Sean and I went together, as usual, to 12:15 Mass and slid into the rear pew, hoping nobody would notice we were late for Mass again. It was Father Ryan, who could usually be counted on to wrap things up in forty minutes, sermon and all.

I generally dozed or daydreamed through Father Ryan's sermons—William Jennings Bryan he wasn't. He'd usually pick some scriptural passage and babble on for fifteen minutes until he got to the important part of the Mass, passing the collection basket around.

Father Ryan walked to the pulpit, and as my eyelids dropped low and I prepared to doze off, he said, "For my sermon today I am indebted to our fine girls' Catholic high school, Immaculate Heart, and to the school newspaper, the *Marian Messenger*.

My eyelids popped up like a broken window shade.

"This issue features an article on a saint from whom we can learn many things."

"Oh shit!" I said, sotto voce. Sean looked at me. I was not usually foul-mouthed in church.

"A man of God, a man of the Church, who speaks to us over the ages from a small medieval province in the fourteenth century."

I put my hands to my mouth to keep the giggle from escaping. Sean looked at me.

"You're up to something," he said.

I nodded, still trying not to laugh.

"St. Leon of Skorytt," Father Ryan intoned.

"Who the hell is he?" Sean asked.

"What?"

"St. Leon. Who is he?"

69

"Con made him up."

"*What!*"

Heads turn our way.

"Shh! We're in church!"

"What do you mean, made him up?" Sean whispered.

"Con got tired of the old saints, so she made up a new one."

"Oh Jeez," Sean said, and he started to giggle too, and he buried his head in his missal so no one would notice.

Father Ryan told St. Leon's story, quoting verbatim from Con's article. He even read the stirring speech to the peasants: "You have naught to lose but the fetters that bind you!"

Sean looked at me suspiciously. I knew what he was thinking. I had typed his junior history paper for him, "The Rise of the Godless Communist State."

"And for his efforts to bring peace," Father Ryan said, this holy man was brutally murdered. Felled by his former comrades in arms, by a vicious blow to his head with an ax."

Sean stared at me, his mouth agape. "Leon Trotsky! It's Leon *Trotsky!*"

"Shhh!" I said, pressing my lips together.

Sean's head went down into his missal again; I heard little choking sounds and then he suddenly slipped from the pew and ran out of the church.

Mrs. Petersen, sitting next to me, stared and I whispered, "He's coming down with the flu," and I left too by the back door. I found Sean collapsed with laughter on the steps.

"You're going to *do* it," he said. You're going to go down as the greatest *Messenger* staff in history. Leon Trotsky. Jesus, Mary, and Joseph—Leon *Trotsky!*"

Father Ryan was so impressed with St. Leon that he announced he was sending the *Messenger* piece to the *Catholic Herald*, asking them to reprint it. That caused a quick emergency meeting in the *Messenger* room.

"What do they do to people who invent a saint?" Mollie asked.

"They have this rack," Con said, "and they keep turning it and turning it until you look like a pretzel."

"They don't do that anymore," I said.

"For us, they'll bring it out of mothballs," Con said. "The *Marian Messenger* at Immaculate Heart High School will single-handedly bring back the Inquisition."

We sweated like mad for a while, but nothing showed up in the *Catholic Herald*, and that made us giddy with relief, and triumph. We were pulling it off! We were golden! Everything we touched was magic. Con announced that she was starting a journal, a historical document so that our deeds would live forever. We would set the standard. No one would match us, ever. But we had to go forward. *Excelsior* was our motto. We had to climb higher.

"We're going to get a boy into the Big Sex Talk!" Con announced.

Each year, before Thanksgiving, the whole school went on retreat; classes were cancelled for two days, and we spent our time praying, meditating, and going to special assemblies. The grand finale of the retreat was the assembly on Christian Marriage, known to the student body as the Big Sex Talk.

The Big Sex Talk was usually given by Father Thomas Milliken, a small, diffident man who referred to screwing as "The Marriage Act" and who liked to tell little stories to illustrate his point. His big finish was the one about Catholic couple, John and Mary. It went like this: Catholic girl Mary goes out with Catholic boy John, and they fall in love on the first date. He wants to kiss her good night at the front door, and she *really* wants to kiss him back, but she sees the shadow of the Holy Spirit overhead, and she draws back and says, "I am a child of Mary."

And John goes away and joins the Foreign Legion. He doesn't see Mary for five years. Mary is sure she's lost her true love. But then one day, John appears on her doorstep and asks her out again. Once again, she really, *really* wants to kiss him good night, but guess who flutters overhead? Right. The old reliable Holy Ghost. So Mary steps back again and says, "I am a child of Mary!"

And John embraces her chastely and says, "Thank God! I was testing you! If you had kissed me, I would have gone away forever. But now I know you are the woman I want to be my wife and the mother of my children!"

Of course, we all wondered how this red-hot couple was ever going to produce any kids. By the time they worked their way up to it, they'd be in Holy Family retirement home.

"How can we get a boy into the Big Sex Talk?" I asked Con. "Hide him in the heating ducts?"

"No, we'll dress him up as a girl. Get him a uniform, the works. It'll be a gas!"

"Just which boy did you have in mind?" I asked. I thought I knew the answer.

"Sean's already said he'd do it."

I thought a stunt like that would appeal to Sean's sense of the absurd. Sean had certainly been busting out senior year; the zany side of his personality had all but eclipsed the moody, mystical side. I wondered if Sean wasn't trying to pack a whole lifetime of silliness into the months before the door of childhood closed on him so inexorably. The rest of us had a bit more time to act like kids—if not to be them. The boundaries of childhood were more elastic with us. Sean, as a priest, had to be sober and good, had to set an example for all of us who were not in a special relationship with God. A priest had to act with dignity—he couldn't crack up and horse around; a priest who did that would surely be a scandal to the laity. When he was a priest, Sean couldn't ever be crazy again.

It was easy enough getting Sean into Immaculate Heart. Kids from Sacred Heart were in and out all the time, delivering messages. We just got Sean a courier pass and when he came in the front door, we hustled him upstairs to the *Messenger* room. We had everything in readiness. Con locked the door and Mollie pulled a shopping bag out from under the table.

"Strip down to your shorts," Con ordered.

"Here?"

"Well, you certainly can't do it in the girls' john."

Mollie pointed to St. Theresa. "If she can hang out in her bra, you can stand around in your shorts," she said.

"What the hell," Sean shrugged, and he peeled of his clothes, until he was standing there in only his socks and his jockey shorts. I tried, dutifully, not to stare at a bulge in a strategic spot.

Con gave Sean an appraising look. All that weight-lifting he had done junior year had broadened his shoulders and developed the musculature of his torso. He was lean, but well formed. He straightened his shoulders and let his muscles ripple, showing off shamelessly, I thought.

"This is a first!" Con exhulted. "A naked man in the *Messenger* room!"

"I am *not* naked."

"Well, almost."

"O.K., if you *really* want something for your journal," he said, and hooked his thumbs in the waistband of his shorts.

"Don't you *dare!*" I gasped. Even Con seemed thrown off balance a little.

"Flashing in front of the Little Flower is a No-No," Mollie said.

Sean looked at me, and he had that impish grin I knew so well on his face.

"Course, it's nothing new to Peg," he said.

Mollie and Con stared at me. I felt myself turning eight shades of red.

"We played doctor," I explained.

Con raised an eyebrow.

"We were five years old, for heaven's sakes!"

"O.K., let's get the show on the road," Mollie said. She reached into the bag, pulled out a bra, and strapped it onto Sean's chest. The cups hung loosely against his skin.

"We've got to pad him," Con said.

"If I'm going to have bazooms, I want big ones," he said.

"Like father, like son," I muttered.

"Stuff him with Kleenex," Con ordered. We rolled up balls of Kleenex and stuffed them into Sean's bra until he started to look like Jayne Mansfield.

When we had him finished, I stepped back to look and burst out laughing. The Kleenex-stuffed bra, against Sean's hairy chest, was the most ridiculous thing I'd ever seen. Sean grinned and struck a pin-up pose. "Eat your heart out, Betty Grable!" he said.

"God, Sean, if I didn't know you were such a straight arrow, I'd say you were a born transvestite," Con said.

"A what?"

"Transvestite. Guys who like to dress up in women's clothes. They have whole shows full of them in Paris. Guys wear gowns and furs and sing and dance."

"That's weird," Sean said.

"Well, Sean, if you're going to be a priest, it could be a big money saver," Con said. "You could be Father McCaffrey in the morning and Mother Superior in the afternoon."

"Ho, ho, ho," Sean said. "Where's the dress?"

With a lot of struggling, we finally got the uniform dress on Sean. It was a bit tight in the shoulders, but otherwise it fit O.K. Mollie got out the black curly wig the drama club had used for *Charley's Aunt*, and I put it on Sean's head and combed the curls into place. Then I put on a touch of lipstick and rouge (we weren't supposed to wear any makeup except clear pink lipstick, but everybody did) and I told him to look at the ceiling while I put eyeliner under his eyes.

When I stepped back to appraise my work, I was astonished. Sean, as a girl, was a knockout. With his even features, those green eyes, and the long, silky eyelashes, he was actually beautiful.

"You're gorgeous!" I said.

"Lemee see." I handed him the mirror. "Not bad," he said. "I think I will ask myself to the prom."

"That's really depressing," I moaned. "I go out with a guy that's prettier than I am."

"There's only one problem," Con said. "Get a load of those legs."

We looked. Sean certainly wasn't very feminine from the knees down.

"My God, Sean, you look like King Kong," Con said.

"Can I help it if I'm hairy? Everybody in my family is hairy."

"We'll have to shave his legs," Mollie said.

"Oh no you don't. Nobody's shaving my legs. People will call me a fairy."

"Sean, you'll give the whole thing away with those legs."

"Nobody gets near me with a razor."

"I got an idea," Mollie said. She disappeared for a few minutes, and came back with a pair of knee socks. "I had to promise to do Sally Gimbel's math homework for a week to get these," she said.

Sean pulled on the knee socks, and we gave him Mary Mulloy's extra pair of oxfords—she wore size thirteen and had to get them specially ordered.

"You look great, Sean," Con said. "Just follow us and for God's sakes, don't cross your legs."

The Big Sex Talk was scheduled for two o'clock, and by the time we came into the auditorium most of the students had already assembled. Con, Mollie, Sean, and I took seats in the back row. Some of the girls turned to stare at Sean, who seemed utterly cool and calm.

"You're too damn pretty," I said. "They're jealous."

He reached over and pinched my thigh. "Lesbe friends!"

"Sean, cut that out!"

He chuckled. He was really getting into the spirit of the thing. If we could pull this one off, immortality was within our grasp.

We sat there waiting for Father Milliken to come out, but we got a big surprise. Father Milliken wasn't going to give the Big Sex Talk. Instead, it was to be Mr. Ralph Kasten, the author of a book called *Straight Talk for Teens*.

Sister Robert Mary walked out onto the stage with Mr. Kasten, a rather short, squat man with dark hair and glasses. I didn't like him right away, because he looked like Joe McCarthy.

Sister Robert Mary left the hall—the nuns never stayed for the Big Sex Talk—and Mr. Kasten started in. He rambled on for a while about the sanctity of Christian marriage, and I yawned, thinking he was going to be even duller than Father Milliken. But then he said, "Girls, I want to be frank with you about men. They have animal instincts. Men are animals."

That perked us all up, especially Sean. He growled like a bear. I hit him. "Shut up!" I hissed.

"Men have these chemicals inside them, chemicals that drive them, forces they cannot control," Mr. Kasten said. "And these drives can be for the good. It is why men are sea captains and architects and pilots and women are not. Women don't have these same drives, not as intensely," he said. "But these same forces that enable men to create civilization can also turn them into brutes. As women, it is your duty to control these drives, to keep them in the confines of Christian marriage.

"Inside marriage, these drives are good. They propagate the race. And as Catholic wives, you must submit to these drives. I must warn you of them, for some girls weep or faint when they first encounter the male drive. On your wedding night, the man you thought you knew will be another person. He will rip the nightgown from your body. He will seem like an animal, but he cannot help himself. It is all part of God's plan, because it will enable him to place inside your body the seed of another life. Women are vessels to carry the male seed, which is called sperm, until a new human life emerges."

I looked at Sean. If I married him, would he rip the nightgown off my body in a frenzy of animal lust? I began to feel a little tingly in a place where I shouldn't. Mr. Kasten sure had Father Milliken beat by a country mile.

Sean looked at me and the impish grin was back on his face. When nobody was looking, he leaned over and bit my earlobe.

"Ouch!"

"I can't help it; I'm just an animal!"

I giggled and Con jabbed me in the ribs.

Then Mr. Kasten went on to tell us that we girls were responsible if boys sinned, and he ran through the familiar list of No-Nos: don't ever sit on a boy's lap, no tongue kissing, no parking, no sleeveless dresses, no open-toed shoes (that was a new one), no touching below the neck. And Mr. Kasten said he would be happy to see girls for individual conferences in the teachers' room.

After that, the sophomore class put on a skit, yet another saga of the thrilling life of Mother Marie Claire, and then the girls started to leave the auditorium.

"Peg, I have to pee," Sean said.

"Can't you hold it?"

"No, I really can't."

"O.K., come on."

I walked with him to the girls' john in the corridor outside the auditorium and checked to see if it was empty.

"O.K., all clear."

Sean went into the bathroom and I stood guard outside

the door. Just then Sister Robert Mary turned the corner and saw me.

"Oh Peggy, will you do me a favor, please?"

"Uh, yes Sister."

"Take this note up to Sister Claudine for me."

I took the note and hurried off. I knew I'd never make it back before Sean came out. He was a fast pee-er.

I was right. When Sean came out of the bathroom (he told me later) he felt a stab of panic because I wasn't there. He figured he'd just go on up to the *Messenger* room, but as he was walking down the corridor, he felt a thin, bony hand grasp his shoulder. He jumped and let out a gasp. It was Sister Justinian, and no wonder he jumped. She had fingers like talons, and when she got you in that special shoulder grab of hers, you felt as if you had been carried off by some prehistoric bird and were about to be eaten alive.

"Why are you out of class?" she demanded.

"Uh, Sister, I—" Sean stammered.

Then Sister Justinian relaxed her grip. "Oh, you must be going for a conference with Mr. Kasten."

"Yes, Sister," Sean said with relief, "that's where I'm going."

"Come along, then," she said, and Sean found himself being propelled down the hall by Sister Justinian's sinewy hand.

"Not many girls are coming for conferences," she said. "That is impolite, with Mr. Kasten generously donating so much of his time."

She didn't know it, and neither did Sean, but nobody was coming because the word was already out on Mr. Kasten. Victoria Grabowski went for a conference, and she said he asked her all sorts of questions about what she did with her boyfriend.

"He even asked me if my boyfriend put his hand under my blouse," she said. "Father Milliken never asked anything like that. Not even in *Confession*!"

Sean and Sister Justinian got to the door of the teachers' room, and Sister Justinian just stood there, her eyes glittering like a bird of prey. Sean prayed that she would go away, but she didn't and Sean knew he was trapped. There was nothing he could do but go in.

"Hello," said Mr. Kasten as Sean entered. He was sitting on the couch in the corner, and he beckoned for Sean to come sit down beside him.

"What's your name, young lady?"

"Shirley," said Sean.

"Well, Shirley, do you want some Straight Talk for Teens?"

"Yes, sir."

"Now, what is your problem?

"My problem?"

"These things are hard to talk about sometimes, but you can relax with me." He gave a hearty chuckle. "I've heard it all."

"You have?"

"Oh yes. So you see, there's nothing to be ashamed of. Just feel free to tell me everything."

"Well, I, uh—"

"It's your boyfriend, right?"

"Yes, sir, it's my boyfriend."

"What's his name?"

"Sean."

"Do you love him?"

"Oh yes, sir. More than anybody else in the world."

"Sean. A nice Catholic name. But he too has drives, isn't that so, Shirley?"

"Yes, sir, he sure does."

"And he is pressuring you to do things? Things you don't want to do?"

"Uh, well—"

"Sexual things. Let's. Let's have some Straight Talk for Teens."

79

"Yes, sir."

"Now what does he want you to do?"

"Well, he, uh, wants me to neck."

"And does he want to touch you improperly, Shirley?"

"Yeah, that's right."

"Well, that's understandable, Shirley. Boys have drives. And you are a very beautiful young woman."

"I am?"

"Oh yes. Beautiful women carry a special cross. They ignite the passions of men the way their plainer sisters never do."

"Oh," Sean said.

"May I ask you a personal question, Shirley?"

"Sure."

"Did you develop early?"

"Develop?"

"Yes. You are quite—developed, you know. And girls who are developed have a special obligation to help keep men pure."

Sean stared down at his Kleenex-stuffed chest.

"Sir, I just developed—fairly recently," he said.

"Ah," said Mr. Kasten. Sean looked at Mr. Kasten's ruddy face, and noticed that the man seemed to be starting to sweat.

"Now tell me, Shirley, just what it is that your boy-friend wants you to do?"

"Feel me up," Sean said.

"I see. *Exactly* what does that mean to you?"

"Well, you know, touch me."

"Where?"

"Here," said Sean, pointing to his chest.

"And does he unbutton your blouse?"

"Uh, yeah, sometimes."

"Now, Shirley, do you understand what such touching does to a young man physically?"

"I have a good idea," Sean said.

80

"It causes a rush of blood to his organ. You know what I am talking about?"

"Yes, sir."

"And it releases a force in him which he cannot resist. You must resist for him, see that his body remains a temple of the Holy Spirit."

"Yes, sir."

Mr. Kasten, Sean noticed, had moved closer to him on the couch.

"You certainly are a pretty girl, Shirley. Do you know, I think you are the prettiest girl I have seen at Immaculate Heart High School."

"Oh, I don't think so, sir."

"Yes, oh yes, no question about it. Now, what else does your boyfriend do, Shirley?"

"Well—"

"I understand how hard this is. I will help you, with Straight Talk." Mr. Kasten reached out a sweaty paw and patted Sean's hand. "Does he put his hand under your panties?"

"Uh—"

"You can be frank with me, Shirley. I'm here to help."

"Well, yes sir, sometimes." Sean tried to edge further away from Mr. Kasten, but he found himself wedged against the arm of the couch. Mr. Kasten seemed to be inching closer and closer.

"What does he do then?"

"Do? Well, you know."

"Please tell me exactly, Shirley. I have to know so I can help you."

"Well, he sort of plays around."

"Does he ever try to insert his fingers into your sexual aperture, Shirley?"

At this point, Sean told me, an evil spirit must have taken possession of him totally. He looked at the beads of sweat on Mr. Kasten's lip, and the bulge that had grown in the crotch of his pants, and Mr. Kasten looked so utterly ridiculous that Sean couldn't resist jerking his chain, like he always did to his father.

"Yes, sir, he sure does."

"How many?"

"Ten."

"Ten?"

"Oh yeah, he gets 'em right up there, both hands. And the other stuff, too."

"Other stuff?"

"Oh yeah. Hairbrushes, playing cards, Coke bottles. Even once, a monkey wrench."

"A wrench! Shirley, do you allow him to perform these perversions on you?"

"I wasn't crazy about the wrench. All the motorcycle grease, you know. He sort of kept turning it around and around."

"Good God!"

"I liked the Coke. It tickled, you know it's all fizzy."

"There was *Coke* in the bottle?"

"Yeah, Coke is very clean. Kills germs. They used to use it for cough medicine."

"Shirley, did you take *pleasure* in these things?" Mr. Kasten was breathing real fast.

"The garden hose was not great. I liked the banana."

"Shirley, my child, you need help! Let me help you!" And Mr. Kasten planted his hand on Sean's thigh.

Jeez, Sean thought to himself, what have I gone and done?

"Mr. Kasten, I think I have to go now."

Mr. Kasten was breathing faster, and his hand moved up another inch on Sean's thigh.

"You need my help more than any girl I have ever met, Shirley," he said. "We must have more conferences. Now, what else has this beast made you do?"

"More girls are waiting," Sean said, nervously.

"Oh Shirley!" Mr. Kasten moaned; he made a grab, and his hand landed squarely on Sean's scrotum. Sean let out a yell, and leaped off the couch, and Mr. Kasten's jaw fell practically to his knees; and he stared at Sean, not able to utter a word.

"You've been a big help, Mr. Kasten," Sean said, backing toward the door. "I'm going to be a temple of the Holy Ghost from now on, I promise!" he said.

"Shirley!" Mr. Kasten called out with a strangled cry as Sean ran out of the teachers' room and made it up the stairs two at a time. He banged on the door of the *Messenger* room; we opened it and he came running in and dropped in a chair, out of breath. He took a deep gulp of air, and exhaled, slowly.

"Where in God's name were you?" Con asked. "We thought the nuns had grabbed you!"

"Worse than that," he said. "The author of *Straight Talk for Teens* just copped a feel."

"What!"

"When you weren't there," he said to me, "Sister Justinian grabbed me and made me go to a conference with Mr. Kasten."

"And he tried to *touch* you?" I said.

"Not tried. Did."

"You mean he grabbed your boobs?" Con said, astounded.

"Nope. He went right for the Big V."

"Jesus, Mary, and Joseph!" Con said.

"He got more than he bargained for," Sean said. "You should have seen his face when he grabbed me, right by the balls."

"My God, the man is a *pervert*!" I said.

"He can't go around to high schools feeling people up!" Mollie said.

"He sure is a strange one," Sean said.

"We have to do something," I said.

"What?" Con said. "We can't very well march down to Sister Robert Mary and tell him Mr. Kasten just felt this girl up, only it wasn't a girl, it was Sean in drag."

"Look, we've got to stop this sex fiend," I said. "I grabbed Con by the hand. "Come on."

We caught up with Mr. Kasten just as he was walking down the front hall to the door. He seemed to be in something of a hurry.

"Mr. Kasten, we're the editors of the *Messenger*, and we'd like to thank you for coming," I said.

Mr. Kasten didn't break his stride. "Thank you, girls," he said.

"Yes, I said, "Our friend Shirley said you were such a *wonderful* help!"

"Shirley?" Mr. Kasten said. He blinked.

"Yes, she's going to write a letter to the archbishop telling how helpful you were," Con said.

"Maybe to the cardinal," I said.

"The *pope!*" Con said, cheerfully.

Mr. Kasten took one look at us and practically flew out the front door.

The next week, Sacred Heart had its retreat, and all the boys were excited about the Big Sex Talk, to be given by the author of *Straight Talk for Teens*. But at the last minute it was announced that Mr. Kasten wasn't coming. He was too busy with his new book to do any more lectures at high schools. So poor old Father Milliken was dragged out of retirement. Sean went to the assembly, and he reported that when Father Milliken got to his big show-stopping story—"You are the woman I choose to marry and have my children!"—half the school was asleep.

SIX

Naval Operations

The year was going too fast. It was already time for the Thanksgiving dance, The Turkey Trot. I had asked Sean to be my date. Actually, I hadn't asked him; we just started talking about it as if he assumed he was going with me, and so did I. I was trying to get things sorted out in my head about me and Sean. Not as Best Friends, we would always be that, but the boyfriend–girlfriend stuff. We were back to the old Illuminated Map of Sin rules—with a few new twists—because we were both pretty scared about what happened that night in the parking lot. I didn't used to believe the stuff the nuns handed out about being swept away by carnal passion, but I had to admit there was something to it. We weren't just kissing that night; Sean had his tongue right up against my tonsils and the Natural Wonder right up against my you know what and we were right on the verge of getting swept away. We knew we had to be careful. Sean was better at that than I was. I tried, but I kept forgetting.

One night, when we were out in the Caddy, we were taking a break from kissing and Sean was stretched out on the back seat and I was lying on top of him, very comfy, my head resting on his chest. I started kissing the nice soft spot in the hollow of his neck, and he sighed, and then I guess I started moving a little. I didn't mean to, but all of a sudden there it was, the old Natural Wonder, pressing against my jeans. I just kept moving and Sean said, sternly, "Peg!"

"Umm."

"Stop *moving*."

"I wasn't. I was just trying to get comfortable."

"Well, stop."

I stopped, immediately. "Can I just lie here, like this?"

"I guess that's O.K. See, I can control myself if you stay still, but if you move around, I can't."

"O.K. I'll be real still." And I just nestled against him, liking the feeling of that pressure in a certain spot, just letting it make me feel tingly.

"Is this nice?" I asked.

"Oh yes," he said. "It really is."

He gave a little sigh, and then another, and we just rested that way for a bit. But then something was moving up against me, and it wasn't me moving this time.

"Sean?" I said.

He didn't stop. He just kept moving, and his eyes were closed.

"Ohhhhhh," he said. "Ohhhhh!"

"Sean!"

His eyes popped open. "Oh shit!" he said, and he scrambled up and jumped out of the car, dropped on his face and started doing push-ups. He did thirty-five of them, very fast, and when he got up he was sweaty, but the Natural Wonder was back down again.

"Jeez, that was a close one!" he said. "I don't know, I think my self-control is going all to hell. I used to be pretty good at it."

"Oh Sean," I sighed, "sometimes I wish we weren't Catholic. It's so *hard*."

"Well, we are. We just have to be better than other people because we have informed consciences."

"I guess so," I said. I thought of all those Protestants at Hoover High who could just grope each other in the back seats of cars without a care in the world. It didn't seem fair.

"Come on," he said, "I got a civics midterm tomorrow."

"I'd rather stay here."

"So would I, Peggy, but look"—and at this point his voice sounded a little plaintive—"I think I've exercised all the self-control I can for one night."

"I'm sorry, Sean. I guess it's harder for guys than it is for girls."

He looked at me. "Is it *hard* for you, Peg? I mean, when I kiss you, does it, does it—"

"Oh yeah, drives me crazy," I said. "I just don't have any self-control at all when you kiss me, so I'm glad you're strong."

He grinned at me. "Like really wild? Like you can't help yourself?"

I nodded. "Only with you, Sean. No other guy affects me like that."

He sat up a little straighter, and he looked smug, and I'd swear he was preening a little bit. He said, solemnly, "You are just very lucky, Peg, that it's *me* who drives you crazy. Because I won't ever take advantage even though you can't resist me."

"Thanks a bunch, Sean."

He grinned again. "Even if you come at me and start tearing my clothes off, crazed with lust—"

"Crazed with lust? Did you say, 'Crazed with lust'?"

"Yeah. That's what Brother Peter says, all the time."

"In school he says this?"

"Oh yeah. He says it's what happens to guys who— uh—jerk off, you know." He says they go crazy."

"Crazy? Like insane?"

"Yeah. Bonkers."

I felt a sudden cold chill, right around my heart. Could that happen to *girls*? "You think it's true?" I asked.

He looked thoughtful. "I don't think so. I looked it up in a medical book and it said that it was just natural and you wouldn't go crazy. 'Course, it's a sin, but it doesn't make you nutso."

"Well, that's a relief."

"It is?"

I was glad it was dark so he wouldn't see that my face was beet red.

"Well, I'd just hate to think of all those poor Catholic boys going bonkers. Just for—you know."

"Yeah, it's probably no fun being crazy."

I really wanted to ask Sean if he ever did it, but I'd be too mortified to say any such thing. When we were little, we used to like to watch each other pee. We did it way deep in the woods, because we figured that would really make Dr. McCaffrey foam at the mouth. It was fun, and very naughty. Once, we peed on the same anthill and drowned a whole colony of ants, but we felt like murderers afterward and never peed on sentient beings again—except an old, slow-moving box turtle, and we didn't hurt him, just sort of gave him a shower. As we got a little older, Sean got embarrassed about it, and he'd tell me not to watch when he'd go behind a tree. I did, anyhow. That was one of the problems of growing up, you couldn't do some of the fun things you did as a kid. Grown-ups didn't go around peeing on things together, and I felt that was a great loss. There probably would be fewer murders and wars and stuff if they did.

He kissed me good night at the door, not the old quickie like he used to, but a long, lingering, tingly kind of kiss. I just wished he wouldn't stop. I'd gotten to the point where I wasn't even interested in kissing anybody else anymore, and I used to be. I used to look at guys and speculate about how they'd kiss, and I'd have them rated in my head, from Nauseating to Divine. I wondered if you could get addicted to kissing one person, so that nobody else would do. That could really be a problem since Sean was going to be a priest. What if I found out that I was hooked on his kisses, the way some people get strung out on heroin? I'd have to follow him around everywhere he went, to get my daily fix; I'd have to hide behind the water font in the sacristy and spring out at him when he came in from the rectory to say six o'clock Mass, kissing him madly while he put on his alb and his chasuble. He'd get sick of that pretty quick:

"Kiss me! Kiss me, Father, I got to have my fix!"

"Get away from me, you disgusting junkie!"

"Please, just this once! I promise, after this, I'll go cold turkey."

"Don't you have any pride?"

"Oh God, just one smackeroo. Please, Sean, don't make me beg!"

"Oh, all right. But if you're here again after the eleven o'clock Mass, I'll have you thrown out on your ear."

"Oh bless you, Father! Now pucker up!"

Con was on my back all the time about my dating Sean.

"How long have you been going out with him?"

"Since we were freshman. But I met him when I was two."

"Peg, why don't you go out with other guys?"

"I do."

"How many?"

"Three."

"How many times?"

"Once. Each."

"What are you afraid of?"

"Me? I'm not afraid of anything."

"I think you're afraid of men. I think you're repressed."

Con was always quoting Sigmund Freud, whom I'd never heard of before I met her. One day in junior year Sister Justinian mentioned him; she said *he* said that children had dirty sex thoughts and so of course he was a pervert. And an atheist. But Con was very high on Freud.

"Peggy," she said darkly," you may even be frigid!"

"I don't think I'm frigid," I said. "I like kissing Sean a whole lot."

"That's no sign. A lot of frigid people like to kiss."

"They do?"

"Yes, but then when they get to the real thing, their muscles get all tense and they get paralyzed."

"You mean really paralyzed? Like can't move?"

"Yes. Sometimes they just stay that way for years and years. When you get like that they put you in the frigid ward in the hospital, and they have to feed you with tubes."

"How do you get better?"

"You have to have an orgasm. But that's hard to do when you're paralyzed and have tubes up your nose."

"I guess so."

"There are men in the hospital, too," Con said. "But they have castration anxiety."

"What's that?"

"Remember when Delilah cut Samson's hair and he lost his strength? That's why they have castration anxiety."

"They're afraid of haircuts?"

"No, of course not." Con gave me one of those exasperated looks. "Hair is just a symbol for a penis. The whole story is about the fact that men are afraid women will take their penises away."

"Sister Justinian never said anything about that in Bible History."

"Sister Justinian doesn't know about it. That's probably a good thing."

I agreed. Sister Justinian was certainly the type of person who'd take some poor guy's penis. Heck, she'd do it just for talking in study hall.

"Sister Justinian gives *me* castration anxiety, and I don't even have a penis," Con said. "See, men have castration anxiety because women have penis envy."

"What's that?"

"It's when women want to have penises, of course."

"I don't think I'd want one. I mean, they're nice and all, but what would I *do* with it?"

"Go around sticking it into people, I suppose. That's what it's *for*."

"Well, I don't think I have penis envy. What happens to the men who get castration anxiety? Do they get put in the frigid ward too?"

"With the women? Of course not. Then they'd be really anxious, because they'd be scared the women would creep over at night and steal their penises."

"But if the women were paralyzed with tubes up their noses, how could they do it?"

"Well, they couldn't, of course. But the men would *worry*."

I sighed. "Psychology is real complicated, isn't it?"

"Yes," Con said, "but it's *very* important."

Con certainly wasn't repressed, I thought, enviously. She had a new guy, every dance. She really played the field, and she never cared if guys never asked her out more than once.

"I want variety," she said. "I want small ones, tall ones; I want to break their hearts, use them, and throw them away." But it seemed that Con was always getting fixed up by somebody or other, because she had a lot of blind dates. Then, after she went out with a guy, and he didn't call, she'd say he was a stupid child or a hopeless *naif*. I think Con intimidated people, boys especially. They didn't know what to make of her, especially the Catholic guys. When she started talking about Omar and Freud and Dorothy Parker, they just blanked out. And Con didn't care.

Con was always putting her looks down, too—always saying her hips were too big or her fingers too stubby or her legs weren't long enough. She always did it in a funny way though, making herself the butt of her own jokes.

But Con's attention was focused on me now; she really

had a campaign going to get me over my fear of men. She made me promise I'd go out with other guys besides Sean. I promised, even though I really didn't want to. Besides, Sean's vocation to the priesthood really hadn't been much of a problem before. It had always seemed so far away. Sean had started talking about it freshman year, and then senior year seemed far off in the mists of the future.

I wondered if Sean would really do it, after all. Would he go away to be a priest? One thing I had never asked Sean was if he had gotten a Call. That's what the nuns said happened when you had a vocation to be a nun or a priest; God talked to you, like in a person-to-person phone call, and you just knew it.

I had a near miss with The Call in my junior year. It was at the vocation seminar that Father Millenbarger from the archdiocese gave us every year. Father Millenbarger was a recruiter, but they didn't call him that. He didn't tack up posters saying, "God wants you!" or talk about re-upping. But I thought of him as a sergeant in God's army, and he was very good at his job. He stood up on the auditorium stage, rocking back and forth on his heels, spewing forth a seductive mixture of romanticism and guilt. Nuns' lives weren't drab, he'd say; why, at the Mother House he'd just visited, there was pink toilet paper in the bathrooms. After he said that he stood there beaming at us, as if he expected us to practically have an orgasm over pink toilet paper. You'd have thought he'd just told us that nuns were allowed to go to proms or soul kiss every Thursday. The romance ploy left me cold. I was turned off right away by the fashion question. No way was I going to sweat through life in one of those long black dresses and the icky shoes. Besides, it was rumored that nuns shaved their heads, and no way were you going to get me to do that. I wanted to look like Susan Hayward, not Yul Brunner.

But the guilt stuff kind of got to me, and Father Millenbarger was a specialist in guilt. Still rocking, smiling beatifically, he'd say that anyone who had The Call and refused it would be miserable for the rest of her life, because she had rejected God's plan for her. He seemed to be looking right at me when he said it, and that was when I started to get this churning sensation in my stomach, which was either the Call or the first rumblings of food poisoning from the hot dog I ate for lunch. But I was clever. Just in case it was The Call, I set up, in my mind, a deflector shield like the ones I used to see on "Captain Video," where the good guys aimed the bad guys' death rays right back at them. Except I was aiming my deflector at Ruthie Harrigan, who was sitting in the row ahead of me. Mentally, I aimed The Call smack at the back of Ruthie's head; she wore her hair in two ponytails, one over each ear, and I directed the beam right at the part where a few flecks of dandruff were anchored in her hair.

"Ruthiiiieeee. . . Ruthieeeeeeeee. . . " I called, softly, hoping she would mistake my voice inside her head for the authentic baritone of the Almightly. "It's God calling you. I want you to be a nun. Nun, Ruthie. N-U-N. It's God, Ruthieeee. . . "

I figured Ruthie would be a terrific nun because she was skinny and never dated and got *A*'s in religion. I saw The Call boring through her skull the way my father's drill skewered hardwood, and I thought I could even hear its little whirring sound. A week later I heard that Ruthie had told Sister Robert Mary that she was going to be a nun, and I broke out in a cold sweat. Did Ruthie have *my* vocation? Did I give it to her the way I gave Sean the chicken pox? Would God be mad? Would I be unhappy? But I figured God got a good deal out of the whole thing, because I would have been a rotten nun and Ruthie would be a good one. Thank You, God, for taking Ruthie instead of me!" I prayed.

But still, I wondered about The Call, so one day, when I was walking to Mass with Sean, I asked him about it.

He looked at me, in a sort of embarrassed way, peering out from under those long eyelashes of his, and he said, "You won't laugh at me?"

"No, of course I won't."

"Well," he said, "I did have a Call."

"You did?"

"Um hmm."

"What was it like?"

"Well, I was thinking about how I wanted to do something good with my life. Something really good. Not like my father, who tries to make people do what they don't want to do. I wanted to do something—to help people, you know how I mean."

I nodded.

"Some people," Sean said, "they just spend their whole lives getting rich or trying to be big shots. They don't help people. If I'm a priest, my life will mean something."

Sean was always able to make me feel a little selfish when he talked like that. I could tell myself that I wanted to help people too; that I wanted to be a journalist to right the evils of the world. But it was really the glory I coveted, the byline. I had already pictured the banquet where I'd get my Pulitzer; we'd have steak and French fries—and no peas—and everybody would cheer and cheer. It was the alternate ending to *The Peg Morrison Story*, where I didn't get shot and die in Sean's arms. It wasn't as romantic, but at least I'd get to see the movie.

Sean never could stand to see anything hurt. Before he decided to be a priest, he was going to be a veterinarian. He always dragged home wounded birds and cats and mice. It was probably a good thing he abandoned his plans to be a vet, because while he was well intentioned, he was also clumsy. If the wounded animal didn't die of natural causes, he was sure to croak from Sean's ministrations. Sean usually dropped his patients while he was trying to put iodine on them, and then we'd have a requiem mass in the backyard, with Sean, of course, officiating. Sean had jars and jars of holy water—he filled up at the baptismal font almost as often as his father filled up with Esso—and he'd sprinkle the deceased with handfuls of it. The grass always grew great in Sean's backyard, thanks to the nitrogen enrichment and the sanctification caused by all those little corpses soaked with holy water.

Sean had what I thought of as pain sensors—he knew when someone or something was hurting when nobody else did. Once we walked all through the little woods at the back of my yard because Sean said he heard a hurt animal. I told him he was crazy, but sure enough, we found a bird on the ground flapping a broken wing. Sean took it home—and dropped it on the floor and broke its other wing. At least as a priest, Sean wouldn't be able to injure anybody physically, unless he accidentally stuck a candle in somebody's eye when he was doing the Blessing of the Throats.

Sean explained to me about The Call. He said, "I was walking in the park one morning, and the sun was out and it was warm, and suddenly I knew that God was there, all around me. I felt Him. I saw Him."

"Saw Him? Like at Fatima?"

"No, you know I don't believe in that stuff. Visions. Why should God have to put on a slide show when he can talk to you inside your mind?"

"Did He? Talk to you?"

"I think so. All of a sudden everything just seemed all golden and I had this feeling that God was all through me—inside my bones. It was—I can't describe it, I just never felt anything like it before."

I looked at Sean; he wasn't talking to me, really; he was lost in the memory, and his face seemed to be glowing, as if it were lit up by some inner fire. It seemed to me that he was just shining brighter and brighter, and if I kept looking at him I'd burn out my eyes. It was like staring into the sun.

"I can't tell you how I felt," he said. "It was like—I was

part of everything on earth and it was part of me, and I could never die; I'd just live forever, and I just stood there and hoped the feeling would never go away. It did. But I knew then that God was touching me, calling me."

We walked along in silence for a while, and I thought, Phew! Maybe I hadn't gotten a Call after all, because nothing like that had ever happened to me, maybe it was just the hot dog. I thought of Sean standing by slimy old Sligo Creek and God turning everything golden, and oh, how I envied him, at least for a minute. Nothing I had ever felt even approached Divine Rapture. Masturbating came closest, maybe, because it felt so good, but it was probably a sin just even to *think* about it in the same breath with The Call.

"I wish I'd been there," I said. "I wish I'd felt it too."

"So do I," Sean said. "But I'm glad I told you about it."

"So am I," I said, and I reached out to take his hand and we just kept walking along quietly together. I don't think I've ever been as close to another human being as I was to Sean at that moment. I wanted to take him in my arms and kiss him all over, which seems a strange reaction to having somebody tell you about how he got called by God, but there it was.

After that, it was impossible to pretend to myself that Sean wasn't really going to be a priest, and I decided Con was right; I had to start dating other guys. I told Con I was ready, and she said she'd start working on Annapolis.

Her aunt, the one who was married to the Navy commander, had promised that she'd get Con invited down to the Naval Academy when she turned eighteen. Con had her eighteenth birthday on the first day of December, and her aunt, true to her word, delivered a present. Her husband taught at the Academy, so it was easy for her to get dates for us to the big Winter Hop. Con said that uniforms really turned her on, which seemed strange to me, because the military seemed the least likely institution to be compatible with Con's anarchistic tendencies.

96

"I just can't help it; I see those uniforms and I practically have orgasms," she said. "I just look at them and all I can think of is sex, sex, sex."

"How about I get you a troop of Boy Scouts?"

"Oh, you're quick on the draw these days, Peg. Not Dorothy Parker, but you're getting there."

I told Sean that Con and I were going to Annapolis, and he seemed a little upset about it.

"Look," he said, "You watch out for yourself down there. Most of those guys probably aren't even Catholics."

"Yeah," I said, "one bunny hop with one of those guys and I won't believe in transubstantiation anymore. I will scream across the dance floor, 'GOD DOES NOT LIVE IN THE HOST.'"

"You know what I mean. Those guys don't care anything about sin. Just because they wear those neat uniforms they expect girls to rip their clothes off and come running."

"I promise, Sean, I won't rip my clothes off, even if all the guys look like Tab Hunter."

Sean looked at me crossly. He knew I didn't like Tab Hunter.

"What if one of them looks like James Dean?"

"Then I'll rip *his* clothes off."

"Oh, Peggy, be serious for a second. I mean these guys are older. They know all the tricks for getting girls, you know, worked up."

"Sean, I am not an infant. I have been out on dates with guys who know tricks. Last year I went out with Go-Go Gunderson."

"So?"

"This is the Big Catholic athlete of the year, goes to Mass every day, right? I barely got in the *car* when he stuck his tongue in my ear."

"Go-Go has no class. These guys are smooth. Devious."

"What will they do, stick their tongues in my *eye*?"

"Don't drink anything," he ordered. "They'll ply you with liquor."

"O.K., I won't"

"Don't kiss anybody."

"For Chrissake, Sean, this is really going to be some fun weekend. Maybe I'll suggest we all just say the Rosary for a good time. 'O.K., everybody, let's hear it nice and loud, the fourth glorious *Mystery*!'"

"You don't have to be snotty. I just don't want you to come back—pregnant or anything."

I stopped walking and looked at him. "Pregnant! Sean, four years of high school and I haven't even unbuttoned my blouse! You think all of a sudden I'm going to get pregnant!"

"Well, you're just so—pretty, and—um—sexy, that I think maybe some guys might just get carried away."

"I'm sexy?" I said.

"Oh *God*, yes," Sean said, and he grabbed me and kissed me, right there in front of People's Drug, so hard it made my head spin. All of a sudden I didn't want to go to Annapolis and dance with gorgeous guys in their uniforms; I didn't want to do anything but just stay around good old Crystal Springs and keep kissing Sean. That was when I knew I really was addicted. Half the kids in the school were green with envy because Con and I were going to the Naval Academy. They certainly wouldn't be jealous of me because I kissed a kid from Sacred Heart High School. They could do that any old time.

So the next weekend Con and I climbed on a bus, with our suitcases, heading for Annapolis. I had never felt so utterly grown up in my life. We were going to stay overnight at a "drag house"—dates at the Naval Academy were called drags—and our dates would pick us up there for the hop.

"Nervous?" Con asked, as we lugged our suitcases along the cobbled streets.

"A little," I said. "Are you?"

"Me? Of course not. Remember, they put their pants on one leg at a time."

"It's not their putting their pants on that has me worried," I said. "It's their taking them *off*!"

I have created a monster," Con sighed

When we got to the drag house, a modest two-story building on a quiet street, we went inside and met Mrs. Belcher, who ran the house, and she told us we would be sharing a room on the second floor with two other girls. I dragged my suitcase up the stairs and through the door of the room, and then I stopped short, flabbergasted. A woman, totally naked, was sitting at the vanity bench putting on makeup. I mean, she was *starkers*! She just sat there, calm as you please, with her boobs resting on the table. At Immaculate Heart, all the showers had curtains, and nobody ever walked around just in panties and bra. When we had slumber parties we all wore heavy flannel nighties with little flowers on them. Sister Justinian even told us that when we took a bath we ought to put talcum powder on the surface of the water, so we wouldn't see our own bodies and be tempted to impurity. I tried it once—more out of curiosity than out of concern for purity—and it didn't work very well. The powder turned slimy, and it was like taking a bath in the Johnson & Johnson version of the Great Dismal Swamp.

"Hi!" said the naked woman, "I'm Marianne."

"I'm Dolly," came a voice from the top bunk. Dolly was wearing a bra—that was it. She was just lying around with her pubic hair waving in the breeze (there wasn't any breeze, but you know what I mean) and that shocked me more than the lady who was starkers. I mean, it was pretty mortifying to grow hair down there in the first place, but to sit around flaunting it *had* to be some kind of sin.

"Where y'all from?" said Dolly, in a voice drenched with magnolias.

"Immaculate Heart High School," I said. Con rolled her eyes up to the ceiling, and I knew I had blown it.

"Gawd, a couple of high school virgins," Marianne said, with a sigh.

Con slung her suitcase on the top bunk of the bed opposite Dolly, and she said, "Honey, if there's any virgins in this room, look for a star in the East, because it's a miracle!"

Dolly and Marianne chuckled appreciatively. Con took out a cigarette, lit it, and took a sensual puff, just like Lauren Bacall. I was bowled over with admiration, and proud that Con was my friend.

Dolly laughed and said, "This your first time here?"

"Yeah," Con said, taking a puff. "Giving the Navy a try. West Point's where Peg and I usually hang out."

My blood froze. Con was lying. We'd never been near West Point. I wondered if that could qualify as a Mental Reservation. I didn't quite see how, though.

"How are the guys up there?" Marianne asked.

Con actually leered. I didn't even think she knew how to do it, but she cranked up a genuine leer, like Mae West. "The only problem is that they have all those damn *buttons* on their pants," she said.

"Yeah, but it's worth the wait," I said, and Con flashed me an approving glance. Take that, Dorothy Parker, I thought.

"Peg's been on Flirtation Walk with so many guys they're going to put her lip-prints in cement," Con said. Oh God, she was *brilliant* today.

"If all the guys at West Point who gave me hickeys dropped dead, we'd lose World War Three," I said.

"Yeah," Con said, "the whole Joint Chiefs of Staff of 1980, wiped out in one blow. And speaking of blow, how are the guys down *here*?"

Dolly hopped off the bed and started doing toe-touches, and her boobs jiggled up and down. "A hard man is good to find, and there's a lot of them in the Navy."

100

"I hear they put saltpeter in the food down here," Con said. "That's what they say at West Point."

"Yeah, but it doesn't take," laughed Dolly. "Hardly slows 'em down."

I thought this had to be the most sophisticated conversation anybody had, anywhere, and I was thrilled right down to my toes. I'd probably committed five or six venial sins just *listening*.

Marianne got up from the table and started walking around, picking out her clothes from the closet. The hair on her head was red, but the hair Down There was dark brown. I was stunned; Marianne dyed her hair. I tried not to stare at her crotch, without much success.

Then Con, not to be outdone, stripped off her blouse, and then her bra, and started unpacking just like that, with her boobs showing. She didn't strip any further; Con had a beautiful bust, but as sensitive as she was about her hips, she wasn't going to flash them around. She glared at me—I was still standing there with my coat on and my blouse buttoned up to my Adam's apple. I put my suitcase on the bed, and very slowly I took off my clothes, except for my bra and panties. I had a new lace bra and new panties. My old ones were all cotton, like kids wear, and I was really glad I thought to buy some new nylon ones. Dolly and Marianne would have laughed themselves silly to see me standing there in my little cotton panties from Sears Roebuck with the reinforced crotch and the daisies.

I started unpacking and Con looked at me, expectantly, but this was it, as far as I was going. No way was I going to walk around flashing my tits for these two Scarletts. I wasn't in their league, and I knew it.

"You girls go to school?" Con asked. "Or do you just hang around here screwing Middies?"

"Sweetwater College," Dolly said. "Home of the most beautiful girls in the South. At least that's what it says in the catalogue."

"What are you majoring in?" I asked Dolly politely. Con gave me another look.

"My *Mrs*," said Dolly. "What the fuck else is there?"

Dolly and Marianne finally finished dressing, tottering around on four-inch heels, getting ready to risk a broken ankle on the streets of Annapolis. They went out together, laughing and chattering.

"Oh God, Con, we are over our heads here," I said. "This is the real world."

"We're doing just fine, Peg. Remember, we're the intellectual elite. We don't have to be scared off by a couple of fake Southern belles."

"They're not fake, Con. Not where it counts. I don't think those bodies have *ever* been temples of the Holy Ghost."

Con laughed. "I wonder what they study at Sweetwater College—if anything."

"Well, it sure isn't the Baltimore catechism."

Con started to sashay around, imitating Dolly. "Honey chile, we sho' do know the l'il ole Baltimo' catechism. Ask me that first l'il old question."

"Who made us?"

"God made us—and then there was Freddie, and Billy, and Rhett, and then there was that cute Ole Johnny."

I collapsed on the bed. "Do you think they really do it, with different guys?"

"Oh yeah, they do. We're just faking it, but they're not virgins. You can tell by looking at their eyes."

"Is that really true?"

We both walked to the mirror and looked in.

"Pale, watery eyes," said Con. "A pair of virgins if ever I saw them."

"Don't you want to be a virgin when you get married?"

"I don't want to be a virgin yesterday."

"Con!"

"Well, I don't. What's so great about being a virgin?

Unless you're the Blessed Virgin, and you know what? I think she got gypped. She had to have a baby and didn't have sex. Whose idea is that of a good deal?"

We sat in silence for a minute and Con said, "Don't you want to get laid?"

"Well, sure, eventually."

"Why eventually? And don't give me that sin stuff. You don't believe in it and neither do I."

"Of course not." (Well, I half believed it. Sometimes yes, sometimes no. It was very confusing.)

"So?"

"Well, I just don't want to go out and give it away like it was free passes to the Silver Theater."

"Peggy, you've got to grow up. I mean, you're nearly eighteen years old and you date a guy who's going to be a priest."

"We *neck*," I said defensively.

"You'll just have to come with me to New York, Peg. When I'm a writer I'll have my lovers up to our apartment and you can have the ones I'm not using."

"You're going to have more than one at a time?"

"Why not? Men do it; why can't we?"

"I suppose we can," I said. I thought of having a garret, and Sean could come up, when he took time off from being a priest, and he could be my lover. But I was sure even the Jesuits frowned on that, and they were pretty liberal. Con was right. I could use some experience. Here we were, talking about lovers, and all I could dredge up was Sean, Roman collar and all. I certainly wouldn't want Go-Go Gunderson as a lover. I'd be trying to have a witty, literate conversation and he'd just be trying to stick his tongue in my ear.

"Peg," Con said. "Let's make a pact. A sacred pact. Let's promise that we'll get an apartment in New York together the *minute* we graduate from college."

"Hey, that's a great idea!"

"You'll be writing for the *Herald Trib*, and I'll be writing "Talk of the Town" for *The New Yorker*. All the best men in town will be at our place. I'll be standing there, and a handsome playwright will come up to me with a bag of peanuts, and he'll offer me the bag, and he'll say, 'I wish they were emeralds!' "

I looked at her. "Did you make that up?"

"No. It's what Charles MacArthur said to Helen Hayes the first time he met her."

"Holy shit. He said that?"

"Yeah."

"You're right, Con. We don't meet the right class of men hanging around Immaculate Heart High School." (I remembered what Go-Go Gunderson said when he asked me out. "Hey! You! You busy Saturday?")

"Will you do it? Promise?"

"I promise."

"No matter what happens. Even if Aly Khan asks you to marry him, you'll say no?" Con threw her arms in the air, which jiggled her boobs considerably. "New York or Die!" she cried.

I took the two water glasses from the sink and filled them up. I handed one to Con. "With the Sacred Water of Annapolis, we make our Vow," I said. "New York." We clinked the glasses together. I felt a flow of exultation flow through me. Con was going to be with me, in New York. How could I fail?"

"Hey, look at the time," Con said. "We better get dressed."

We got out our gowns, and we struggled into our Merry Widows—wired and padded like Victorian corsets—and Con put on her peach tulle dress and I slid my blue taffeta over my head. She zipped me up and then I pulled up the zipper on the peach gown; it got caught in the fabric and there was panic for a minute, but I got it free.

Con examined herself in the mirror. The peach dress

showed off her pretty neck and shoulders, and there was enough cleavage to palpitate the heart of the Nemesis of Smut. But she was despondent as she looked in the full-length mirror.

"I look like a cow. A peach-colored cow."

"You do not. You look beautiful."

"Why did I eat that Mars bar? It went right to my hips."

"Con, you look fine."

"You look super. You should always wear blue. It's your color."

"Me and the B.V.M.," I said. I started to sing: "I love a Lady in Blue. . ."

Con chimed in: "And Dear Mother Mary, it's You. . ."

We both piped away, "When I look up to your beautiful face/I see a mirror reflecting God's Grace. . ."

Then we both collapsed on the bed in giggles.

"Ten'll get you twenty it's the first time that number's been done in this place!" Con said.

"Yeah, virgins of any kind are pretty rare around here."

When we had collected ourselves, we went downstairs to meet our dates. First Classman Lee Masters was Con's Middie, and he turned out to be very tall, with a face that I thought was bland and unremarkable, but he did have a wonderful chin with a dimple in it, and blue eyes that seemed merry. Con took one look and couldn't take her eyes away; she was staring at him the way the kids at Fatima must have looked at the Virgin—with a sort of unbelieving wonder. "There's trouble," I thought.

My date, Harry Wexler, a yearling, did turn out to look a little like Tab Hunter. Not really my type, but handsome, and very dashing in his white dress uniform. And he was old, twenty-one at least. He introduced himself, very formally, and then he took my hand and we started down the street toward the yard and Bancroft Hall. My palms were starting to sweat. I mean, he was a *man*. How was I supposed to act? I knew how to act with boys. I grew up with Sean; I knew what he was thinking before he did. With Go-Go, all you had to do was give him a shove every time he tried to stick his tongue in the nearest available orifice. But Midshipman Harold (Harry) Wexler was different.

I thought about an article I had read in the *Ladies' Home Journal* called, "How to Talk to A Man and Make Him Fall in Love with You." I didn't want Harry Wexler to fall in love with me; I just wanted to convince him I wasn't a deaf-mute. The *Journal* said to talk about something you think the man would be interested in, not something you were interested in.

"Uh," I said, "what do you think of Senator McCarthy?" (Men liked politics, I figured.)

"I think he's a real patriotic American," he said. "Don't you?"

I didn't like him at all, even if he was a Catholic and was against communists. He had mean eyes, he was a bully, and he ruined the lives of innocent people. But the *Journal* said you should *never* disagree with a man.

"Well," I said, "he certainly is an American, all right."

So much for politics. We walked along in silence, and my palms were really sweating now. Frantically I searched for a topic of conversation. Hobbies! The *Journal* said to ask about a man's hobbies.

"Do you collect stamps?" I asked.

"No."

"Neither do I."

More silence.

"Do you collect *anything*?" The desperation had to be echoing through my voice.

"No."

"Oh."

"I used to, though."

(Thank You, God, thank You, Jesus, Mary, and Joseph!)

106

"Oh really? What?"

"Bugs. I had a pretty good collection."

"Bugs? You mean like flies, things like that?"

"Grasshoppers. I had eighteen species of grasshoppers."

"I used to like to catch grasshoppers when I was a kid. We used to have jumping contests with 'em."

"We used to pull their back legs off, watch 'em gimp around," Harry said with a laugh.

My blood ran cold. The idea of pulling the legs off a grasshopper made me sick. A shiver ran through me; Harry thought I was cold and he put his arm around me. I looked back at Con, who was still gazing up in a daze at Lee Masters, and I felt very much alone. Con was falling in love with Prince Charming, and I had to dance all night with a man who was into grasshoppercide. I wondered what other things he killed; I hoped he didn't have anything against Catholics.

But then Harry started to talk about the things he was studying, and it occurred to me that maybe grasshoppers were just an aberration. He didn't display any other homicidal tendencies. I had a bad moment when he led me out to the dance floor, and my hands got really sweaty—thank God for the long white gloves—because I was never good at dancing. Guys told me I always tried to lead; too much basketball, I guess. But Harry was a good dancer, and I didn't step on his toes, so I relaxed and even started to enjoy myself a little. Every now and then an image of a grasshopper flopping around in the dust came to mind, but I quickly pushed it away.

One nice thing about dancing with Harry was that you didn't have to talk much when you were dancing; the midshipmen all seemed to be talking to each other anyway. When Harry danced by Lee, he'd say, "COMCIMPAC," and then another midshipman would dance by and say, "COMCONATFT"; it was like dancing with a bunch of Martians speaking a whole other language. Con told me later it

107

was a game with them, that they were making up letters for imaginary Naval Commands and they had to guess what the letters meant.

When the band went out for a break, Con and I went to the ladies' room, and she said to me, "For God's sake, Peg, you should see the expression on your face when you're dancing with Harry. You look like you've just been told you're the next virgin that gets to be martyred."

"I'm having fun, Con, honest I am."

"Flirt with him, for heaven's sakes. Bat your eyelashes."

"Like this?"

"Oh God, no! You look like you've got some nerve disease. Don't you know how to flirt?"

"I guess not."

"Peg, you have to learn how to be *feminine*. You're pretty, but you're a klutz."

"I am not. I have the best jump shot in the league."

"That's what I mean. Men don't like girls who do jump shots. They like girls who are dainty."

I laughed.

"O.K., forget dainty. How about sultry?"

I tried my Marilyn Monroe opened-mouth stare.

"Scratch that one too," Con said. "Peg, looking feminine does not mean you're supposed to look like you've just had a lobotomy."

I got annoyed. "Let's just forget about this whole thing, Con. I am doing just fine!"

"Suit yourself," she said.

The band came back, and Harry and I danced some more, and then we drank some punch, and all in all the evening passed pleasantly enough. Then it was time for the last dance—after which the upperclassmen had two hours to get back to their dorms. I found myself walking very fast through the streets of Annapolis with Harry, and as we rounded a corner we saw a pair of familiar faces—Dolly and

Marianne. Their dates, it turned out, were Harry's best friends, and one of them had a relative with an apartment in town: He was away for the weekend and wasn't using it. I looked back at Con and Lee, who were staring moonily into each other's eyes, and I wondered about the wisdom of going to an unchaperoned apartment. But I figured it would be O.K. since Con was with me, because she could talk her way out of anything.

But then Con, the rat-fink, double-crossed me.

"We're going to walk around for a bit. I want to show Constance around," Lee said. He looked at Con. "How about it, hon?"

Con just nodded dumbly. She would have nodded if he told her he was going to ship her off to a work camp in Vladivostock, that's how smitten she was. So off they went, and there *I* was, alone with two fallen women, their paramours, and a man who pulled the legs off grasshoppers.

We went into the apartment, and Dolly's date got out some beers. Dolly and Marianne didn't waste any time getting kissy-kissy with their middies; Marianne draped herself all over one of the white uniforms and Dolly snuggled up to the other. Her midshipman guzzled his beer, and then very casually, as if it were nothing at all, put his hand right down the front of Dolly's dress.

I nearly choked on a swallow of Miller High Life. Nothing I had ever seen in my whole life shocked me so much; I felt as though I had just been air-dropped into Sodom and Gomorrah. I felt panicky; I wished Sean were there, with his illuminated Map of Sin so he could explain things to Dolly. I wished Con were there. I wanted Sister Justinian to materialize and grab Marianne and Dolly in her pterodactyl grip and explain to them that they were going to wind up toasting like marshmallows if they didn't cease and desist immediately. I even wished for Father Clement Kliblicki to come barging in the door screaming, "Spawn of Satan!"

And then Dolly and Marianne and their dates drifted

off to the bedroom, leaving me and Harry alone on a couch with only one tiny little light on. He put his arms around me and I got as rigid as a corpse. But he just leaned over and kissed me gently, no tonsil-swab or anything, and he smelled of aftershave, a nice clean smell, and his lips were soft and warm and so I let him kiss me. I even unclenched my teeth after a while, and closed my eyes. We kissed like that for a while, and it was real nice, and then I noticed he was making a little humming noise in his throat, and his breathing was getting faster. I was surprised, because I didn't know I was such a good kisser. I opened my eyes, and to my horror, I discovered that Harry had his hands on the front of my dress and was feeling away. I had no idea how long this had been going on. He didn't know it, but he was getting all steamed up from an inch of foam rubber. I couldn't feel a thing; for all I knew, Harry might as well have been groping a Squeegee Mop. I wondered about the theology of it all. It certainly wasn't a sin for me, since I didn't even know it was happening. Was it a sin for Harry, feeling up foam? But then, he was a Protestant, and the whole scale of sin was different for them.

I pulled his hands away, and he didn't protest, just kept on kissing me. He was still kissing very nicely, no caveman stuff, so I relaxed and closed my eyes again—which was my mistake.

I realized I didn't feel his arms around me anymore, but his hands weren't on my foamy chest either, so I wondered where they were. I opened one eye, and I saw, with a terrible sinking feeling in the pit of my stomach, that he had unzipped his fly, and what to my wondering eye did appear but the second actual penis I'd ever seen in my life.

I couldn't help staring at it; it was sticking straight out of his pants, and it was a lot bigger than Sean's five-year-old one (though that must have grown a bit as well) and it looked so funny just sort of jutting through his pants that I couldn't help giggling. Unfortunately, Harry mistook it for a cry of passion.

110

"Oh baby, baby!" he said, and pulled my hand down between his legs. I yanked it away as if he'd been trying to hold my hand against a hot stove.

"For heaven's sakes, put it away!" I said.

"What?" he panted, not comprehending.

"Your *thing* there. Put it back!"

I was reverting to the language of my pup tent days. Somehow, it just seemed absurdly formal to refer to it as a penis in a situation like this. *Ladies' Home Journal* did not deal with this conversational dilemma: "How to Talk to a Man Who Has Just Unzipped His Fly."

"My goodness, that's certainly an interesting penis you have there."

"Why, thank you."

"Not at all. I've always been interested in the subject of penises. Have you?"

"Yes, indeed."

"I've been thinking of collecting them. It might be a nice hobby. Speaking of hobbies, do you collect stamps?"

But Harry didn't seem interested in conversation. He said, "Oh baby, baby, kiss it!" and he tried to nudge my head down in the vicinity of his exposed member.

"Oh My *GOD!*" I shrieked, jumping up and running back behind the couch. Harry looked at me, puzzled. Then he tried to climb over the couch and I doubled up my fist and I said, "Don't you come near me, you—you *grasshopper killer!*"

He blinked and said, "What the hell is going on?"

Just then there was a moan from the bedroom. Dolly's voice. That didn't help things at all.

"You think I'm just going to sit there and let you paw me?"

"Oohhhhhhhhh!" Dolly said, from the bedroom.

"Oh for God's sake, Peg, what's this quivering virgin act?"

"More! More!" Dolly groaned. I wanted to go in and bludgeon her to death with her high-heeled shoes. Let's see if she'd yell "more" as I mashed the high heel into her left nostril. But then the impact of what Harry had just said hit me right in the stomach.

"Act?" I said. "What act?"

"You put out for half of West Point; what the hell's wrong with me?"

"What?"

"Harder, harder!" Dolly yelled.

"Babe, I'll make you forget there ever *was* an Army," Harry said.

"Who told you about West Point?" I asked.

"Dolly told me how you'd been *bragging* about how many of those Army jerks you'd been with. Come on, let me show you how we do things the Navy way!"

"Ohhhhhhhhhh!" Dolly said. Not only was she a harlot but a blabbermouth as well. I thought of stuffing a magnolia down her throat until she choked to death.

"Come on, babe, you'll love it!" Harry said, and he made another lunge at me. I darted away and I said, "Harry, honest to God, I've never been to West Point! I've never even been north of Philadelphia!" I added, "My cousin lives there. Second cousin, once removed."

"Fuck me! Fuck me!" Dolly said.

Harry looked at me, perplexed. His penis had deflated too, I noticed.

"But all that stuff about West Point—"

"We were just kidding."

"You mean you really *are* a virgin?"

I nodded. "Yeah, I am."

"Oh shit!" he said. He looked so miserable that I felt a pang of sympathy for him.

"I'm sorry," I said.

"Well," he said, "I guess you can't help what you are."

"It's not that I don't like you. If I wasn't—you know—I'd do it with you, I really would."

"You sure you don't want to—change your status?" he said.

112

"No, I'm only a senior in high school. I think I ought to stay a virgin a little longer."

"Well, sure, that makes sense," he said. He really was being decent about it. "Come on, I'll walk you back to the drag house."

We walked back in silence, and when we got to the door he said, "I didn't really kill a lot of them. Grasshoppers. And I was only a kid."

"I'm sorry I called you a killer," I said. "I think you're very nice, really."

He leaned over and kissed me goodnight, gently, and then he walked off. I stood there, watching him vanish into the darkness, and then I turned and went into the house. I went upstairs and discovered that Con wasn't back yet; she was probably having a grand old time necking away under a statue of some dead Navy guy someplace. I undressed and climbed into bed, and pulled the covers up to my chin, the way I used to do as a kid when I wanted to feel safe. I was feeling really rotten—lonely and miserable.

I sure had made a botch of it with Harry. No way was I going to get asked back to Annapolis. Calling a guy a killer—even if you apologized—was not one of the conversational ploys suggested by "How to Talk to a Man and Make Him Fall in Love with You."

Let's face it, I was just hopeless at this man-woman stuff. I wasn't dainty; I couldn't flirt without looking terminal; I didn't know how to act when somebody unzipped his fly; I led when I danced; and I had sweaty palms and ear wax. I didn't want to end up on the Frigid Ward, but on the other hand I don't think I could ever be as casual as Dolly, calmly sipping my beer while some guy had his hand down my dress.

Maybe I made a mistake when I aimed my deflector shield at Ruthie Harrigan. Maybe when I got back to Immaculate Heart I should just march up and tell her that she had my vocation and she had to give it back. Nobody cared if nuns had ear wax, and they didn't dance, so leading wasn't a problem, and they probably didn't have to worry a lot about people unzipping their flies.

If it weren't for the crappy clothes, maybe being a nun wasn't such a bad deal.

SEVEN

Defying Decency

Right before Christmas, we scored another coup for the *Messenger* staff, a five-minute interview with Senator John F. Kennedy on a trade bill he was sponsoring. It was our most thrilling interview yet. We had done the Philippine ambassador to the U.S., a center fielder for the Washington Senators, a missionary to the Congo, and a semi-well-known actor who was in a play at the National Theater. The actor dropped hints of a ménage à trois after the play, and Con said that one of the problems with being virgins, was that we couldn't take him up on it.

"I mean, I would have been mortified, really *mortified*, if we were having an orgy and he couldn't get it *in*," Con said. "And then I'd bleed all over the dressing room and, God, that would be *tacky*."

"You mean you'd really do it if you weren't a virgin?"

"Sure. It would be something to put in my novel."

"But he's old, Con. He's old enough to be our father."

"Well, that means he knows how to do it, right? He didn't get that old without learning something."

"I'll never be as sophisticated as you, Con," I sighed.

We both went weak in the knees over Jack Kennedy. He was very nice and polite, and talked to us very earnestly about his trade bill. He wished us good luck in our career as journalists. We walked out into the corridor of the Senate office building, entranced.

"God, what a hunk!" Con said. "I felt like raping him, right there in the office."

"I think that's what's called statutory rape," I said, "doing it with a senator when he's talking about his trade bill."

Con looked at me. "Oh, Peg," she said, "Dorothy *Parker* couldn't have said it better!" and she gave me a hug. I felt wonderful. Con had actually compared me favorably to Dorothy Parker!

We got into Con's black Ford—it belonged to her mother, but Con got to drive it all the time—and Con started back to Crystal Springs at her usual terrifying pace.

"In New York, Peg, we'll knock 'em dead! Look, we're only in high school, and look at what we've done!"

"There's no stopping us, Con. You and me together, we can do anything!"

"Maybe we'll have our own television show, like 'Meet the Press.'"

"And now," I said dramatically, "NBC bring you 'People in the News,' a weekly program of news and information starring Miss Constance Marie Wepplener of *The New Yorker* and Miss Peggy Morrison of the *Herald Tribune!*"

Con hummed the *Washington Post* march. Then she said, "Welcome to 'People in the News.' Our guest today is Senator John F. Kennedy—"

"Who will discuss foreign trade while Miss Wepplener puts her hand on his thigh."

And we went around the curve at Fifteenth and L on two wheels, almost precipitously ending our own lives as well as those of a family of five in a station wagon.

"Oh Peggy," Con said, "I can't wait for the future. So many *wonderful* things are going to happen to us!"

And when she said it, I knew it was true. Con could do that for me, cut away the underbrush of my doubts and fears and make everything seem so easy, so inevitable. Sometimes, at home alone in my room late at night, I'd get scared. I'd break out in a cold sweat, the fear clammy against my skin. *I'll never be able to do it*, I'd think. *I'm just little Peggy Morrison of Immaculate Heart High School.* How could I have the nerve to think of working for the *Herald Tribune* or winning the Pulitzer Prize or ever being anything more than just a little editor on a high school newspaper in a suburb nobody knew about. Nobody I knew had ever become a journalist, especially not a woman. The world was such a big place, and there were so many people smarter and better than I was. How could I ever do it? I never would. I'd just stay in Crystal Springs and probably marry some guy and I'd get old and die and nothing would ever happen to me.

But now, sitting beside Con, those thoughts were blown away as if by a wind from the sea. Beside her in the Black Ford, breaking the speed limit on Sixteenth, I felt the future to be as real and as solid as the buildings, the trees, the sky.

We had it all planned; we'd been talking about it ever since we got back from Annapolis, where we took the sacred vow. We were both going to the University of Maryland, where we'd be editors of the *Diamondback*, and we'd be the staff to go down in history. We'd be immortal. And the offers would come flooding in from all over, but we'd pack our bags and go off to our New York apartment, where we'd meet everybody who was anybody. We'd be as witty as Clare Booth Luce, as brilliant as Rebecca West, have necklines like Faye Emerson.

"We'll be brilliant! We'll be beautiful!" Con said. "I'll be so thin you can hardly see me when I stand sideways." She took another bite of a Mars bar as she said it. She kept a hoard of them in the glove compartment. With her mouth full, she said, "I think my lovers will be Jack Kennedy, Norman Mailer, and Jack Kerouac. How about yours?"

"Can we share Kennedy?"

"O.K."

"Johnny Lujack, Richard Burton, and maybe Sean."

"He's got a great body."

"Burton?"

"No, Sean. What a waste that he's going to be a priest."

"God gets the best and the girls get the rest."

"Well, tell you one thing. I'm not ever going to marry a Catholic."

"You aren't?"

"Not unless he believes in birth control. I don't want to have a kid every year, do you?"

"No." I had already decided that. It was the first major issue on which I decided not to do what the Church said. I knew my parents had used birth control; I found a pack of rubbers in my father's drawer once. And he used to say that it was nobody's business, even the Church's, how many children people had. And he was a good, church-going Catholic, too.

"We can't let anybody tell us what to think, Peggy. That's what the whole Constitution is all about. Even the pope can't tell us what to think. We're Americans.

"Especially us," I said. "We're journalists. We have to ask questions."

"Nobody's ever going to own my *mind*," Con decreed solemnly. "Not ever." She took a bite of Mars bar and grinned, a big chocolate grin. "My body, now that's a different story."

She had someone in mind for her body: First Classman Lee Masters, U.S.N. "Know what he told me?" she said with her mouth full of Mars bar. "He told me I was the kind of woman who looked better naked than with clothes on."

"Con, how does he know?"

"Well, he doesn't, but he has a *good* imagination. He says I have a womanly body, not one of those bodies like a twelve-year-old boy. He hates Audrey Hepburn."

"I think she's beautiful."

118

"Yeah, but she probably looks just awful with her clothes off. Lee said he'd like me just to stay naked for a whole day, just walk around with my clothes off so he could look at me."

"Didn't you people talk about anything except you in your birthday suit?"

"Oh yeah, we talked a lot about J. Edgar Hoover."

"Does Lee want to see *him* naked, too?"

"Very funny, Peg. Lee thinks J. Edgar Hoover is single-handedly saving America from the Red Menace."

I yawned. The whole communism business bored me to death, even though I dutifully prayed for the conversion of Russia like everybody else.

"When are you going down to see him again?"

"I don't know. He said he was going to write to me. He better." Con said that if he didn't ask her back down to Annapolis she was going to start cutting off little pieces of her body, starting with an earlobe.

"He'll like that. When he gets all of you, he can put you together like a jigsaw puzzle, and see you naked that way. Maybe you just ought to send him brownies."

"Oh Christ, *brownies*? I have to be clever, witty, brilliant. I want him to know he's dealing with a sophisticate!"

"O.K., chocolate chip cookies."

"You're a big help."

Con had already decided she wanted to lose her virginity to Lee Masters. "But not right away. I want him to think that I am just irresistibly passionate, not some slut who puts out for everybody."

"Con, you mean you're really going to Do It?"

"Yeah, but I got to get back down there first. It's sort of hard losing your virginity long distance."

Con agonized over strategy. "What can I send him?"

"How about a picture of you, starkers?"

"Not subtle."

"How about a picture of you in your uniform?"

"Oh God! In that thing, I look like a cow that's enlisted."

"We could send him the collected Saints Corner."

"He's not Catholic."

"Yeah, and the story of Lourdes isn't exactly an aphrodisiac."

"Hardly. What guy do you know that gets turned on by the B.V.M.?"

"Mr. Kasten. He would."

"Yeah, she's in big trouble if she appears to Mr. Kasten. He'd try to put his hand up her dress."

We finally decided on a nifty little Dorothy Parker poem to send to Lee Masters. We'd have to wait a while to see if it worked. Christmas vacation was coming up, and Lee was going back to his home in St. Louis, so Con's campaign to lose her virginity would have to be put on hold for a while. And I had a moral dilemma of my own coming up.

It was Legion of Decency pledge time again.

Every year, Dr. McCaffrey came to St. Malachy's, and we all stood and formally pledged with him not to see any dirty movies for another year.

I was against the Legion, on principle. It wasn't that I favored dirty movies, but it was like Con said, I didn't want anybody owning my mind. And the Legion really did dumb things—like condemning *The Moon Is Blue* because Audrey Hepburn used the word "virgin." I'd felt like a real hypocrite standing up the last couple of years, even when I didn't recite the pledge. If I was going to be a journalist, I would have to start standing up for what I believed in. I was going to have to stop being a nice, polite, Catholic girl who did what everybody else wanted.

I walked to Mass with Sean on Legion Sunday, and he noticed that I was quieter than usual, but he didn't ask me any questions. I hadn't told Sean what I was going to do, mainly because I was afraid I was going to chicken out, and I didn't want to have to live that down.

120

Dr. McCaffrey gave the sermon that Sunday, at the invitation of Father Ryan. Wouldn't you know it, he started talking about Jane Russell again. I had really had it with that subject. Besides, why shouldn't I get to go see *The Outlaw*? Jane Russell's boobs certainly weren't a Near Occasion of Sin for me; they left me cold. I wondered what it was that men liked about big boobs, anyhow. I didn't think I'd want things that dropped almost down to my belly button, even if it did mean that a lot of guys would pant after me all the time. I liked to think of mine as perky; they had personality; they didn't just lie there. I stole a look at Sean. I wondered if he liked *perky*. I certainly hoped he wasn't like his father, all hung up over great big ones. And then I realized what I was thinking and I stopped it immediately. Thinking about boobs—perky or otherwise—certainly was not proper at Mass. A venial sin, undoubtedly. I tuned in to Dr. McCaffrey again.

"And we can send a *message* to the moguls of Hollywood—to the panting purveyors of putrid pleasures—that we will not wallow with them in the gutters; we will not stoop to the sewers of slime and seduction! (Seven alliterations in one sentence! A record, even for Dr. McCaffrey.) Catholics of America, will you join with me in hurling a challenge at the silvered gates of Hollywood?"

I started to feel little quivers in my stomach.

"Will you say, with me, Enough! Enough of your filth and your moral decay. We shall destroy you!"

I clenched my teeth and my whole body must have gone rigid. I was about to take a stand in favor of putrid pleasures, of sewers of slime. Sean looked at me and I saw the alarm in his eyes.

I thought about the words of Christ, "Be ye either hot or cold or I shall vomit thee out of my mouth."

"You're not going to take it!" Sean whispered, and I whispered back, "No."

"Jesus Christ!" he said.

"Shhh! He'll hear you."

I saw Sean's fists clench. I knew I had triggered a war inside him. He made fun of the Legion of Decency as often as I did. I looked at him, and the expression on his face unsettled me. It was a mixture of doubt and guilt; he could have posed for a portrait of Judas Iscariot.

"Peggy," he whispered, "I can't! He's my *father*!"

"I know," I whispered back. "Stand up."

He hesitated.

"Sean, stand up!"

He stood, slowly, and I just sat there. Everybody in the whole church had risen except me. I felt my heart beating and my face getting hot. I was sure everybody in the whole congregation could hear the clamorous pounding of my heart. At first, only a few people turned to look at me, but then the whispering began. I could see it spreading like a wind through tall grass, moving through the pews. More people turned to look. Dr. McCaffrey started the pledge.

I opened my missal and started to read: "I believe in God, the Father Almighty, creator of heaven and earth—" My face was really burning now, it felt as if it would burst into flame. I plowed through the Apostles' Creed and started on the Agnus Dei—"Lamb of God, who takest away the sins of the world, have mercy on us."

I have done a few brave things in my life since then—I have been where guns were fired uncomfortably near me in anger and I did my job, did it well. But I never did anything as hard as not getting to my feet in church to recite the Legion of Decency pledge when I was a senior at Immaculate Heart High School.

The pledge just kept going on and on—had they made it longer?—and I could feel hundreds of eyes on me. I thought that when I went home and took off my blouse, I'd have lots of little eye-holes in my skin; the stares felt like lasers.

Then it was done, and Sean sat down beside me and

took my hand. I was shaking, and he squeezed my hand hard. He looked more miserable than ever.

After Mass, Dr. McCaffrey stopped me on the church steps and said, "Peggy, I can't believe it! Was that you? Sitting down during the pledge?"

His tone was incredulous, as if he were asking if that was me, there among the folks nailing Christ to the Cross, just happily tacking away.

"Yes, sir. I didn't stand."

"For heaven's sakes, why not?"

"Because I am a journalist and I believe that the pledge violates the spirit of the First Amendment."

"You are a Catholic, Peggy. That's the important thing."

"No, sir. I'm an American too. And I don't believe that anybody has the right to tell me what I can see or read."

"That's very impertinent," Dr. McCaffrey said.

"Thomas Jefferson was very impertinent," I said tartly. "So was Thomas Paine."

"Thomas Paine was an atheist."

"Yes, sir, he was. But Thomas Jefferson was a Deist."

"Young lady, I'm going to talk to Sister Robert Mary about you!"

"Dad, don't do that," Sean said.

"This young woman has been rude, and impertinent, and she has defied the Catholic Church!"

"She has a right to believe what she wants!"

"Young man, you are being impertinent, do you know that?"

"Yes, sir."

"You are coming home from Mass with me. I don't want you being seen with a young woman who has caused a scandal."

"No, sir."

"What!"

"Sir, I'm walking home with Peggy."

"Sean," Dr. McCaffrey said through clenched teeth, "you are *coming* with me!"

"No, sir," Sean said, planting his feet firmly and letting his lower jaw stick out a little, the way he used to do as a kid.

"*Sean McCaffrey*—" Dr. McCaffrey said, but just then a woman dashed up and grabbed his arm and said, "Oh, Dr. McCaffrey, you were so wonderful at the Sodality last week—"and Sean and I made our escape.

We walked home together, holding hands, and Sean sighed and said glumly, "I let you down. I let you take the heat all alone. And I lied."

"You lied?"

"Taking the pledge was a lie. I don't believe in it. I think it was a sin to stand up."

"But if you didn't stand up, Sean, it would have been like slapping your father in the face in public. It would have hurt him something awful, Sean."

"I know," he said, looking even more miserable. "Shit, all those courses we take on Moral Guidance, and they're not worth diddley-squat. I thought the church would have answers. Maybe the Double Effect."

The Double Effect was a system we learned for making moral decisions. If an action had two effects—one good and one bad—if the good effect didn't *cause* the bad effect, then the act was moral. Take Catholic Aviator Alphonse, for example, one of the examples in our book. Alphonse is flying a mission when his plane gets hit by a shell. He knows he's bought it. Can he dive his plane into the enemy ship, and become a human bomb?

Answer: yes, because the good effect—zapping the enemy—isn't caused by the bad effect—Alphonse's demise, which is going to happen anyhow. But I was always doubtful about deciding what was right and wrong by mathematical formulas.

"Look," I said to Sean, "you think old Alphonse is

really up there with his fuselage on fire, thinking about the double effect? 'Let's see now, I guess I can smack my Hellcat into the Jap carrier, thanks to the Double Effect. So here I go, dirty Nips! I'm blowing you fucking slant-eyes away, but I'm clean with God!'"

That made Sean smile and I poked him in the ribs, playfully. But in a minute he was miserable again.

"I should have known what to do. I mean, I'm going to be a priest, I should *know* what's right."

Being a Catholic kid was a real pain in the ass sometimes. We were always talking about our consciences, and worrying about them. Were they formed right? We had a whole book full of situations where our consciences had to be informed. There was convict Z, who is chained to the wall. A fire breaks out. Can he cut off his foot and crawl to safety, or is that a sin of self-mutilation? And Catholic father Leonard, whose kids are starving. Can he steal meat for them on Friday, or will he go to hell for stealing and eating meat on Friday? And Catholic girl Maria—can she slice up her face so the enemy soldiers won't want to feel her up? And Catholic boy Gerald: The communists are telling him that if he doesn't Deny His Faith, they are going to put lighted matches to his father's feet. What does Gerald do?

Protestant kids didn't have to worry about these things. You never heard them, over sodas at People's Drug, debating about convict Z.

"I think he *should* cut his foot off. Better a gimp than burned to a crisp."

"Yeah, well, what about Gerald? Would you let them toast your father's tootsies?"

"It's Catholic aviator Alphonse who's really in deep shit."

Why did we have to worry about all these people? Why did we have to get our consciences informed all the time and be on the lookout for sin, as if it were a mugger behind

125

a bush? Why couldn't we just grow up, and do algebra, and ride around in cars, and neck, just like other kids, without having to worry about theology? Being a Catholic kid was sometimes very hard.

"Sean," I said to him, "I think you *did* know what was right. You knew you couldn't do that to your father." Then I added, "Even if he is a jerk."

"I guess," he said.

"I think you know what's right, in here—" I pointed to my heart—"and you don't need any old double effect to tell you."

"But what's more important, my father's feelings, or the truth?"

"What feels more important?"

"My father."

"See."

He sighed, a deep sigh; it was the sound a grown-up makes, not a kid, I thought.

"If I'm going to be a priest, I have to take a vow of obedience. That's not something I'm real good at."

"I noticed. What'll he do to you?"

"Ream my ass. I'm used to it. But what if some superior tells me something and I don't think it's right? And I've taken a vow. A holy vow."

"I don't think anyone should go against his conscience. Vow or no vow."

"But what if my conscience isn't formed right? What if I'm wrong?"

"It doesn't matter. You have to listen to what it says is right."

"Hitler probably thought he was right too."

"Sean, you're not Hitler."

"Invade the Sudetenland! Crush France! Sieg Heil!"

I giggled. "Your father, maybe he's Hitler, but you're not."

"Yeah, my father and his blitzkrieg against cleavage.

Why can't he be like other fathers, interested in baseball or bowling or running around with women?"

"I'm really in the doghouse with your father now. He never did trust me, not since the business in the tent. He keeps looking at me like he thinks I'm going to pull your pants down and start messing around again."

"Well, I wouldn't mind that," he said with a grin.

Sean's father never did get around to giving him a beating, because Sean said that since he was going to be a priest his flesh was probably holy, and it would probably be at least a venial sin to whomp an almost-priest. I figured Dr. McCaffrey took a look at the muscles Sean had grown and decided it wasn't very smart to mess with a kid who could break him in half. He never did talk to Sister Robert Mary, either, and I learned a valuable lesson. If you stood your ground, people would bluster and bluff, but in the end, more often than not, they'd back down.

Sean didn't even get grounded over vacation, and I sure was glad of that, because Christmas was a lot of fun, with parties and movies and a lot of just hanging around. But Con wanted vacation to be over with, quick. Con never was one for hanging in groups; she was a loner, really. She was waiting for Midshipman Masters to get back from St. Louis so she could get the antivirginity campaign on the road. She said the parties and the goofing around we did over Christmas were just "kid stuff."

She had his address in Missouri, and she was agonizing over whether to send him another Dorothy Parker poem. She had three of them selected, and the second night of vacation she called me, and I told her I'd come over to her house and give my considered literary opinion.

I drove my mother's car over to Con's house, and when I got there I saw that the front door was open, so I just walked in. But when I got into the front hall, I heard, from upstairs, a terrible scream. It stopped me in my tracks and it froze my blood; I'd never understood the expression until I heard that scream, because it really did feel as if all the blood in my body had stopped pumping and had turned to ice. I heard a moan, and then another. I was sure somebody was being murdered.

"Con! Con! Where are you?" I called out.

She came out of the kitchen, and the expression on her face was the most terrible I have ever seen on a human being—except for my mother's face the day she learned that my father had dropped dead. Con's eyes were cold, empty, and her face was all squeezed up into little bubbles of pain.

"Con!" I said. "What—Shall I call the police?"

She shook her head.

There was the sound of a slap from upstairs, and another cry.

"It'll stop in a minute," Con said.

"Stop? What is it? What's happening?"

"My father is beating the shit out of my mother."

"What!" My mouth gaped open.

"It's nothing new," she said.

And then Con's father came tearing down the stairs, his face all flushed red, and he didn't even look at us, just stormed out of the house and slammed the door.

Con's mother came halfway down the stairs, crying out, "Frank! Frank! Don't leave me!" and I stared at her, not believing what I saw. A trickle of blood was running out of one side of her mouth, and the whole side of her face was red and raw, as if someone had been using it as a punching bag. She saw me and quickly turned around and hurried back up the stairs. I heard the sound of a door closing.

I just stood and stared at Con, not knowing what to say.

"Home sweet home," she said. "Want a beer?"

"Con—why?"

"Come on," she said, and I followed her into the kitchen and she handed me a beer. "Now you know. Our dirty little family secret."

"I won't tell anybody," I said. "But Con, how long has this been going on?"

"A long time. He gets drunk and slaps her around. I used to scream and get hysterical when it happened." She shrugged. "Now I'm used to it."

"God, Con, I'm sorry."

"So am I."

"Does he really hurt her?"

"Oh yeah, sometimes. Once he broke her jaw and another time he broke two of her fingers. The fucking bastard."

"Oh, Jesus!"

"Yeah, that's why we moved from Long Island. All the neighbors knew. My father stopped drinking when we moved down here and it was really great for a while. But it just started all over again."

"Con, why does she let him do it? Why doesn't she call the police?"

"Because that would be so *embarrassing*. My mother wants to keep up appearances. She wants people to think we're this nice little family, just like everybody else."

"But your father, Con, he seems so normal. So nice."

"He is, when he's not drinking." She turned away from me. "When I was little he was the nicest father; he'd take me on his lap and read to me—but all the time he was beating up on my mother. I hate her!"

"You hate *her*?"

She turned around and her eyes were filled with tears, but they were tears of anger.

"I hate her for letting him do it to her. I hate her for being such a fucking—*wimp*!"

I didn't know what to say; but I did know I would carry inside my head the echo of that scream for years to come.

"Con, can't she get help?"

"I've asked her to. I've begged her to. She just says to me, 'You don't understand these things, you're just a child.'"

"Oh shit!"

"And then he sobers up and we all pretend it never happened. We just go on pretending we're a normal family. I even get to believing it myself, and then it's Jack Dempsey time again. And she still loves him. That's the dumb thing."

I couldn't imagine loving a man who beat me up and broke my fingers. I couldn't imagine not fighting back. What did that have to do with love? It was all very puzzling.

"I'm getting out of this fucking house, Peggy, and I never want to see them again. When I graduate, it's goodbye, and I don't ever want to come back to this fucking house again. When we're in New York, I don't even want them to come and visit me."

"Con, let's go to a movie or something." I could tell she needed to get out of the house. I think I knew, too, why she'd been so much of a loner. She had this secret, and she had to carry it around with her, all the time, and she was still only a kid, really, and that was an awful lot for a kid to carry.

"Yeah, let's go to a movie," Con said, and we went out together to my mother's car.

I was growing up fast, I thought, too fast. How many secrets were there in the adult world, dirty little secrets I knew nothing about? So many wonderful things are going to happen to us, Con said, but what about the things that weren't so wonderful? They could happen to us too.

I tried not to think about that as I watched Tyrone Power making love to Rhonda Flemming, kissing her madly when they both weren't fighting off an irate tribe of Zulus somewhere in Africa, but I kept hearing in my head the sound of Con's mother's screams, and seeing her face, the way it had looked when she said, "Frank! Frank!"

With an effort, I forced my thoughts back to the screen. Everything would end up fine in the movies; it always did. Life, I thought, was a lot less predictable.

EIGHT

The Kissing Priest

*T*he altar was resplendent with poinsettias; at Christmastime, St. Malachy's always took on a festive air, with the red flowers matching the red vestments of the priests, and the sweet scent of incense wafting across the church, curling up inside your nostrils, and staying there for hours. Later, that smell would belong not only to Catholics, but would also become the equivalent of Lysol spray for potheads, the incense mingling with the even sweeter smell of marijuana. But while others associate the sweet, sandalwood aroma with turning on in somebody's pad, it always reminds me of God. If God smells like an acidhead, so be it.

I knelt in the pew, inclining my head at the small, icy sound of the bells, and thought that it was my last Christmas as a high school kid—my last as a kid, really. People were right when they said that when you get old, time rushes by. I thought of something we had read in English class. Dr. Faust, waiting for the dawn when the devil would come to claim his soul, crying out, *Lente, lente curritus equus nocte! Run slowly, slowly, horses of the night.* I wanted to call it out, as the bells rang for the Offertory—"Run slowly, slowly!" I wanted this year to stretch into infinity. Next year, it would be different. All of us, the seniors at Immaculate Heart and Sacred Heart, would be spread out across the map, some to college, some to work, some to get married. Some girls would even be mothers by next year. Maybe we'd come back to St. Malachy's for midnight Mass, but it would never be the same.

After Mass, I walked home with Sean, wearing on my wrist the silver bracelet he had given me, with our two names inscribed inside a heart. He wore the silver miraculous medal I had given him, with the word *Sean* etched below the feet of the Blessed Mother. We walked hand in hand, and the sky above us seemed ablaze with stars and the moon was a silver crescent, like a tree ornament, floating in the blackness. Christmas night had always seemed enchanted to me; it was a pagan sort of magic. The Christmas story and the fables of Rapunzel and Rose Red seemed cut from the same cloth—within them, the laws of man and nature were suspended, and marvelous things could happen.

The moonlight, cold and white, washed across the sidewalk and only heightened the sense of otherworldliness. I looked at Sean. His face in the moonlight seemed not to be solid, but ever shifting; he was ephemeral as the night. One minute he seemed the boy I'd always known, his face the same gentle, childish one I once held down in the sandbox until he came up gasping, his eyelashes encrusted with sand and his whole face looking like a sculpture of Childhood. (He stuffed a handful of sand in my mouth for that, nearly choking me.) But I'd look again and it was a man's face I saw: the line of the cheek was more angular, not sweet and round the way it used to be, the jawline squaring off, but the hollow of the neck, the spot I loved to kiss, still as sweet and vulnerable as ever.

Suddenly I had the feeling that I wasn't there, not really, but a long way off in the future, looking back at the two of us. I was trying to reach back, through time, to touch the cool silver of Sean's cheek, and I couldn't reach him, couldn't touch him. "Sean," I called. "*Sean!*" But he couldn't hear me; he just kept walking in the moonlight, beyond my grasp.

Sean and I spent a lot of time that Christmas hanging around with Mollie and her boyfriend, Davy Parelli. Con wasn't much in evidence. She had picked up a guy at People's Drug, a sophomore from U.S.C. home for the holidays, and she was going to parties where everyone drank bourbon, not beer, and got drunk and passed out on the floor. With that kind of adult entertainment available, who wanted to hang around with a bunch of high school kids?

Mollie and I had sort of an easy rapport. We didn't talk a lot, the way Con and I did; Con was so aggressively verbal that we talked all the time, but Mollie and I were good at just being quiet together. Mollie had even features and the blonde good looks so popular then (and now), but she had cool, smoky gray eyes that tended to keep people at a distance. "I am my own person," they seemed to say, and she was. Mollie had a way of looking purposely deshabille before it became chic. Her red uniform ties were always faded, her blue dress a bit threadbare, her oxfords scuffed, but it always looked deliberate, not just sloppy. Mollie was a wizard at math, and she was going to be an engineer. When people told her that women just didn't become engineers, she merely shrugged. Who cared what other people thought?

Mollie's parents had a fit about her going out with Davy, and that wasn't surprising. I thought Sean was mercurial, but compared to Davy he was an island of tranquility. Davy's highs were manic; his laugh sometimes had a knife edge of hysteria in it, and when he plummeted to the depths you just stayed away from him, because he was withdrawn or mean. I think it was this roller-coaster quality of Davy's that intrigued Mollie. There was something in Mollie that seemed drawn to the edges of things. When the eighth-grade class at St. Malachy's went to New York for the class trip, Mollie was the only one of us who tried to lean over the rail fence on top of the Empire State Building, looking into the eye of the abyss. I sensed that Mollie had a recklessness inside that would put Con and me to shame, but it rarely showed on that cool facade of hers.

Mollie liked Davy a lot, though they rarely held hands or gave any display of public emotion. Davy had been thrown out of Sacred Heart freshman year, and was now almost flunking out of Hoover High, which seemed to concern him not in the least. Sean said to him, "I'll never forget how you used to go out the window in the middle of algebra. Brother Michael would really get pissed. He'd keep screaming, 'Somebody stop that boy!' Shit, no one was going to try to stop you from going out the window. We knew you'd just do it all over again."

"Yeah," Davy said, "The fucking brothers!" and that was it, as far as he was concerned, for an entire order of clerics.

We'd never met Davy's mother. She worked as a clerk at a Kresge's downtown someplace, and his father had lit out years ago. The only time Davy ever mentioned him was to say, matter-of-factly, "If my old man ever shows up, I'll cut his fucking throat."

Other than Mollie, Davy cared for only three things as far as we could tell: cars, clothes, and movies. He was what we called a "rock," or sometimes a "drake." He wore peg pants with zippers at the bottom and pink shirts and "Mr. B." collars—named after singer Billy Eckstine—and had the most perfect duck's ass haircut I'd ever seen. It looked as though it had been oiled, and not a hair was out of place.

But what really distinguished Davy from any other kid I ever met was the fact that he had tried to kill himself—three times, in fact. Once he slashed his wrists with a penknife in the boys' bathroom at Hoover. I was fascinated with his wrists, and would stare at the crisscrossing of small cruel canals of scar tissue, some of it old, white, and faded, and some of it a reddish color.

"Does he really want to kill himself?" I asked Mollie.

"Sometimes," she said.

"Can you make him stop doing it?"

Mollie shrugged. "You can't make Davy stop doing something if he wants to do it," she said.

When he wasn't trying to kill himself or tinkering with his car, Davy went to movies. He saw everything: adventure films, three-handkerchief Bette Davis specials, Biblical epics. If he liked a movie enough, he'd see it so many times he'd memorize the dialogue, and he'd do complete scenes for us, with background music. For some reason, he was intrigued with a circus movie called *The Greatest Show on Earth*, about acrobats, and he'd seen it thirty-two times.

"Fucking good movie," he said.

He made that critical comment one night when we were all at Sean's house watching T.V. Dr. McCaffrey and his wife were out at a banquet someplace.

"Come on, let's do the movie," Davy said.

"Which one?" Sean asked.

"The Greatest Show on Earth, natch."

We were all pretty bored, so we said O.K. Davy assigned us our parts. I got the Betty Hutton role as an acrobat, and Mollie got to be an animal trainer.

"You got to look the part," Davy said to me. "This has to be authentic."

I said I had a bathing suit I could use for a costume, so Davy sent me to my house to get it. It had a picture of a duck on it, and Davy said the duck was really ugly, but it would do. Sean got the Jimmy Stewart role of the clown who never takes off his makeup. (Turns out he was really a doctor who had performed an abortion as an act of mercy on an unmarried girl, and was wanted for murder.) Sean thought it was a juicy part; Mollie and I painted up his face with lipstick, and he put on his flannel pajamas, which was as close to a clown suit as he could get. He also dug up an old pith helmet someone had given to his father for Mollie, the animal trainer.

Davy, of course, got the most dramatic role—the Cornell Wilde part as the star trapeze performer. He called himself The Great Zoltan, because Davy had seen a sci-fi flick with a character named Zoltan, and he thought the name was really cool. Zoltan was obsessed with doing a stunt no one else in history had ever done—a triple somersault.

Davy stripped down to his undershorts and declared that he, Zoltan, was going to do the triple, without a net!

"No, Zoltan, you can't!" I sobbed. "You'll be killed."

"Zoltan, don't do it!" Sean implored.

"You'll be all over the floor—splat," Mollie said.

"The Great Zoltan knows no fear!" Davy cried. "No fear!" Then he said, "Oh shit, wait a minute." He disappeared into the kitchen and when he came back he looked as if he'd just made a quick trip to a leper colony. His whole arm was pale white, thanks to the fact that he has just dipped his arm in Mrs. McCaffrey's ten-pound sack of flour.

"Zoltan knows no fear!" he repeated, and climbed up on the arm of the sofa. I climbed up on the arm of a chair across the room.

"Hey, this is fun," Sean said.

"Beats the shit out of the Life of Mother Marie Claire," I said.

"Doctor," Mollie said to Sean, "if Zoltan falls, can you save him?"

"Not me" said Sean, "I'm a urologist. If he breaks his back, tough shit, but if he has trouble peeing, I'm your man."

Meantime, Zoltan was flexing his muscles, way up at the highest point of the Big Top, and he reached up to catch his imaginary trapeze.

"Ladies and gentlemen," I cried, "your attention please! The Great Zoltan is going to attempt a stunt never before performed successfully in any circus, anywhere. He is going to perform the triple somersault—and without a net!"

Zoltan reached up, put both his hands on the trapeze, and bent his knees slightly. (We had piled all the couch pillows up on the floor, so our Zoltan wouldn't land as hard as Cornell Wilde had.)

"Dum Da Dum Dum!" Sean hummed.

"Silence, ladies and gentlemen! Silence, please!" I said dramatically.

Zoltan drew himself to his full height, flexed his legs, and swung out, way out, into space. His body twisted into a pretzel, trying for the vaunted triple, trying, trying—but he missed the bar and plunged like a falling star to the earth. Zoltan let out a horrible scream as he plunged earthward, and then he lay groaning, his arm a twisted claw beneath him.

I screamed.

Mollie screamed.

Sean screamed.

Mrs. McCaffrey screamed loudest of all.

I whirled around and saw them standing there: Mrs. McCaffrey, Dr. McCaffrey—and His Excellency, the Reverend Matthew Hanlon, archbishop of the diocese of Washington and Baltimore.

"Oh *shit!*" I thought.

Dr. McCaffrey had gone white as a fish's belly. He took one look at me, standing on the arm of the chair in my bathing suit, at Sean with lipstick all over his face, and at Zoltan lying on the floor in his underwear, and he looked as if he were going to pass out, right there on the spot. The archbishop just stood there, his mouth gaping open in a most unecclesiastical way.

"Sean!" his father croaked. "*What* is the meaning of this!"

137

"Oh hi, Pop. Mom. Your Excellency. We're doing, *The Greatest Show on Earth*."

Davy got up, his arm still twisted into a claw. "Hi, I'm Zoltan. Zoltan the Great."

"Davy, this is my mom and dad. And Archbishop Hanlon."

"Hi, Your Honor," Davy said.

"Excellency," Sean corrected him.

"Whatever," Davy said.

Davy stuck out his floured hand to shake the hand of the prelate.

"Sean, you are in your pajamas!" Dr. McCaffrey hissed. His eyes had narrowed to slits. I was sure that if he had had a machine gun in his hand at the moment, he'd have mowed down all of us, starting with Sean.

"Oh, I'm a clown," Sean said. "I'm really a doctor, but I'm wanted for murder."

"It's a B movie," I said. "It's not condemned or anything."

"Want to see it? From the top?" Davy asked, his eyes bright with anticipation.

Dr. McCaffrey turned faintly green, but the archbishop said, "I'd love to see it," and he turned to Dr. McCaffrey and said, "I think you are to be congratulated, Liam. It's nice to see teenagers getting interested in something as wholesome as dramatics."

Your Excellency, I thought, *you have saved our asses!* So we ran through it, from the top, and the adults all applauded when Zoltan made his final, terrible plunge—Dr. McCaffrey loudest of all. After all, the archbishop had said we were all right, had put his imprimatur on us, and that was that as far as Dr. McCaffrey was concerned. We could have been standing there stark raving naked, but if the archbishop had approved, he would have clapped just as loudly.

After that, Davy started hanging out with Sean a lot.

Dr. McCaffrey wasn't too happy about it, because he said Davy looked like a juvenile delinquent, but he just grumbled a bit. One night, when Sean and Davy were watching T.V., Sean asked him, "How come you always used to go out the window?"

"I dunno. I felt like it. Sometimes I feel fenced in, y'know, like in *Flash Gordon*. Y'know those walls that move in on you? I feel like that. Then I got to move. I can't stand it when that happens."

"You going to college or anything, Davy?"

"Nah. I was thinking, I might drive out to Hollywood after I graduate, get some kind of tech job in the movies."

"That would be cool."

"I dunno. After a while, I'd probably feel just like I feel here. Maybe I'll bum around for a while."

The future didn't exist for Davy; it seemed to be like some formless, floating cloud. He was so different from most of the boys at Sacred Heart, who had already started to draw the maps that would carry them into the future: college choices, careers selected, dreams already born. Davy was a creature of the present, and he was like the sea, moving, restless. He couldn't be still, but motion didn't seem to bring him joy. Sean was drawn to him, and with those finely honed pain sensors of his, he picked up Davy's inner turmoil.

"I feel bad for Davy," he said.

"Why?"

"He doesn't seem to belong anywhere. And he knows it. But he can't do anything about it."

"Lots of kids are like that; they get straightened out."

"No, I don't think that's it with Davy. I think he's like—a Martian would be. Always out of place."

"You mean there isn't any place for him, anywhere?"

"I don't know. I asked him why he tried to kill himself."

"You asked him? And he didn't get mad?"

"No. He says that when he gets to feeling like he did when he went out the window at Sacred Heart, he has to get out, only there aren't any more windows."

"Except one."

"I guess so. He says he can't breathe, even the air hurts, and he has to bust out."

"He's a kid, Sean. He'll grow out of it."

"I hope so."

But Davy was pretty up all through vacation, and we had a lot of fun, going to movies and parties. Toward the end of the two weeks, just having fun started to pall, as it always did. That's why I was glad that Con dropped back into our lives again. The U.S.C. sophomore had gone south, and she regaled us with tales of life in the fast lane.

"I passed right out on the couch!" she said. I mean, *everybody* passed out. It was a blast!"

"Con, you shouldn't pass out. I mean, somebody could rape you!"

"Everybody was too drunk to rape anybody. Oh, did I tie one on!"

Sean turned to me and said, "Were you ever drunk?"

"Oh yeah. At Suzie Meadows's slumber party. We drank her father's stuff. I think I put a lampshade on my head."

"I've never been drunk," Sean said glumly.

"Well, that's something to be proud of," I told him.

"I ought to know how it feels, at least. They don't let you get drunk in the seminary."

"They don't let you do anything fun in the seminary," Con said.

Sean began to brood about the fact that he had never been plastered. "I've never even been high," he said. "I'm a wimp!"

He went on and on about it until Con and I finally got fed up and Con said to him, "Sean, you want to get drunk, we'll get you drunk. You can get plastered among friends."

140

"Would you?" he said. "Really?"

So, the last night of vacation, Sean and Con and I climbed in the black Ford and drove to Sligo Creek Park and Con pulled out a whole bottle of bourbon and we all got in the back seat. Con handed Sean the bottle. "Better you than my father."

Sean took a big swig of bourbon. "Ugh!" he said.

"Haven't you ever had hard liquor before?" Con asked.

"Sure. But my father drinks Scotch. I never had bourbon before." He glugged down some more.

"Careful, that's hundred proof," Con said. "You're not supposed to swill it like beer."

"I don't feel anything," Sean said. He chug-a-lugged some more bourbon. A quarter of the bottle was gone.

"Feel it?" Con asked.

"Nothing," Sean said. He tipped the bottle again. "I don't feel a thing."

"God, Sean, you're a sponge," Con said. Sean drank again. Half the bottle was gone now.

"Oh damn," Sean said. "I bet I'm immune. I bet I can't even *get* drunk." He took two more swallows. "Wait a minute, I think I'm starting to feel warm."

I put my hand to his forehead. "A little bit."

"Kiss me!" he ordered. I kissed him.

He took another drink. "Ummmm," he said, "do it again." I did.

"Oh this is swell," Con said," a ménage à trois and I'm not even the trois."

"A what?" Sean asked.

"Three people having sex," I said.

Sean giggled.

"He's getting high," Con said.

"O.K., *you* kiss me," he said to Con.

"Why not?" She leaned over and kissed him. Then he took another big swallow.

"Sean, I think you're having too much of that stuff, too fast," I said.

"Shut up and kiss me again," he said. I did, and then he tipped the bottle up again. "Now you," he said to Con. He gave her a long, lingering kiss—and he opened his mouth, I noticed.

"Hey!" I said. Sean giggled again.

"He's a good kisser," Con said.

"Yeah, he is."

"Too bad he's going to be a priest."

Sean giggled. "The kissing priest, that's me!" he said, and he grabbed me and kissed me again, hard.

"He's a sex fiend," Con said.

"Umm. Sex fiend." Sean took another swallow. His words were starting to slur, I noticed. "Both kiss me," he said.

"You're a degenerate, Sean," Con said, but she kissed him on the earlobe and I kissed him on the neck, and he let out a sound that was half a moan, half a sigh.

"More," he said.

"More what?" Con said. "Booze or kissing."

"Both," he said, and giggled again.

"Let's give him what he asked for," Con said, and she pushed him down against the armrest and she started to nibble on his ear while I kept kissing him on the lips.

"More more more," he said, and giggled again. And Sean was definitely not a giggler.

"Con, he's getting schnockered," I said.

"That's not all he's getting," she said, nodding in the direction of Sean's trousers.

Sean burped, then giggled. "We're having a manage, a manage—what are we having?"

"Let's get him out in the fresh air," I said.

Sean took another swig of bourbon and started kissing my neck.

"Come on, Sean," I said, "we've got to get out," and

Con and I literally dragged him out of the car. He just stood there, leaning against the fender, his eyes unnaturally bright.

"Shit, I'm drunk," he said, and then he giggled again. "I did it."

"How does it feel?" I asked.

"Drunk." He let out a hoot. Then he giggled again, and said, "Can't catch me!" and he took off at a zig-zag run across the park.

We walked quickly after him. "He drank practically the whole bottle," Con said. "No telling what he'll do."

"Yeah, we better get him home."

"Let's go to the *beach*!" Sean yelled, and before we could get to him he had pulled off his shoes and socks and waded into the filthy, frigid waters of Sligo Creek. He just stood there, grinning at us, up to his knees in water.

"Sean, come back here!" I yelled.

He hopped around in the water. "*The beach*!" he giggled.

"Peg, if he stays in that cold water too long, he could get pneumonia."

Now he was flapping his arms like some kind of big, goofy bird, stomping around and giggling.

"Sean, please come out of there. You'll catch your death of cold," I called.

"Death of Cold," he chuckled. He was grinning, and then he started dancing around, splashing and chanting in a crazed version of a Gregorian chant, "Death of cold, death of cold, death of cooooolllldddddd—"

"I guess I'll have to go in after him," I said, so I pulled off my sneakers and socks and rolled up my jeans and waded out into the cold water. I advanced toward him, my hand extended.

"Come on, Sean. we're going home."

"No we're not!" He giggled.

"Come on, Sean."

"Death of Cold. Co-oh-ohohoh-oh-oh-oh-oh-ld."

I made a grab for him, but he giggled and hopped away.

"Sean, stop this!"

"Death death, death, cold, cold cold!"

I made another lunge and he tried to jump away again, but his foot slipped and down he went, face first in the freezing water.

"Oh *God*!" Con shrieked, and she plunged in too, shoes and all. Between the two of us, we dragged him up and helped him stumble to the bank. Sean was shivering as the cold air hit his soaking body. I ripped off my jacket and put it around his quivering shoulders.

"Quick, back to my house!" I said, and we helped the stumbling Sean back to the car and shoved him in. His eyes were glittering. "I don't feel good," he said.

Con made it home at breakneck speed, and we pushed Sean, still shivering, out of the car and marched him around to the back door of my house. I called upstairs to my mother, "Mom, Con and I are going to be in my room playing records."

"All right, dear, just don't forget to lock the back door," she called down.

We hustled Sean into the bathroom next to my bedroom and then stripped off all his wet clothes except for his underpants. We shoved him into the shower stall and I turned on the hot water.

"That'll warm him up," I said, and I went into the bedroom and put nice warm wool socks on my freezing feet. I went back to the shower and peered in at Sean. He was leaning against the wall, his eyes closed, and his skin starting to turn lobster red from the hot water.

I turned the water off. "Sean, come on out."

He just stood there, his eyes closed." Ohhhhh," he moaned, "I'm dying!"

"Sean, you are not dying."

"Yes I am. Ohhhhhh!"

Finally Con and I had to grab his arms and pull him out of the shower.

"Going round," he said. "Everything."

I took a big towel and dried him off. He just stood there, swaying and moaning.

"Ohhh, I feel awful," he said. "Going to barf."

I pushed him towards the toilet and he collapsed over it and began to vomit, his whole body heaving as everything in his stomach came up. He kept vomiting until nothing more came up, and then he got the dry heaves, his whole body shaking.

"Ohhhhhhhh. Dying," he moaned.

I wiped his face with a wet towel.

"Want to die!"

"Poor baby," I said, wiping his face again.

"Come on," Con said, "Let's get the Kissing Priest back to the bedroom."

We helped Sean back to my bedroom and I said to Con, "He shouldn't have those wet underpants on, he could get chilled," and she said, "O.K., get him a pair of yours."

I went to my drawer and pulled out my last clean pair of panties, blue nylon ones with yellow daisies on them. We wrapped a towel around Sean's waist and I said, "Sean, take your shorts off."

"Want to die. Now," he said. I reached up under the towel, and managed to drag the wet underpants down his legs. Sean stepped out of them. Then Con held the daisy panties down by Sean's feet.

"Step!" she commanded. He obeyed her.

"Other foot." He put his other foot in the leg of the panties.

"Pull them up, Sean," I said.

"Up," he repeated. He just stood there.

"Oh for heaven's sake!" I said, and I bent over, and

145

with a lot of pulling and hauling, I got the panties up, under the towel.

"Now what?" Con said.

"He can't stay here. We've got to get him home."

"And just how do we do that?"

"His bedroom is on the first floor in the back. The window's never locked."

"O.K., let's do it."

We wrapped Sean in a blanket and I put an old pair of slippers, pink fuzzy ones, on his feet and we propelled him down the back hall to the door.

"Where we goin?" he slurred.

"Home. Be quiet, Sean."

"Dying."

We walked him through the backyard to the back of his house, looking like a scene from *The Ransom of Red Chief*, and I quietly lifted the window to his bedroom as far as it would go. Sean's bed was right by the window; we shoved his torso through the frame until his head and shoulders were resting on the bed, but his feet were still on the ground.

"Sean, crawl through!" I ordered. "Come on!"

"Drunk," he said. He closed his eyes. He didn't move.

"We can't leave him like this!" Con said.

"We'll have to drag him through. Come on."

Con and I crawled over Sean, into the room; we dragged Sean's legs through the window and turned him around on the bed so that he was lying in it the right way.

"Ooohhhhhh!" he moaned.

"Sean, shut up!"

"Oohhhhh! Don't feel good!"

Just then we heard a noise in the hall outside the bedroom. "Sean? Sean, is that you? It was Dr. McCaffrey's voice. His footsteps moved toward the door to the room. Con and I took one look at each other, and we were both thinking exactly the same thing. We made a dive for under the bed and smacked our heads together as we did. Con just managed to drag her foot under the bed as the door opened and the light snapped on.

"Sean? Sean, what on earth—Mary, Mary, come quick!"

"Ohhhhhh!" Sean moaned.

"Sean, are you ill? his father asked. Sean had wrapped both hands around his pillow and shoved his face into it.

Sean's mother's footsteps moved into the room.

"What is it, Liam? Is Sean ill?"

We saw Dr. McCaffrey's feet move close to the bed. We heard him sniffing the air, as well.

"Young man, what's the meaning of this!"

"Dying," Sean said.

"Look at him. *Look* at him!" Dr. McCaffrey said to his wife. "Mary, he's as drunk as a lord!"

"Oh, *Sean*. My baby!"

"What is he wearing. What *is* that he's wearing?"

Now we could see Sean's mother's tiny feet as she too moved close to the bed.

"Panties," she said. "He's wearing girls' panties."

"On my GOD!" said Dr. McCaffrey.

"Sean, darling, why are you wearing girls' panties? And slippers? Look, Liam, girls' slippers."

"He smells like a brewery and he's wearing *panties*! Young man, where the hell have you been? Answer me!"

"Doan feel good," Sean moaned.

"Dear, I don't think he's in any condition to discuss this right now."

"My boy," Dr. McCaffrey said plaintively. "My little boy, what's happened to you?"

"Sean, dear, I'm putting your covers on," his mother said.

"He was such a good child," Dr. McCaffrey said. "So quiet. So polite. And now he's dead drunk and he's wearing *panties*!"

"They grow up so fast," Sean's mother said.

"That Morrison kid," Dr. McCaffrey growled. "I bet she has something to do with this."

Con jabbed me in the ribs. Meantime, I was struggling to ward off a sneeze—the dust under Sean's bed was getting in my nose and I wanted to sneeze more than anything in the world. I practically strangled myself holding it in.

"I'm going right over to that house and I'm going to get to the bottom of this!" Dr. McCaffrey announced, and he stormed out of the room.

"Goodnight, dear, sleep tight," Sean's mother said as she left the room and closed the door.

Con and I dragged ourselves out from under Sean's bed. Sean moaned again.

"The kissing priest is going to have one hell of a hangover," Con said, looking at him.

"Jeez, Con, let's go. He's halfway to my house by now!"

We both scrambled back out the window and ran as fast as we'd ever run in our lives back to my house. We got inside, dashed into my room, turned on the record player and tried to steady our breathing down. There was a rap on my door, and my mother, in her bathrobe, said, "Peggy dear, Dr. McCaffrey would like to talk to you. He says it's important."

Con and I walked out into the front hall to confront Dr. McCaffrey.

"Have you been with my son!" he thundered.

"With Sean? No, sir."

"We've been here playing records," Con said. "Is something the matter?"

"Is anything the *matter*? I'll tell you what's the matter! My son is lying in his bed dead drunk, that's what's the matter."

"Sean?" I said, trying to look shocked. "Drunk? Oh, I can't believe it."

"It's true. Drunk as a lord!"

"Everybody knows Sean doesn't drink," Con said, her eyes wide and innocent. "Why, he's an *inspiration* to the other boys at Sacred Heart."

"You weren't with him?"

"Oh no, sir," I said.

"That Davy kid. What's his name?"

"Davy Parelli?"

"That's the one. The juvenile delinquent. I bet he's the one who got my boy drunk."

"I don't know, sir."

"Well—" he said. "Well, goodnight," and he stomped off.

"Poor Sean, Con said. "If only we hadn't put the panties on him. He's really going to get it."

"Yeah, he will, this time."

"It's partly our fault."

"I know. But he nagged us, Con, he really did."

"Well, he'll have one hell of a story to tell in the seminary. Except I guess they don't let you tell those kinds of stories there."

"I wouldn't think so."

"He's a crazy kid, Sean."

I laughed. "Yeah, he is."

Con looked at me. "Peggy," she said, "how the hell is Sean going to turn into a priest?"

"Beats me," I said.

NINE

In Hoc Signo Vinces

"We must smash communism!" Con announced.

"Yeah, sure," I replied, writing the last line of an editorial on school spirit (nonexistent at Immaculate Heart, I decreed).

"Peg, you don't take the Red Menace seriously enough. Don't you listen to J. Edgar Hoover?"

Con was always a little to the right of me, politically. I couldn't figure out how anybody who wanted to be beautiful and damned could wear an Eisenhower button, but life, I was learning, was full of contradictions.

"This, from the person who canonized Leon Trotsky?" I said.

"That was just a joke. This is *serious*. . ."

"Yeah, the Red Hordes are all the way down Sixteenth Street," I said. "They just took over Morris Miller Liquors."

"It's people like you who will be sorry when we're on our knees before Joe Stalin."

"You really are on an anticommie kick lately. How come?"

"Lee and I talked about it a lot last weekend. He opened my eyes. There are Russian spies everywhere, Peg. J. Edgar Hoover has drawers full of reports on them."

I groaned. "How does Midshipman Masters know what's in J. Edgar Hoover's drawers?" I chuckled at my own double entendre. "Get it? J. Edgar Hoover's *drawers*!"

Con didn't crack a smile. Maybe it was a shame that Operation Middie had worked so well, if Con was going to be such a bore on the subject of communism. It figured that Lee Masters would be a commie baiter; any guy who had a blond crewcut, dimples in his chin, and came from St. Louis was bound to think Alger Hiss was guilty as hell.

"Librarians," Con said.

"What?"

"Do you know how much harm one communist librarian in a public school could do? Hundreds of American kids could get caught in The Web of Deception."

"I always did have my doubts about Sister Conception Rose," I said, "ever since I wanted to take out *Saints Are Not Sad* and she made me take out *Das Kapital* instead."

But Con would not be jollied. She was dead serious about her new crusade, and her weekends at Annapolis weren't making things any better. I didn't know how she planned to lose her virginity, when they seemed to spend all their time talking about J. Edgar Hoover. I pictured them, sitting close together in the drag house, underlining all the dirty parts in *I Was a Communist for the FBI*.

Con had even taken to hanging around the classroom of Sister Immelda Mary, who was Immaculate Heart's numero uno booster of Joe McCarthy. Sister Immelda was behind a one-woman campaign to get the pope to consider Joe McCarthy for sainthood, a prospect that made me want to barf. I could just picture tail-gunner Joe, roaming around heaven looking for commies. "I have in my hand a list. . ."

It really blew my mind to see Con and Sister Immelda so chummy, because the two of them had had a big dust-up sophomore year when Con announced she believed in the theory of evolution.

Sister Immelda was shocked. "Constance, do you really

want to believe that your ancestors hung by their tails from trees?"

"Why not? It's scientific. You don't expect me to believe that story of Adam and Eve. It's right out of *Grimm's Fairy Tales*."

"Miss Constance Wepplener, you are blaspheming!"

"No I'm not. I just believe in Natural Selection, Survival of the Fittest."

"You said that Adam and Eve was a—a—*Fairy Tale!*"

"Sort of," Con said. "A fable, like the Epic of Gilgamesh—that's Hindu."

"Hindu! Miss Wepplener, do you mean to tell me you read things written by *heathens*!"

"Hindus aren't heathens, Sister. Their religion is a lot older than ours is."

"You march yourself right down to the principal, Miss Smarty Pants, and we'll see about this!"

The whole thing blew over when Sister Robert Mary told Con it was O.K. for her to believe in Darwin if she also believed in God. Con said that she did, and she also promised not to debate the point with Sister Immelda, who took a rather literal view of things Biblical. She believed that there *was* an apple, probably a MacIntosh. She also told us that black people bore the mark of Cain. When Cain killed Abel, the Bible said, God put a mark on him so that everyone would know, and that mark was black skin. The N.A.A.C.P. would have thrown a fit over that one; fortunately, Sister Immelda's theology didn't have a very wide circulation. But then, Sister Immelda also said that Mary Magdalen had a part-time job tending goats, and *that* was why the snobby people in the Bible didn't like her.

Lately, however, the Great Monkey Battle between Con and Sister Immelda had apparently been forgotten because the two of them were thick as thieves. They were hatching something, but Con was circumspect and wouldn't tell me anything about it. I think she suspected I'd go straight to the Russian embassy. So I didn't meet Count Orlov until the day he came strolling into the *Messenger* room, right behind Con. I could hardly believe my eyes when I saw him. He was six foot seven if he was an inch, and he had to hunch down to get through the doorway. He wore, over his dark business suit, a black cape with a red silk lining and ermine trim, which he said had once belonged to Tsar Nicholas. I had my doubts; it looked as if he'd lifted it from the property room at the Metropolitan Opera.

"Peggy, this is Count Vladimir Illyich Orlov," said Con. "He's Russian."

I was going to say that I really wasn't about to mistake him for the exalted leader of the Ancient Order of Hibernians, but I thought better of it when I looked at the count. He didn't seem like a guy with a big sense of humor.

"The count is speaking at an assembly next week and we're doing a story on him," Con said.

The count bowed gravely to me, and I stuck out my hand, democratic style. I didn't hold with this royalty stuff. The count sat down in a chair and started to explain the subject of his talk, but every time he looked right at me I felt a chill run up and down my back. The count had large, wide, hypnotic eyes. They seemed vaguely familiar to me and I wondered where I had seen such eyes before. Then it came to me—in our history text, the Mad Monk Rasputin. Or maybe it was Eddie Cantor. Anyway, he had weird eyes.

The count, it turned out, was a Russian nobleman (so he claimed) who had heard a voice from God commanding him to reclaim Russia in the name of the Holy Virgin. He was going to do it by holding bake sales and raffling off a new Buick. I tried to imagine his conversation with God:

"Count Orlov! Count Orlov! Up here!"

"What? What? That voice! From whence does it come?"

"Up here, on the left, by the grease spot on the ceiling. It's God talking."

"My God!"

"Right the first time."

"What can I do, My Lord?"

"I am calling you on a sacred mission. Reclaim Russia in the name of the Blessed Mother."

"But how, oh Lord? Where are my legions, my weapons?"

"Tollhouse cookies."

"I beg your pardon?"

"And sponge cakes and brownies and (you should excuse the expression) devil's food. Go forth and hold bake sales."

"I am your humble servant, Lord!"

"And while you're at it, pick up a '56 Buick, hydromatic drive, white sidewalls."

Count Orlov was promoting something called Smash Godless Communism Day, which was to be a giant rally on the monument grounds, and in which a hundred thousand Catholics were to gather and pray like crazy at the same time, sending a huge tidal wave of Hail Marys against the gates of the Kremlin. Count Orlov actually seemed to think that would bring the walls tumbling down. I figured one well-placed ICBM would do it better, but it would take a hell of a lot of bake sales to buy one of those.

I walked home from school with Sean the day Con brought the count to the office. Sean had survived the whole panties episode pretty well. He had been really hung over the next morning, but his brain was working well enough to come up with a good story. He said that a bunch of the "wild" kids at Sacred Heart had made a bet that they could get Sean drunk, because everybody knew he didn't drink. They gave him liquor in orange juice, and when he passed out, they took his clothes and put the panties on him as a gag. Dr. McCaffrey wanted to make a big deal out of it with the brothers, try to get those awful boys expelled, but Sean begged him not to, because he said he'd be branded as a squealer and he wouldn't have any friends.

154

As we were walking, Sean said to me, "There was a really weird guy at our house last night."

"Oh?"

"Big guy, with wild eyes, and he was wearing this *cape*. Scared the shit out of me when I walked in. I thought he was Dracula."

"Count Orlov!"

"Yeah, that's the guy."

"Sean, what was Count Orlov doing at your house?"

"I don't know. He was talking to my father about some rally. I could hardly understand the guy. He talks like Boris Karloff."

"This is *not* good news," I said. I explained to him about who Count Orlov was and what he was planning to do.

"He's going to *pray* the Kremlin into little pieces?"

"He says the prayers of a hundred thousand Catholics will create a resonance in the upper atmosphere that will cause winds of a thousand miles an hour in Red Square."

"He said that? With a straight face?"

"Yeah."

"I'll huff and I'll puff and I'll blow your house in?"

"That's the general idea."

"My God, my father is going to do it *again*!" Sean moaned.

"It looks that way."

Sean sighed, another one of those grown-up sighs he'd been doing lately. "Why does he attract loonies? What is it about him?"

"You'd think he'd have learned something after Father Clement Kliblicki and his modesty crusaders."

"My father doesn't seem to learn things. He just keeps on smacking into one wall after another."

"Look at it this way, Sean. Your father isn't *dull*."

"That's for sure," he said glumly.

Sean hoped that the count would simply fade out of his father's life—maybe just turn into a bat and sail off into the

155

night—but no such luck. Smash Godless Communism Day was scheduled for a Saturday in March, and the planning went on at a feverish pace. The count and Dr. McCaffrey spent hours together, huddled around the dining room table, and Dr. McCaffrey started to get that expression of demented enthusiasm in his eyes again. The *Catholic Herald* ran a big story about the rally, although there was no mention of thousand-mile-an-hour winds. The count was playing it close to his chest on that one.

The day of the rally dawned bright and clear, and we all rendezvoused at Sean's house. The count was decked out in his most splendid finery. He was not only wearing his cape, but on his breast sparkled a Byzantine Cross encrusted with rubies, and he wore at his waist a white leather scabbard with the hilt of a sword protruding from it. The hilt of the sword glittered, like the Cross, with precious stones. I was mightily impressed. The count's sword made Excalibur look like a carving knife.

We all set off for the monument grounds, with Dr. McCaffrey driving the white Caddy, Count Orlov beside him, and Sister Immelda beside the count. Sean, Con, and I were in the back seat, and Davy and Mollie were following, in Davy's car.

"Oh, Count, this will be a historic day!" cooed Sister Immelda.

"Today we begin the march to victory!" Count Orlov said.

"I hope they don't forget the portable toilets," Dr. McCaffrey said.

"Yeah, it's hard to pray good when you have to pee," Sean said. Con jabbed him with her elbow.

We rode in silence for a while, and then Sean said, "Hey Count, how many people do you think we'll need to pray to get the winds up to a thousand?"

I shot him a warning glance, but his face was as innocent as a choirboy's.

156

"It will depend," the count said, "on how fervently our people can pray. If our hearts are pure, if we are not Doubting Thomases, God will send the power of nature to assist us in our cause. But if we cannot gird our loins, if we are not pure in spirit, surely then we will fail."

"Yeah, if we only get'em up to thirty-five miles per hour, we'll just stir the dust around and aggravate their allergies a little," Sean said.

This time I jabbed him in the ribs. I looked at the profile of the count: the strong aquiline nose under the heavy brows. This was a guy who did not kid around. He really was ready to pray the Kremlin to its knees. I wondered if the people in the politburo were quaking in their boots.

"Brace yourselves, Comrades. The Catholics in Bethesda, Chevy Chase, Crystal Springs, and maybe even Alexandria, Virginia, are praying up a storm."

"We have them on our radar now. A squadron of Hail Marys."

"Hail Marys? That's *it?*"

"No, there's a few Our Fathers and some other stuff thrown in."

"Where are they now?"

"Coming in over Leningrad, on a wing and a prayer."

"Ten seconds to impact. Five, four, three, two, one—"

"Oh, my God!"

"You can't say that. We don't believe in Him."

"Damage report, Comrade General."

"Lenin's tomb has just taken a direct hit from an Apostles' Creed."

I was going to write a story about the rally for the *Marian Messenger*, so I guessed I'd better start my work. "Uh, Count, do you really think we can do it? I mean, knock down the Kremlin?"

"More things are wrought by prayer than this world dreams of," he said.

157

"Yeah, but wouldn't a lot of innocent people get hurt? Just ordinary people, not communist bigwigs."

"God swept his fiery sword across Sodom and Gomorrah!" he declaimed. "He destroyed the world in a flood when the people knew not God!"

"The Blessed Mother sent us a warning, at Fatima," said Sister Immelda. "She told us that Russia must be converted or terrible things will happen."

"Let a tidal wave of blood sweep from the Urals to the sea!" the count thundered. "Let the blood of the Godless drench the fields, flow through the cities, let the Virgin crush the heads of atheists as she crushed the head of the serpent!" He took the ruby-encrusted Cross that hung from his neck and raised it above his head: "*In hoc signo vinces*. In this sign, you will conquer!"

"I bet they won't have enough hot dogs," Dr. Mc-Caffrey said. "If we get a hundred thousand, we'll run out of hot dogs for sure."

"I love hot dogs," Sister Immelda said. "We don't get them much in the convent."

"They have no hot dogs in Russia," said the count. "I too like hot dogs."

"When Russia is converted, then they'll have hot dogs," Sister Immelda said with conviction.

Sean reached over and took my notebook, the one I had brought to take notes for my story. He took out his pen, and made a quick sketch of a hot dog in a bun—Sean was a good drawer—and underneath he printed the words, *In Hoc Signo Vinces*.

I had to shove a knuckle in my mouth to keep from laughing outright. Then I whispered to him, "Our secret weapon!" and I took his sketch and I wrote on the hot dog, "B.V.M. Franks." Underneath, I wrote:

> Mother dear, Oh pray for me
> Whilst far from heaven and Thee

        Just one bite of a B.V.M. frank
        Is a taste of Eternity.

We both giggled quietly, and Con threw us a disap-
proving glance. I handed her the sheet of notebook paper
and she looked at it, her face set in a hard anticommunist
line. But then I noticed the corners of her lips tugging upward; even the militant Con, the red-baiting, J. Edgar
Hoover-loving Con, couldn't resist a funny line. She fought
it, but in a minute she was stuffing her knuckles in her
mouth like I had, trying not to crack up.

When we got to the momument grounds, everything
was in readiness for the rally. The portable bathrooms had
indeed arrived, the hot dog stands were doing a brisk business, and a stage had been set up for the speakers. It was
draped in blue bunting, with a banner featuring the Blessed
Mother, in her usual blue-and-white color-coordinated en-
semble, draped across the top of the stage. There was another banner on the far side of the stage, which depicted a
huge Cross, landing like a buzz bomb on a hammer and
sickle, smashing it into tiny pieces, under the words *In Hoc
Signo Vinces*.

A good crowd had already begun to gather, nothing
like the hundred thousand that Count Orlov said was
needed to polish off the Kremlin, but there did seem to be
several thousand people milling about. Sean, Con, Mollie,
Davy, and I wandered around for a while, and then we
noticed that little knots of people were gathered around
what appeared to be informal speakers in several areas of
the grounds. We ambled over to see what was up.

In the center of one group was a man in white priests'
robes, surrounded by a small group of men and women
who were dressed in a similar manner. But the women, although they wore nunlike garments, didn't wear the standard head coverings, but long mantles like the Blessed
Mother wore in her pictures. The men and women all wore

some kind of a chain around their waists, which served as a belt, and large red cloth hearts about their necks. In the center of the group, the man who was speaking was gesturing with his hands; he was a small, rather mild-looking man—I'd have thought he was maybe a G.S-five in the commerce department—except for his eyes, which had a Count Orlov glitter to them. One of the women was holding a hand-lettered sign saying, "Slaves of the Immaculate Heart of Jesus."

"Protestants! Jews!" the man was saying. "Accept the One True Church, before it is too late. The gates of heaven are barred to those who do not accept the Holy Roman Universal and Apostolic Catholic Church. It is the only true Church. Listen and be saved!"

The man threw his arms in the air, a gesture of appeal to heaven.

"Holy shit," Sean said. "It's Father Frank Feeley."

We'd all heard stories about Father Feeley, the brilliant scholar and poet who had simply gone round the bend one day and decided that everybody went to hell but Catholics, an opinion that many of his fellow religionists might have agreed with privately, but didn't like to say out loud, especially if their bosses were Jews or Methodists. The hierarchy kept trying to get Father Feeley to soft-pedal the hell business, but Father Feeley was adamant about that, and he had gathered his own little band, which went about the East Coast preaching.

"Who's he?" asked Davy. The Reverend Frank Feeley was not as well known a personage at Hoover High as he was at Sacred Heart.

"He's been excommunicated," Sean told Davy.

"No kidding? Tossed out on his can?"

"Yep."

"How come?"

"He says Protestants can't get to heaven," Mollie explained.

160

"Can they?"

"Yeah, if they're sincere in their beliefs," Sean said.

"No shit," Davy said. "I didn't know that."

We listened to Father Frank Feeley for a while, but it got boring pretty fast. Besides, most of the people listening to him were Catholics, so nobody tried to punch him out, which happened a lot to Father Feeley. I guessed that his new life—getting smacked in the teeth in shopping malls and parking lots—was a lot more exciting than his old one, sitting in a classroom and lecturing on medieval poetry.

Over the loudspeaker system came the announcement that the glee club from Visitation Convent would perform for the multitudes, and the clear, piping voices of female singers started in, inexplicably, on "I'm Looking over a Four Leaf Clover."

"What's going on over there?" Con asked, and we walked in the direction she had pointed, where another small group had gathered. Holding forth there was a young man, who looked, I thought, a little bit like Lee Masters with his blond crew cut, and who was wearing brown pants and a brown shirt, and some kind of strange officer's cap. It had a skull and crossbones on it, and an American flag. Four other young men, dressed in similar fashion, stood with their arms crossed and legs spread, Benito Mussolini style, peering malevolently out at the crowd.

The young man, his chin thrust out aggressively, was saying, "Are you going to let the niggers and the Jews take over the country? Commies want the niggers to take over. They want them to marry your daughters and produce a race of little brown bastards to take over the country and give it to Karl Marx."

Davy looked at Sean. "Did this cat get excommunicated too?"

"I don't think he's a Catholic."

"Oh," Davy said. "With those uniforms, I thought they might be from St. John's."

161

The young man, we discovered, was Commander Raymond G. Blanton, from the Fighting American Patriots and Heroes, of Upper Marlboro, Maryland, and his Thunder Troopers.

"Thunder Troopers?" Con said. "Those guys don't look like they have the brains to come in out of the rain."

"They all have acne," I said. "You ever hear of an Aryan superman with acne?"

"Kill the niggers! Kill the Jews!" Commander Blanton screamed.

"I guess he isn't big on Brotherhood Week," Sean said.

"We ought to get him for our assembly next time," I suggested. "He's a lot livelier than the life of Mother Marie Claire."

"Yeah, and I bet *he* gets canonized before Mother Marie makes it," Con said.

The Visitation Glee Club switched to "I Want a Girl Just like the Girl Who Married Dear Old Dad," and we wandered over to the third little group that had gathered in another part of the grounds.

There were about twelve people holding signs in this group, printed signs tacked to wooden slats: FREE ALGER HISS. DOWN WITH FASCISM. IMPEACH MCCARTHY. DOWN WITH FRANCO.

The speaker here was a tall, gaunt man clad in jeans and a work shirt, who had a flamboyant mane of silver hair, and who still retained in his speech traces of a boyhood in Dublin. He was Seamus O'Flaherty, president of the Socialist Progressive People's Worker's Party.

"They're commies," Sean announced.

"How do you know?"

"Anything with *People* in it is a communist front."

"People's Drug Store?"

"Well, almost anything," Sean said.

The people around Seamus O'Flaherty were a fairly unkempt lot, also clad in work clothes, and they applauded wildly every few minutes. Everybody else just stood around quietly.

"He's Irish, and he's a communist?" I said to Sean.

"He's from New York."

"Oh," I said. Strange and wonderful things happened in New York that didn't happen anywhere else in America—somebody with a name like Seamus could be a real, live communist. I wondered if I *really* wanted to go there. You could probably Lose Your Faith real easy in New York. (That was always the big warning to Catholic kids who were tempted to stray off their own turf—like to a state university. You could Lose Your Faith. The nuns always said it that way, with capital letters, as if faith was like a clutch bag, which could just slip through your fingers and onto the sidewalk before you even missed it.)

"Did you think we defeated fascism when we destroyed Hitler, vanquished the Roman legions of Benito?" Seamus O'Flaherty asked, in a deep, musical voice. "Oh no, my friends, no! Fascism is in flower here, in the very citadel of democracy. It is not only in the fascist countries that people are thrown into prison, hounded into exile for their beliefs!"

The Visitation Glee Club switched to a musical version of Joyce Kilmer's "Trees":

I think that I shall never see
A poem lovely as a tree—

The crowd around Seamus O'Flaherty and his group started to get larger as the word spread that there was a communist, in the flesh, on the monument grounds. It wasn't every day you got to see a commie, close up.

"There is blood on the hands of Franco, and we pay for his bloody terror by the aid and comfort we give—"

Suddenly there was a stirring around the edges of the crowd, and then it parted like the Red Sea, and storming

163

through the opening, Rasputin-eyes flashing, was none other than Count Vladimir Illyich Orlov.

"Swine!" he thundered, taking one look at Seamus O'Flaherty and shaking his fist at the sky.

Seamus O'Flaherty looked at the count and spat contemptuosly on the ground.

"Tsarist pig!" he hissed.

"I think they know each other," I said to Sean.

"Scum of Satan, filth thrown up from the bowels of the sewers of Sodom!" growled Count Orlov.

"Oppressor of the masses, running dog lackey of the Wall Street bloodsuckers!" countered Seamus O'Flaherty.

A Tree who may in summer wear
A nest of robins in her hair—

"Seed of Lucifer, bastard son of Beelzebub, excrement of the Jew pig Karl Marx, slime of the earth!"

Antisemite, Nazi murderer, pig who would violate the sacred womb of your mother in the unholy name of Capitalist avarice!"

"They sure have good vocabularies," Sean said, admiringly.

The crowd was growing larger by the minute, and it now included Father Frank Feeley and his Immaculate Slaves and Commander Blanton and his Thunder Troopers; the commander, in fact, was standing right next to me.

"May God strike you down in the filth where you stand!" roared Count Orlov.

Commander Blanton nudged me on the shoulder and asked, "Is he a Ruskie?"

"Yes," I said.

"He's a commie, then."

"No, he's a White Russian."

"They have *niggers* in Russia?" the commander said, astonished. *"Damn!"*

"God is a myth, invented to oppress the masses. Opium of the people!" yelled Seamus.

Upon whose bosom snow has lain—

Father Frank Feeley had been watching, and, seeing himself fatally upstaged, decided to remedy that situation by stepping between Seamus and the count, throwing his arms in the air, and crying, "Accept the One True Church and be saved!"

"Who's he?" the commander asked.

"Father Frank Feeley. He was excommunicated."

"And he *lived*!"

"Usually they do," I said.

"*Damn!*" the commander said in wonderment.

I noticed that Dr. McCaffrey had worked his way into the crowd, had struggled up to Count Orlov, and now was tugging tentatively at the count's cape.

"Count, we'd better get started. Count?"

Now Father Feeley spotted Commander Blanton, and he stepped in front of him and shrieked, "Do you accept the One, Holy, Universal, Apostolic, Roman Catholic Church?"

"Hell, no," said the commander, "I'm a Baptist."

"Then you will face the fires of hell. Repent and be saved!"

"Shut up, you fairy, or I'll beat your face in," yelled the commander.

Intimately lives with raaaaiinnnnn—

"Depart this holy place at once!" screamed Count Orlov, shaking off Dr. McCaffrey's hand and glaring at Seamus. "Slink away to your sewer, communist pig!"

"Do you think you frighten me, you—you *gigolo*! Have you never heard of the Constitution and free speech?"

165

"Have they free speech in the wastes of Siberia? Have they free speech in Lubianka prison?"

"Is there free speech in America, when honest men tremble before the pig, McCarthy?"

"Hey, Count," said the commander. "You want we should break their heads open?"

Dr. McCaffrey had resumed tugging at the count's cape, and Father Feeley, always on the lookout for converts, grabbed Sean's father by the lapels and said, "Do you accept the One, Holy, Universal, Apostolic, Roman Catholic Church?"

And Dr. McCaffrey, upset because the rally was already twenty minutes late getting started, lost his temper and yelled at Father Frank Feeley, "Of course I do, you stupid twit!"

Sean chortled. "Way to go, Pop!"

Then Father Feeley turned to Seamus O'Flaherty and said, "Do you accept the One, Holy, Universal, Ap—"

"Take your mumbo jumbo somewhere else," Seamus roared. "Opium of the masses!"

Poems are made by fools like me—

"Depart now, or know the wrath of God!" Count Orlov decreed, taking a step toward Seamus O'Flaherty.

"Take your prayers and your phony Virgin and stuff them up your—" Seamus began, but all at once the count let out a mighty roar, one that could be heard clear over on the other side of the monument. With a flourish, he ripped his sword from the scabbard, and as people screamed around him, he raised it high over his head. The sunlight glinted off the silver of the blade, and he stood that way for an instant, then he waved it in a circle and advanced on Seamus, like a mad cossack in full charge.

"No, Count, don't do it!" Dr. McCaffrey screamed, but the rest of us just stood there, frozen, as the count advanced on Seamus O'Flaherty with decapitation clearly in mind. Fortunately, the treasurer of the Socialist Progressive People's Worker's Party had the presence of mind to do something. She clobbered the count, right on the back of the head, with a FREE ALGER HISS sign. The count went down in a crumpled heap on the ground.

And then pandemonium broke loose. It swirled all around me. Father Frank Feeley, apparently getting even for all those times he'd been rapped in the mouth, decked Commander Blanton with one good right to the jaw. Communists started hitting slaves of the Immaculate Heart; slaves started hitting Thunder Troopers; Thunder Troopers started hitting communists; then communists hit slaves, and slaves hit troopers, and troopers hit slaves, and slaves hit communists. People in the crowd started hitting all of the above, just for the sport of it. It was a mess.

"What a story!" I yelled to Sean, just as an IMPEACH MCCARTHY sign, wielded like a poleax by a commie, caught me on the side of the head. I literally saw stars, and I felt myself starting to fall, but Sean caught me, and carried me away from the fray, and laid me down on the grass.

"Peggy! Oh Peggy, are you all right?"

I put my hand to my head. "I'm O.K. Oh Sean, I bet Maggie *Higgins* hasn't ever seen this much fighting! I've got to take notes."

But Sean wouldn't let me get up. "You can take notes from right here. You could get killed in there!"

"Sean," I said remembering something. "Your father! He's in there! Somebody might really hurt him!"

"Oh Jeez!" he said and he got up and ran toward the boiling mass of humanity. At that very moment, Dr. McCaffrey, who had been trying to revive the count, was engaged in a tug of war with one of the slaves, who had pried the sword out of the count's hand. Sean's father, who realized that the slaves were not the most stable people in the best of times, could imagine what one of them could do armed with a broadsword: decapitate a dozen people, at least. That would really put a damper on the rally.

Just then, the metropolitan police descended on the melee, in force. Now slaves were slugging troopers who were slugging commies who were slugging cops.

A burly D.C. policeman lifted Seamus O'Flaherty right off his feet.

"Fascist! Nazi!" screeched Seamus.

Commander Blanton, still stunned, got carted off next. Father Frank Feeley was thrown against a paddy wagon and handcuffed. He asked the cop who was fastening the cuffs, "Do you believe in the One, Holy, Universal, Apostolic, Roman Catholic Church?"

"Anything you say, pal," said the cop.

Sean was still trying to struggle through the brawlers to reach his father. A Thunder Trooper tried to knee him in the groin so Sean smacked him one and the trooper went down like a rock. Just as Sean had almost reached his father—who was still hanging onto the jeweled hilt of the sword for dear life—Dr. McCaffrey was lifted by his feet and his shoulders by four cops. He was carted off that way, still clutching the sword, looking like a medieval warrior who was being carried from the field of battle by his compatriots. Well, he almost looked like one, since most medieval warriors didn't wear a three-piece suit and Hush Puppies.

"Pop!" Sean called out, in dismay.

The Visitation Glee Club had gone back to "I'm Looking over a Four Leaf Clover."

"Sean," Dr. McCaffrey hollered as the cops opened the door of the paddy wagon, "Sean, do you have your keys?"

"I got 'em, Pop!" Sean yelled back.

"I'm at a two-hour meter. I don't want to get tagged!" he called out, and then he disappeared, sword and all, behind the doors of the wagon. The driver turned the siren on, and the wagon pulled off, heading for the D.C. jail.

Sean walked back to me. I had struggled to my feet and was watching as the cops broke up the remnants of the crowd, and people started to drift away to other parts of the grounds. Sean sighed and leaned wearily against one of the portable toilets.

"I don't believe it!" he moaned. "My father is in the slammer *again!*"

"At any rate he's going, Sean, your father is going to spend more time in the big house than James Cagney."

"What'll we do about the rally? I think he'd want us to do something."

The Visitation Glee Club kept singing, their high voices now clearly showing signs of strain

First leaf is sunshine, second is rain—

"How can there be a rally when the two major speakers are in the can?" I said. "Unless you want to make a speech about smashing communism."

"No," he said, "I don't think I want to do that. I guess they'll just have to call it off," he said glumly.

"Come on, Sean, I'll buy you a B.V.M. frank, and then we'll go down and bail out your father."

"I guess the Kremlin can relax," he sighed.

"Are you kidding?" I said. "The Nemesis of Smut still has lots of fight left in him."

"I suppose."

"Let's look at it this way," I said, trying to cheer him up: "He who fights and gets thrown in the slammer/Has another day to clobber the sickle and hammer."

"Peggy," he said, "would you do me a favor?"

"Sure, Sean. What?"

"Just shut up," he said.

TEN

The Lenin Ball

"*A*nd then he pulled his sword right out of the scabbard, and raised it over his head, and he *charged*. You should have seen him! It was magnificent. *Magnificent!*" Dr. McCaffrey's eyes were glowing at the memory. "The man is a hero, a true hero of Catholicism."

"Wow!" said Bill, Sean's older brother, who was sitting at the right hand of his father at the dinner table. Bill was home from Holy Cross for spring break, and Sean had invited me over to dinner to hear Bill's tales of campus life. But first, Dr. McCaffrey was reliving the saga of the rally.

As usual, the scenario had changed quite a bit in the retelling. Dr. McCaffrey's part had grown quite heroic. In fact, it seemed he had single-handedly saved dozens of lives by wresting the sword from the hands of the slave, crying out, "Unhand that sword, you miserable heretic!"

He didn't mention that the Hero of Catholicism had been charged with two counts of attempted homicide, assault with a deadly weapon, and inciting a riot. Count Orlov had taken his Smash Communism crusade off to Milwaukee, where he didn't have a police record. But the charges against Sean's father had been dropped. True to form, he had come off clean as a whistle.

"But enough about me and my mundane life," Dr. McCaffrey said. "Let's hear about Holy Cross." He turned to me. "Peggy, did you know that Bill was named to *Who's Who in American Colleges and Universities*?"

"Oh that's great," I said. Bill nodded, modestly.

"And he's been playing varsity baseball all four years. Bill, you're really tearing up the track at Holy Cross."

"I'm doing O.K." Bill said.

"O.K.! Bill, you're being modest. Did you know, Peggy, that the school newspaper did a story on Bill and called him, 'the Renaissance man of the senior class'?"

"Oh Dad," said Bill, "you're going to bore everybody to death."

"Hey, Bill," I said, "did you know that Sean practically saved my life at the rally? And you should have *seen* him when he slugged that trooper. The guy went down like a *rock*!"

Sean flashed me a grin, sheepish but proud.

"*Sean* slugged somebody?" Bill said. "No kidding."

"Yeah," Sean said. "This nerd tried to knee me in the groin, and I—"

Sean's father cut him off with a gesture. "That's hardly anything to be proud of, Sean, brawling in a public place!"

Sean's face deflated. I nearly choked on my soup. This, from a guy who'd been thrown in the slammer twice in the past six months for behaving like the Manassa Mauler?

"Now, Bill. Let's hear about this *Who's Who* business. How did you get picked?"

Bill went on to explain that the whole student body had voted; he told the story in a way that was becomingly modest, but not overly so. It was as if he simply expected good things to happen to him, so they came as no surprise.

I looked at him as he talked. Unlike Sean, Bill was starting to look like his father: his torso was getting fuller, his face more square than it had been in boyhood. I tried to figure what it was that bothered me about Bill, who seemed a nice enough young man. But there was a—a what? A blankness about him, a lack of perception. I thought of him as one of those comic book characters who walk blithely through disaster, unscathed and unaware. Safes crash into the pavement six inches behind them; airplanes fly into buildings right over their heads; the earth cracks under their feet, and they just go on about their business. Shades of gray were invisible to Bill. He simply didn't see them, the way some men can't tell the exact color of their socks. His landscape was a desert vista, where the sun always shone bright and the air was warm and clear.

Dr. McCaffrey was turned to Bill the way a plant turns to the sun; only in this case it was he who was sending out the ultraviolet rays of love and approval, so intense that I felt I could almost see them. Sean, on his father's left, sat in shadow, like the dark side of the moon. I had a sudden, awful thought. Was Dr. McCaffrey giving Sean to God because he was—expendable? Would he ever have given Bill, who was going to go through life picking up trinkets just as his father did, only bigger, shinier ones? Was Sean the throwaway?

I looked at Sean surreptitiously while I ate my dinner; he wasn't aware I was watching him. When he knew someone was watching, he'd let those green eyes chill, so no one had any idea what was going on behind them. But now, unaware, he was looking at his father with such an ache of longing in his eyes that I couldn't stand to see it and I looked away.

"My brother always does things so easy," Sean once said to me. "And I'm always second string." Sean was never the last kid picked for the baseball game—but he was never the first—or the second, or the fourth. He always tripped on his own feet. Bill never practiced at anything, but he was always good at whatever he did. Sean worked and worked, but he was always second string.

But if Sean was clumsy physically, he had a grace of spirit that was obvious to me. He had a mind that skipped like a stone skimmed across the surface of the water from one idea to another and a heart that could reach out to embrace all of God's creatures—and even if he did kill a few of the smaller ones off, it didn't mean he didn't care about them.

I looked at him. He was so different from the rest of his family members, more exquisitely wrought. He was like a piece of fine china in a closetful of dimestore dishes. And I looked at his father, seemingly unaware of Sean beside him, and I wanted to shake the man until his ears rattled. *Why haven't you ever looked at him! Why can't you see him? Why don't you know what you have? How can you throw him away so easily—throw him away to God!* It seemed to me that Sean's father had been talking about the priesthood for him for a long time, but not for Bill—never for Bill. I wondered whose voice it really was that Sean heard that golden morning. Was it God's? Or just the echo of a voice that to a child often sounds like God. A father's voice.

Since Bill was home, he had the use of the Caddy all week, so Sean and I couldn't go park. We sat on the couch in my living room, and after my mother had gone up to bed, Sean stretched out with his head in my lap and I curled the tendrils of his brown, wavy hair in my fingers, and then ran my fingers across his lips. He was so beautiful it was hard for me to keep my hands off of him. I just liked touching him.

"Sean," I said, "maybe you ought to go to college first and then go into the seminary afterward."

"The seminary is a college."

"No, I mean a real college, where you can go to parties and go out on dates and stuff."

He was quiet for a minute. "But I had a *call*, Peggy, you know that."

"Well, who says you have to answer it right away? The call will still be there after you graduate from college."

"I don't think I'd be strong enough," he said. "I think

I'd get to like the secular life too much. And I wouldn't answer the call, and then where would I be?"

"Maybe that wouldn't be so awful."

"Oh no, I'd be in the wrong place. 'Our hearts are restless, Oh Lord, and they will not rest until they rest in thee.'" He was quoting St. Augustine; it was that damned mystical side of him again. He saw himself pursued by the Hound of Heaven down all the corridors of his life. But what if he had mistaken whose voice he had heard? Wouldn't he be in the wrong place then, too?"

"I think a call isn't very strong if it can be drowned out by a few frat parties," I said.

"Oh, some guys, they could do it. But I'm not *good*. I'm not worthy. I mean, I really like driving the Caddy. I shouldn't like material things so much. I like—doing crazy things, I don't follow rules very well. I'm just not—*good*."

"So you figure being a priest will make you good?"

"Well, the seminary will be like a fire, a purifying fire, you know? You put steel in a fire, and it tempers it, makes it strong."

"Do you want to be a priest or the human torch?"

"Ho, ho ho. You know what I mean."

"No, I really don't. I mean, maybe it's too easy."

"Easy? The priesthood is the hardest life there is."

"Yeah, but it's like. . . " I struggled to find the words I wanted. "It's like putting on a uniform. Like when you put on an Immaculate Heart uniform, you know a lot about what you're supposed to be. You're polite, and you're a lady, and you polish your shoes, and you don't sass grown-ups. It gives you something to be. You don't have to go out looking."

"You mean I'm running away from life, copping out, by wanting to be a priest?"

"Maybe. You're just a kid, Sean."

"No I'm not. I'm eighteen. I'm a man. People my age go into the Army."

"Yeah, but in the Army they don't take vows of poverty, chastity, and obedience." I thought about that for a minute. "Well, maybe poverty and obedience, but certainly not chastity."

Sean was quiet for a minute, staring at the ceiling. "Oh shit!" he said.

Then I felt real bad about what I'd been saying, even though I thought it was true. He'd been miserable enough all evening as it was. His brows were knotted, his gentle mouth pulled up in a scowl. I leaned over and kissed him and I said, "That's just for being a great person. You are, you know."

That seemed to cheer him up, and we just kept on kissing until my mother called down, "Peggy, it's getting late. You have school tomorrow."

Reluctantly, we pried our lips apart, and I walked Sean to the back door. He reached out his hand and touched my cheek, gently, and I saw something in his eyes that hadn't been there before. Something older. I wondered what it was.

The next day in school, I plunged back into the business of being part of the greatest *Messenger* staff in the history of the world. I tried to get Con inspired, but her heart just wasn't in it.

"Come on, Con, we've got to pick up the pace. We've got a reputation to live up to, you know."

"I'll think of something. Give me time."

"Time is what we haven't got. The year is really zipping by, in case you hadn't noticed."

"Why don't you or Mollie think of something immortal? Why do I always have to do it?"

"O.K., I'll work on it. Listen, on Saturday, we'll do it together. Maybe a fake stigmata. That would be a gas. (Now and then you'd read about people who would miraculously get the stigmata—the wounds of Christ.) If we

175

could pull off a fake stigmata, we'd really go down in history. "Who could we get to do it?"

Con thought for a minute. "Maybe Ruthellen Mirden. She'll do anything you tell her to. But Ruthellen is so dippy she'd probably get a real stigmata. Hysterical suggestion."

"You mean a person could get it just by thinking she would?"

"Sure."

"How do they get better? Do they put them in the Frigid Ward?"

"Of course not. You can't mix Frigids with Hysterical Stigmatas. Peggy, you really should learn about psychology."

"Well, what do they do?"

"Give them some Band-Aids and tell them to take these pills that make stigmatas go away."

"And do they? Make it go away?"

"How do I know?" Con said, crossly. "I have enough trouble with my periods; I don't need the stigmata too!"

"I guess we ought to scratch the stigmata bit, then. I'd hate to see Ruthellen with tubes up her nose and Band-Aids on her hands. She'd miss the prom."

"Probably," Con said.

"So come over to my house on Saturday, I've got a new album, and—"

"Peg, I won't be here Saturday. I'm going to Annapolis."

"Again? You were there last weekend."

"Lee likes me to come down as often as I can."

"When we get to New York, I know who one of your lovers will be. But he'll probably be an admiral by then."

"Oh Peg, it takes *years* to get to be an admiral. You have to play it just right, get the right assignments, the right commanders, not get stuck in some little jerkwater place with someone who sits on your promotions."

"You sure know a lot about it."

"Well, Lee talks about it a lot."

I looked at her. "Hey, Con, you're still going to go to New York, aren't you? A sacred vow, remember?"

She looked up and said, "Sure," but she hesitated just an instant before she said it.

"Have you been going out with other guys?" I said, suspiciously.

"Of course."

"Who?" I demanded.

"Chuck, from U.S.C."

"That was *Christmas*."

"Yeah, well—"

"You're always on my back all the time for only going out with Sean."

"This is different."

"Yeah? How?"

She looked up at me with a wicked gleam in her eye. "Lee Masters is not going to be a priest. That's for *damn* sure."

I leaned over to peer into her eyes. "Still a virgin."

"You can tell?"

"The eyes really show it."

"Just you wait," she said with a grin.

"Big talk, no action."

"Wait," she said.

The next day Con came up to me and said that Sister Immelda had nominated her to be Immaculate Heart's delegate to the regional Catholic Youth Against Dialectical Materialism conference coming up in two weeks. Kids from all over the East Coast were coming. With Con's interest in the Web of Deception, she'd be perfect, I said.

"It's on a Saturday. I won't be here. Want to go?"

"Me? I've had my fill of smashing commies, thanks."

"A lot of cute guys," she said.

I reconsidered. My kissing addiction to Sean was getting worse, and here was my chance to bust out. Lots of cute guys, all Catholics, gathered under one roof to fight communism.

"O.K.," I said, "I'll go."

But as it turned out, Sean was the delegate nominated from Sacred Heart, so we drove together to the conference, at the Shoreham Hotel, in the white Caddy. Sean was all dressed up in a new suit, and he wore a lime-green shirt that matched his eyes, and he looked at least twenty. I thought that the other cute guys would really have to go some to be cuter than Sean.

The conference, though, turned out to be really dull. My workshop was on Marx and Engels and the dialectical process, taught by a Jesuit who really knew his stuff, but who droned on and on and drew lots of complicated charts on the blackboard. I began to feel nostalgic for Count Orlov and his ermine-lined cape and his sword. He sure would have livened things up a little bit.

In the afternoon, there were more boring workshops, and an assembly at which the keynote address, "How Catholic Youth Can Destroy Marxism at Home," was given by Donald Tolsen of St. Stanislaus High in Philadelphia. Then there was a dinner, and afterward a special treat—a dance in the Blue Room with a real orchestra and fruit punch and cookies. The kids had already dubbed it "The Lenin Ball."

Sean and I went in together to the ballroom, and I said to him, "We have to meet people, Sean; we can't just hang around together and not talk to anyone else."

"Why not?"

"Because we are here to meet other Catholic leaders," I said.

"I guess so." His face looked as if I had just told him we were going to be thrown to the lions with all the other Catholic leaders.

"Oh, Sean, don't sulk," I said.

"I will if I want to!"

When he got into one of those moods, there was just

no dealing with him, so I went up to the table to get myself some punch. I poured myself a cup of raspberry glop and suddenly Donald Tolsen, in the flesh, from St. Stanislaus High in Philadelphia was standing next to me.

"Want to dance?" he said.

"Sure."

I was flattered. Donald Tolsen had been chosen, from all the Catholic kids in the East, to give the keynoter. He gave a very forceful presentation, and some of his ideas were quite interesting. I wasn't too keen on the one where he said that Catholic Youth should march into libraries, seize left-wing books, tear them into shreds, and hurl them in the gutter. But then he smiled at me, and he had two wonderful dimples on both sides of his cheek; I decided I could ignore a little incipient fascism in a boy who had dimples like that.

He led me to the dance floor, and held me close right away. As we twirled, I saw Sean, standing by the punch bowl. He looked at me and his face had that hurt look he always used to get when we were kids; like the time I stepped on the seven-story parking garage he had spent three hours building in the sandbox. I did it just to be ornery. But I wasn't trying to be mean to him now. Con was right, I needed to get to know something about men. I had certainly bombed with Harry Wexler. Maybe I was repressed. I was *obligated* to try again.

Don twirled me around again, and I looked for Sean, hoping I hadn't hurt him too badly. I'd dance with him next, I promised myself. And then I saw him, the rat fink! He was dancing with just about the cutest little blonde I ever saw, and she was gazing up into those cool green eyes as though she'd never laid her peepers on anything so gorgeous. And Sean, the future Father McCaffrey, was flirting with her like mad. He was laughing, and he turned up the wattage in his green eyes until they all but knocked her over on her ass.

179

I thought about tearing her eyes out. I pictured the headline in the *Washington Daily News*:

CATHOLIC GIRL SCRATCHES
EYES OUT OF PA TEEN
IN LOVE DUEL OVER PRIEST

Of course, she didn't know she was dancing with the Hero Priest of the Amazon, but I did. I noticed again how good looking he was, and thought about how I liked to kiss that wonderful, sensitive mouth, a Montgomery Clift mouth, and then he pulled the blonde close to him and whirled her around and I asked God to send a plague of frogs to pee on her bleached head.

I moved even closer to Don, and he bent over and kissed me, right on the dance floor, and I let him do it. I looked over at Sean and saw he was watching me. Defiantly, I kissed Don on the cheek. *Take that, faithless wretch!* I thought.

But then, when Don twirled me around again, I saw Sean kissing the blonde, right on the side of the neck. I was shocked. Sean, my Sean, kissing a blonde strumpet, and in public too. I asked God to let the frogs pee on his head too.

It kept going like that—me kissing Don and Sean kissing the blonde, and then Don asked me if I'd like to come to his room for a drink and I said, "I'd love to!"

I flashed a look at Sean that said, *Eat your heart out, you Judas*, as Don and I walked off the floor. I had a momentary second thought, but I figured, what the hell, this wasn't Go-Go Gunderson, fastest tongue in the East, or a man who pulled legs off of grasshoppers; this was the Catholic Youth who was going to smash Lenin. How could I be safer?"

We went back to Don's room and as soon as we got in he pulled open a drawer and took out a bottle of Scotch. He poured some in a water glass and glugged it right down. "Better than the fucking punch," he said. "Want some?"

"No thank you."

"Puts hair on your chest."

"Just what I need."

"Your chest is just fine like it is," he said, leering at me. "You got a great body."

Somehow, I hadn't expected that kind of talk from the Catholic Youth who was going to smash Lenin. I wasn't sure what the correct response should be. Con would have known; something fast and snappy, like, "Yeah, read the small print. No trespassing. This means you." But I just didn't say anything. Don gulped down the Scotch, poured himself another glass, and drank it in one gulp. Then he grabbed me.

"Come here, woman!" he said.

I guessed he meant me, because we were the only two people in the room. I didn't feel like a woman; I had hardly gotten "girl" figured out yet.

Then he started kissing me, and in between kisses he'd take another swig of Scotch. The fumes were really starting to be overpowering. I thought to myself, *This is really sophisticated*, but I'd have liked it better if he were drinking banana daiquiries; his mouth would have smelled better.

Then zap! out came the tongue, and I wondered if it was going to be Go-Go Gunderson all over again. But at least he didn't try to put it in my ear, so I was ahead of the game. I wondered why I liked soul-kissing with Sean and it was kind of weird with other guys. Maybe because I'd known Sean's tongue so long. We used to lick cake pans together after my mother baked, and we'd slurp each other trying to get at the chocolate.

"Oh baby, you are some kisser!" Don said, slurring his words a little. "Oh, I like kissing you."

"Thank you," I said. That sounded dumb, but polite. He was starting to make little noises in his throat that reminded me of Harry. I wondered if my kisses really were something special. Did I really drive men wild with passion? And if so, why? I was five feet eight, had curly brown hair, was a great jump shot, and had nice legs. That did not, in my mind, add up to a femme fatale. Harry, of course, had a reason to start humming in his throat. He thought I had screwed half of West Point, and that he was next in line. But Don knew I was just your average Catholic high school girl who was against Dialectical Materialism. Maybe it *was* my kissing. Maybe I just had the Kiss of Fire, and men just couldn't help themselves.

Suddenly, Don stopped kissing me and said. "Be ri' back!" and stumbled off into the bathroom. I looked at myself in the mirror. My hair was a mess and my lipstick was smeared all over my face—I looked like I'd just gone three rounds with an eggbeater. In the movies, women always got just a touch mussed after they kissed a lot. Why did I took like Tugboat Annie?

I was studying myself in the mirror when Don came out of the bathroom.

"Hi," he said, and I turned around and nearly had a coronary. He was standing there, wearing nothing but his shirt. Oh God, it was happening *again*.

All these years, and I barely knew what a penis looked like, and now they seemed to be sprouting all around me like mushrooms. Why did guys want to take off their pants when I showed up? Was it me? Did I have it printed in big, invisible (to me) letters on my forehead: UNZIP!

Before I could say anything Don made a flying leap, knocking me over on the bed and landing on top of me. He started tugging at the buttons on my blouse.

"Stop that!" I said, pushing his hands away. Then he tried to get his hand up under my skirt.

"Come on, babe, you're hot, real hot!" he said.

Hot was the one thing I absolutely was not. Ready to throw up from his breath, yes. Feeling my ribs splintering into little pieces, yes. That did not add up to passion.

"Oh babe, oh babe!"

"Stop it, you animal!" (I wondered if he'd heard Straight Talk for Teens.)

"Oh, I love it when you talk dirty!"

He had me on the bed, pinned down. He was a big sucker, too. I knew a way to get him off, but I didn't want to resort to that yet. I thought of Father Milliken and tried another tack.

"I am a Child of Mary," I said.

"Oh bullcrap," Don said.

So much for the religious approach.

I flexed my knee. "Don't say I didn't warn you," I said, getting ready to give him a good one.

Just then I heard a knock on the door.

"Peggy, Peggy, are you O.K.?" It was Sean's voice.

"Not exactly," I called back.

"Do you need help?"

"That would be nice."

Sean came barreling through the door like Elliot Ness and the Untouchables. He stopped and gaped open-mouthed at Don, who still had me pinned to the bed and was moving his body up and down.

"You bastard!" Sean yelled. "You fucking rapist!" He dragged Don off the bed, to his feet. Don, who by now was too drunk to know exactly what was happening, grinned.

"Hi!" he said. "We're fucking."

Sean reared back and gave him such a vicious upper cut that it knocked him half across the room. Don collapsed against the wall and slid down it.

"Are you all right?" Sean said to me.

"Yeah, I'm O.K.," I said, tugging at my blouse and trying to wipe the lipstick off my face with my hand. I went over to Don. "He's breathing," I said. "He really did give a nice speech, too."

Sean grabbed my hand. "Come on, I'm taking you home!"

In the car, we rode silently for a while, and then Sean said, "Peggy, why did you go off with that creep?"

"What do you care? You were so busy making eyes at the Catholic Sandra Dee you didn't even notice what I was doing."

"I *noticed*," Sean said. "I noticed when you were practically necking with him on the dance floor."

"What were you doing with the blonde? Making a novena?"

We were quiet again for a while and then I said, "Oh, dammit, Sean, I'll never get the hang of this man–woman stuff. I mean if you don't kiss guys, they say you're frigid, and when you do kiss them, they take their clothes off."

He burst out laughing.

"It is *not* funny," I said

"Sorry," he said, but he was still laughing.

"I think I just meet weird guys. I mean, you don't take your clothes off when I kiss you."

"That doesn't mean I don't *want* to."

"You do?"

"Sure."

"You just have more self-control, right?"

"Right."

"Oh, I wish all boys were like you. Then girls would be *safe*!"

He looked at me strangely, a little crossly, I thought. But why should he be mad? I meant it as a compliment.

He drove for a while, and then he pulled the Caddy into Rock Creek Park, and parked it in a secluded spot under a tree. We climbed in the back seat, and I was ready to settle in for an hour or so of necking with good old reliable Sean and his Illuminated Map of Sin. I closed my eyes, and then I felt a hand on a part of me that was of the most interest to the Nemesis of Smut. Sean had his hand on the front of my blouse—and it wasn't even the prom.

"Sean?" I said.

184

He didn't say anything, but then he gave me an even bigger shock. He started unbuttoning my blouse.

"Sean, what do you think you are doing?"

He still didn't say anything, but doggedly kept working on the buttons. I thought of how I'd been ready to maim Donald Tolsen for life, and here I was letting Sean unbutton away, and I wasn't even lifting a finger. I was starting to feel tingly inside, which was an even better indicator of sin than Sean's illuminated map—which by now must be lighted up like the War Room when a flight of Russian ICBMs passed over Nome.

My blouse was all unbuttoned, and I knew I should be thinking about sin, but I was thinking, Oh shit, I didn't have on my lacy bra but the old one I wear for basketball that was really ugly and stained and smelled of Clorox because it got gray and my mother had to pour on the bleach to get it clean.

And then Sean had his hands on the clasp of my bra and was tugging on it. I was still undecided about what to do. I knew I should slap him, but on the other hand nobody had ever seen my boobs but me, the bathroom mirror, and Dr. Parkinson, which seemed like a real waste. I was really proud of them, and it seemed to me to be in much better taste to give a good friend like Sean a peek at them instead of flaunting them around in the drag house in front of a couple of fake Scarlett O'Haras.

Finally, the clasp came open and Sean just pulled the bra away gently and looked at me. He looked, that's all, for a long time and finally he said, "They're really beautiful." Then he shocked me out of my socks by leaning over and kissing me gently, on each nipple, and if that wasn't big-time sin I was Pope Pius the Twelfth. I tried to think about sizzling in hell, like Sister Justinian said I should, but all I could concentrate on were these little shivers that were going through me, because Sean had his hands under my breasts and was taking turns nibbling gently on the right

185

one and then the left one, and it occurred to me that if he would just keep on doing that, it might be worth a few eons in hell. I wondered if he had been reading *Savage Warrior*, because even Soldred couldn't do it any better, and Soldred did it every ten minutes or so, it seemed. All of a sudden one big shiver went through me, and then another. I knew what it was all right, but I didn't think you could get one of *those* this way. Suddenly I was very grateful to my hormones for coming up with the boobs, however belatedly.

I must have sighed, loudly, because Sean looked as pleased as punch, sort of the way he looked when he won the seventh grade spelling bee: very happy and a trifle cocky. He kissed me again, with a new air of authority, I thought, and then he pulled me down on the seat beside him and drew my hand down between his legs. I started to rub it gently—it was, after all, an old friend, and he moved his hand up under my skirt. I figured we were already way past venial sin, so what the hell, in for a buck, in for a quarter. It wasn't long before I was on the roller coaster again, and I let out a little whoop, which really felt good, because I couldn't do that when I was in bed pretending to study, with *Savage Warrior* stuck behind my geometry book. Sean was lying on the seat, moaning softly, and I thought I ought to return the favor. I reached down and unzipped his fly, and got my first look at the Natural Wonder since it was five years old. It had grown up a bit in the intervening years, and it certainly wasn't soft at the moment, but I liked it as much as ever. I thought I detected the faint smell of canvas.

I was very solicitous of my long-lost friend, and Sean moaned a lot more and then he rolled over and I guess he aimed, because he unloaded right on the floor of the Caddy, a perfect shot. I was enthralled, and for a minute I felt a surge of genuine penis envy. But then I remembered the boobs, and I decided I wouldn't trade them, not even for something that could be shot off like a bazooka.

Then we curled up in each other's arms and I felt good and warm and safe with Sean. It was funny, I was supposed to be feeling sinful and wretched, because I'd just done most of the sinful things I'd ever heard about with Sean—except for actually Doing It of course—and I just felt good all over.

He went right off to sleep in my arms; Sean had always been able to do that, even when we were kids. He'd just curl up in the sandbox and he'd be asleep before I could finish a sentence. I ran my finger across his lips, and I kissed his cheek, the way I always used to do when he fell asleep in the sandbox and I thought he wouldn't know I was doing it. I had known him my whole life, I thought, and I couldn't imagine a time when he wouldn't be there. He was like a twin, part of me. I felt so awful inside, empty and aching, when I thought of him going away, that I decided not to think about it; I closed my eyes and went to sleep too.

When I woke up Sean was already awake, and looking very serious and thoughtful. I sat up and hooked my bra and buttoned my blouse. He looked at me and said, "I just want you to know I really respect you."

It sounded so ridiculous that I started to giggle and Sean looked puzzled for a minute and then the absurdity of it hit him too, and he cracked up. We both just kept laughing and laughing—I laughed so hard I almost peed in my pants. When we simply couldn't laugh any more, Sean peered down at the floor of the car and said, "Yuk."

"We've got to clean it up," I said.

"Peggy," he said, "did you think it was—disgusting or anything?"

"Oh no," I said, "I thought it was neat. Really. Course, after the stuff lies around for a while it probably gets rancid, you know, like old hamburger." I fished around in my purse. "Here, use this hanky. You can just tell your dad somebody spilled Coke in the back seat."

Sean did his best to tidy up the floor of the car, and then he tossed the hanky out the window. He put his arms around me and said, "Peggy, are you sorry?"

"No," I said, "I'm not. Are you?"

"No," he said. "I'm not." I noticed he didn't say anything at all about sin. We just sat there, quietly, close together, and I thought it's only April; we have two months before Sean has to go away. Two months. I rolled the words around in my head, trying to make it sound like a long long time. Two months.

Run slowly, slowly, horses of the night.

ELEVEN

Kidnapping Christ

"*L*ook into my eyes!" Con commanded. We were sitting in the *Messenger* room, under the Little Flower with her boobs half out.

I looked. They *were* different, smokier, I thought, sensuous, sultry.

"Oh my God! You did it! Con, you're a *woman*!"

She smiled enigmatically, and I looked at her in awe. I felt a great chasm open up between us, like the San Francisco earthquake splitting the very floor under our feet. Con wasn't a virgin anymore. Con was a woman. I was still a girl.

Suddenly, I felt shy and tongue-tied. So did Con, a little bit at least. We just sat there and looked at each other, not knowing what to say.

"Well," I said, "you did it!"

"Yeah," she said, "I did it."

"Well. . ." I said. I supposed I shouldn't pry. After all, it was her body. What right did I have to get nosy. But this was *Con*. I couldn't stand not knowing.

"Shit, Con, what was it *like*?"

"Well," she said, "I'm not sure it's all it's cracked up to be."

"It isn't?" I said. I must have looked terribly forlorn, because Con added hastily, "The first time, I mean. They

189

say after that it just gets better and better. It's just that at first it's a little, ah, difficult."

"Yeah? Like how?"

"Well. . ." she said.

It seems that Con was alone with Lee in the Annapolis apartment where I'd seen my second real live penis, and they had been talking about The Red Menace. That always seemed to turn Lee on, Con said, because after they talked about J. Edgar Hoover he'd get real passionate. (I wondered if that would work on most guys. I wondered if some guy was being real cool and aloof, and I just whispered in his ear, "Herbert Philbrick! Pumpkin Papers! Roy Cohn!" he'd throw me down on the couch and kiss my earlobe.) They started necking real hot and heavy and Con thought, "What the hell, why not?"

She told this to Lee, who was delighted, but she informed him that she was a virgin and no way was she going to get pregnant, and he had to use something.

So he put his pants on and ran out into the night, only it took him forty-five minutes to find a drugstore that was open, while Con waited anxiously in the apartment, certain that Lee had been run over by a car, and that her insatiable lust had murdered the man who was destined to deflower her, so she might as well become a nun. (When things were going badly, Con always declared she was going to be a nun. She thought of the convent as one big Valium.)

By the time Lee got back, Con had cooled down considerably, so she suggested maybe they should go to a movie instead. But Lee looked so crestfallen—he'd run a half mile back to the apartment with the rubbers clutched in his hand like a relay runner's baton—that Con didn't have the heart to insist.

If she'd been using her head, Con said, she'd have done the whole thing differently, because when she saw the dimensions of Lee's equipment, she began to worry. This was the girl who couldn't get a junior tampax in without a sledgehammer. Lee might have been thinking of *The Song of Songs*, but Con could only think of *The Charge of the Light Brigade*.

"See, I could have gotten it stretched," she said. "Then I would have been O.K."

"You can do that?"

"Sure."

"Where?"

"A doctor's office."

I thought of my pediatrician, Dr. Norman Parkinson, who'd been my doctor ever since I was born, and who would put on bunny ears sometimes to make me laugh. I couldn't imagine saying to him, "Doc, the bunny ears are a blast, but how about stretching my vagina?"

"How do they do it?" I asked Con, momentarily diverted from her story. Con knew lots about medicine.

"How? They have machines. Stretching machines. All doctors have them. You just have to make an appointment to use the stretcher, you know, like an X-ray."

"All doctors have them? Like even foot doctors?"

"I don't guess a foot doctor would have a vagina-stretcher," Con said grumpily. She was eager to get back to her saga.

Anyhow, Con said, she was in the bedroom, lying on the bed, starkers, and the big moment came and she closed her eyes, expecting this awful pain. But nothing happened.

She opened her eyes and there was Lee, pushing away, but every time he tried he kept bouncing out of her. It was like he was on a trampoline, Con said, going Boing! Boing! Boing!—bouncing further away each time.

"I swear, honey," he said somewhat breathlessly, "you certainly are—*strong* down there."

Great, Con thought, *most girls got eeny weeny pieces of skin. How come I got the Iron Curtain?*

"Lee, just keep on going. I know you'll do it!"

191

And Lee went back to work, plunging away like a pile driver, but not making much progress.

"Honey, I don't know how much longer I can keep this up!" Lee said, plaintively. He was sweating like a native bearer in the Congo, and Con was bouncing up and down on the bed from his frantic efforts. Con resorted to praying. "Please, I'll do the nine First Fridays, I'll say the Rosary for twenty decades, only please, *please* let him get it in."

Maybe the prayers did it, because Con felt this little tearing sensation inside—like a Band-Aid being ripped off, she said—and then Lee said, "Thank *goodness!*" and he moved around a little, then more, and then he lay still.

Con was too exhausted to feel anything but relief. But she thought she would be real sophisticated and lie there naked, smoking a cigarette, basking in her new-found status as a woman. There was only one problem. She was bleeding.

"Like a *pig*," Con said.

"Oh no!" I couldn't suppress a giggle. Con was a big bleeder. She once had a nosebleed in Bible History and you'd have thought the Holy Innocents had been massacred right there in Room Five. The whole floor was awash with blood.

Con lit her cigarette and tried to be real cool, but that is hard to do, she said, when you are pumping fluid like an oil well that's just come in.

"Honey, are you O.K.?" Lee asked, and Con placed a towel in a strategic place and kept smoking, until Lee said, alarmed, "Honey, you are *still* bleeding."

She went through three towels and a blanket, and that's when she started to get worried.

"What would they say in my obit? 'Constance Marie Wepplener, 18, died suddenly of screwing too hard.' I'd be *mortified!*"

"Oh Con, what happened?"

"They took me out in an ambulance," she said. "An

ambulance! Oh, I was *mortified!* And Lee was so nice, and so worried. He just sat beside me and held my hand and told me everything was going to be all right. Then we got to the hospital and this old biddy of a nurse asked me, real snotty, 'What's wrong with you?' And I said, 'I'm bleeding to death, you asshole!' That sort of shocked Lee, because I don't swear around him; he thinks it's vulgar. But the doctor who treated me was real nice, and he said not to worry, I was going to be O.K. I just clot slow. It's pretty rare, like one person in 100,000, but he could give me some stuff to help."

"Oh Con," I said, "everything happens to you! You just *have* to be a writer."

"This one I could write for the *Journal of the American Medical Association,*" she said.

I was worried for a while that the new, nonvirgin Con would be a lot different from the old one. I thought she wouldn't want to run around and do crazy stuff and crack jokes and write blasphemous things about saints in the *Messenger* room. I had this idea that women who weren't virgins sat around a lot in black negligees on red satin couches and thought about sex. I mean, I thought about sex too, but I did it while I was supposed to be translating stuff about the Punic Wars.

But the nonvirgin Con seemed to dig doing the same stuff the virgin one did—like batting around in the black Ford with Mollie and me. We liked to do that a lot, just climb in the car and head off for no place in particular at night after dinner. Sometimes we didn't really go anyplace, just drove around and we'd sing and swear and tell filthy jokes, like the one about the guy who had the blow job and wondered if he'd broken the Communion fast. We'd behave in all the ways that nice Catholic girls weren't supposed to. But we never picked up boys. That was taboo, because we wanted it to be just us, together. We felt so free, zipping along in the Ford, as if we'd simply flown off into the blue ether someplace where the rules for girls had been outdistanced and the rules for women didn't yet apply. We had dreams as grandiose as any boys might have had—Con, the New York writer; me, the war correspondent; Mollie, the engineer who wanted to put things in space.

When I think of us, as we were then, I marvel at how vulnerable we were, and how brave; how little we knew of the world out there that would do its best to crush our spirits, break our dreams as if they were walnuts, herd us back into the tiny pens that were the part of the world that belonged to women. But for the moment, we were young, we were free, and we had each other.

One night as we were zipping along in the Ford, I took a swig of beer and started to sing, "Roll me over, in the clover—"

And Mollie and Con joined in: "Roll me over, lay me down and do it again."

"Amen!" Con said.

And then inspiration struck. "Hey," I said, "let's steal the flag from Sacred Heart."

"They have to take it down at night," Mollie said. "It's the law."

"No, not the American flag. The Sacred Heart banner. The new one. They don't take it in, because it's waterproof."

"Holy shit," said Con, "that would really do it. The Sacred Heart banner! The brothers would have *orgasms!*"

"Yeah, we'd go out in a blaze of glory," Mollie said.

"*Immortality*," I said, "in our grasp."

"Let's *do* it!" Con whooped.

The banner that hung from the roof of Sacred Heart High School was so long that it covered nearly the top two stories of the facade. It was a gift from a wealthy alum who had made a pile in electrical circuits and wanted to show his gratitude to the brothers. He commissioned the banner, which showed Christ, opening his chest to display his Sacred Heart crowned with thorns and pierced with a sword. The artist wasn't very good at drawing organs, so the heart looked more like a liver, and the expression on Christ's face, which was supposed to be one of pained rapture, looked more like sexual transport. It caused a great deal of comment when it was hung in a special ceremony two months ago, but I thought it was tacky to have a two-story Christ having an orgasm right there on the front of the school. Sean thought it was ugly too.

"Did you get a look at Christ?" he grumbled. "He looks like Tony Curtis with a beard. And his clothes, for Chrissake!"

"Well, Sean," I said, "maybe Jesus really did wear chartreuse. Maybe he was a snappy dresser."

Con, Mollie, and I drove over to the boys' high school and cased the joint. We drove around the grounds three times to make sure the coast was clear. There were no signs of life anywhere. The brothers lived in a house half a mile away, so there was no danger of them spotting us. They all had to be in by nine.

We parked the car on a side street, out of sight, and made our way to the base of the fire escape by the side of the building that led to the roof.

"I'll stay here and be the lookout," Con said.

"Oh no you don't," I said. "We're going to need all three of us to get that thing off the building."

"Oh *shit*!" Con moaned.

Mollie and I climbed up the fire escape quickly, while Con climbed slowly, step by step, sweating and keeping her eyes riveted on the step above. When we reached the roof we hunched over and moved quickly and quietly to the front of the building.

"Hey, this is neat," Mollie said. "Like John Wayne."

"Lieutenant," I said to Mollie, "did you bring the dynamite?"

"Yes, sir."

"The Nazis think we don't *know* about their secret weapon."

"Yeah, but they don't know about us commandos."

"Trained killers."

"It's a suicide mission!" I said. "We know we'll never come back."

Mollie started to sing, "Off we go, into the Wild Blue yonder—"

"That's the Air Force," I said.

"I don't know the Trained Killer anthem."

"Oh for God's sake," Con said, "I ought to have my head examined! What am I doing on the roof of Sacred Heart High School with two girls who think they're John Wayne and Errol Flynn?"

We crept over to the front ledge of the building, to examine the manner in which the banner was fastened. It was tied, with rope, to two pipes on the roof, so we wouldn't have too much difficulty getting it loose. We decided to haul the banner up to the roof while it was still fastened; we didn't want to risk dropping Christ four stories to the ground.

We started to pull it up, very slowly, but ran into a problem. One edge of the banner caught on a drainpipe about two feet below the top ledge. We pulled at it, but it wouldn't come. We were afraid that if we tugged too hard, the banner would rip.

"We'll have to free it by hand," I said.

"Good luck," Con muttered.

"I can do it," I said. "I can just reach out with one hand and pull that edge free."

I lay on the ledge, on my stomach, and I wrapped part of the rope that held the banner around my wrist, just as a precaution. I stretched my free hand down to grab the edge of the banner. I shook it once; it stayed. I shook it again and it moved a bit.

"I think I've got it!" I said. I gave one big pull and the banner came free. But in doing so—since I was leaning so far out over the ledge—I shifted the balance in my body and rolled right off the edge of the building.

I found myself, an instant later, dangling four stories up by just a rope around my wrist. If I'd moved my foot just a little bit, I'd have kicked Christ in the teeth.

It happened too fast for anyone to react, even scream. Suddenly there I was, hanging from the roof of Sacred Heart High School.

"My God!" Con said, peering over the edge of the roof. "What are you doing down there?"

I wasn't scared really. It happened too fast for me to be scared, and there was an air of unreality about the whole thing. I still couldn't believe I was dangling there, four stories up, in front of the Sacred Heart.

"I am down here for my *health*, Con, you idiot," I said. "For God's sakes, pull me back *up!*"

I had this sudden fear that Con and Mollie would panic and run off, leaving me hanging there through the night, and when the kids from Sacred Heart came in for first period, there I'd be, strung up above Christ's left molar. For punishment I'd be left hanging there, and eventually nothing but my skeleton would remain, dangling from the rope. Parents would ask about it when they came to visit the school to see about enrolling their kid:

"What is that—skeleton up there?" they'd ask.

"That? Oh, that's just Peggy Morrison. *Was* Peggy Morrison."

"What's she doing up there?"

"She tried to steal the banner of the Sacred Heart, so we just left her up there to starve to death."

"Brother, we're going to enroll our little Freddie right

now. You certainly don't get discipline like that in the *public* schools!"

Con and Mollie grabbed my arms and started to pull. "Ow," I said, "you're ripping my arms out of the sockets."

"Shut up, Peggy," Mollie said, "we're saving your life."

They finally got me back up on the roof again. My legs buckled under me and I had to sit still to collect my wits. Meanwhile, Con and Mollie pulled up the banner and untied the ropes that fastened it. Then we all rolled the banner up, and half-pushed, half-pulled, half-dropped it down the fire escape. We got it down to the second floor and Con said, "Enough of this. Let's drop it down."

"O.K.," I said, "you get down on the ground and I'll drop it over."

Con climbed on down and I shoved the rolled-up banner over the edge of the fire escape.

"Bombs away!" I said, wondering how blasphemous it was to drop Christ like a cluster of incendaries over the Mitsubishi plant.

After we had dropped him, we picked him up and carried him on our shoulders to the Ford. We put the banner on top of the car and tied it with the ropes that were still fastened to its edges.

"We did it!" Con exulted. "We did it!"

"Now what do we do with him?" Mollie asked.

We looked at each other. We hadn't thought about that.

"We have to hang him someplace where people can see him," I said. "That's the whole point."

"I'm not climbing on any more buildings tonight!" Con said, "And that's that!"

"We could leave him spread out somewhere," Mollie suggested. "Like in the park."

"What!" Con said. "Leave Christ in the park? Dogs would pee on him."

"Yeah, we have to be respectful," I said. Then I had an

idea. "Let's get Sean. He has good ideas on things like this, and he's a good climber, too."

We drove to Sean's house and he came out and looked at the black Ford, quizzically.

"What've you got there?"

"Actually, it's Christ," Con said.

"What?"

"The banner. From Sacred Heart. We stole it," I said.

He looked at us with what can only be described as awe.

"Holy Shit! Off the building?"

"Yep."

"You *kidnapped* Christ!"

"In a manner of speaking," I said.

"You've heard of grand theft, auto," Con said. "This is Grand Theft, God."

"The question is," I said, "what do we do with him?"

"It has to be respectful," Mollie said.

Sean looked at the rolled-up Christ tied to the top of the car. "This is respect? He looks like a rug."

"We could put him on Immaculate Heart," I said.

"Are you kidding?" Con snorted. "We'd be the first ones they'd grab. Round up the usual suspects."

"The Baptist Church," Sean said.

We looked at each other. Of course. Why hadn't we thought of it?

There was bad blood between St. Malachy's and the First Baptist Church. The Baptist Church stood at the far end of St. Malachy's parking lot, and on many Sundays, Catholics coming to Mass couldn't get a spot because they had been usurped by Baptists. Not only did the lot belong to St. Malachy's, but the parish had just coughed up 1,200 bucks to blacktop it—which brought in even more Baptists, since now they didn't have to worry about getting a muffler ripped off by a rock.

Father Ryan had done his utmost to keep the parking

lot safe for Catholicism; he'd put up signs saying "Catholics Only" and he'd put sawhorses at the entrance. But the Baptists ignored the signs and removed the sawhorses. Tensions were running high.

We drove the Ford over to First Baptist, and we found it was much easier getting Christ onto the Baptist Church than off of Sacred Heart. The Church had a low roof overhang, so Sean and I climbed up on the roof, and Con and Mollie handed Christ up to us, and we tied him to a pair of stanchions on the steeple. The first thing Father Ryan was going to see in the morning, when he came in to say six o'clock Mass, was the Sacred Heart, proudly draped over enemy headquarters.

We stood back, looked at our handiwork, and broke out a six-pack.

Mollie raised a can. "To us!"

"To the Greatest *Messenger* Staff in history!" I said.

"To *immortality*!" Con said.

Sean raised his beer. "To not getting thrown in the can for the next twenty years. Let's get the fuck *out* of here."

We were still feeling euphoric when Con dropped me and Sean off in front of my house.

"What a night!" I said to Sean.

"Wanna go park?"

"It's pretty late."

"You're right. I have a test tomorrow."

"I have to study too."

"So I'll see you tomorrow, right?"

"Right."

"See you tomorrow."

"Sean?"

"Yeah?"

"Let's go park."

And so, a little while later—how much later I wasn't exactly sure—I lay in Sean's arms in the back of the Caddy and sighed, a contented sigh. The Illuminated Map of Sin had been junked, permanently, since the night of the Lenin ball. We were lying there, naked as jaybirds.

We hadn't meant to get that way, not really. It was just with all the unbuttoning here and there, it just ended up like that. I was glad it did. I loved the feel of Sean's body against me, loved the way it looked in the faint glow that drifted in from a distant street light. I was delighted by its feel, its textures, the hard and soft parts that trembled under my fingers like some finely tuned musical instrument. We weren't Doing It really, just coming as close as we possibly could without technically losing our respective virginities. Sean's conscience was bothering him, of course.

He put his lips against my hair and said, not very convincingly, "I guess we shouldn't be doing this."

And I sighed and said, "I guess not," as I ran my finger down his bare chest.

"But we're really not doing IT, right?"

"Right."

"So maybe it's only a venial sin."

"Right," I said, not really worrying about sin, just thinking how much I liked the lean hardness of his body against mine. Sean's definition of venial sin had grown as elastic as a rubber band lately. I was certain that all the huffing and puffing and panting and moaning we'd been doing a few minutes ago felt much too good to be *venial*. I was on the verge of a major revision of my ideas about sin, anyhow. The things that Sean and I did together were lovely and loving; they brought us closer together than we'd ever been before. Touching his body, giving him pleasure, and taking my own didn't *feel* like a sin. I mean, when I did something wrong, I knew it. Nobody had to give me a written report.

He put his hand against my face and said, "I wish I could stop time and we'd just be here like this, forever and ever."

"So do I."

We didn't talk about the fact that he was going away in a few weeks. I tried not to think about it, because I simply couldn't bear to. He was so precious to me—all of him, his face, his body, that gentle and loving soul—that to think of losing him was like thinking of ripping off my right arm. So I just lived in the present, relegating the future to the far recesses of my peripheral vision. I felt like a woman in wartime, pretending that only the present was real, that tomorrow simply didn't exist. He felt the same way, I think.

Sometimes, we just lay in each other's arms, feeling our heartbeats, and time drifted out of sight; I didn't know whether an hour had passed or five or twelve—and I didn't care.

Run slowly, slowly.

The Sacred Heart Caper (that's what Con called it in her journal) raised even more of a ruckus than we expected, as it turned out. Father Ryan and Reverend Mackie practically got into a slugging match in front of First Baptist the next day. Father Ryan accused the Baptist minister of engineering the heist because, deep down, he wanted to persecute Catholics.

Reverend Mackie replied heatedly that somebody who had a degree in theology from Yale would not go around stealing pictures of Christ off of Catholic schools. Especially ugly ones.

"Ugly?" Father Ryan bristled.

"He has teeth that look like they came from a Colgate ad and a *chartreuse* robe," the Reverend snapped. "This is art?"

Father Ryan intimated that Reverend Mackie's taste was somewhat lacking and the Baptist minister said he'd never buy a painting for his church that looked as though it belonged on a cigar box.

That's when Father Ryan tried to slug Reverend Mackie.

Only the intervention of a couple of Baptist deacons

and of Father Mulloy, the assistant pastor, saved the day. The police were called in, and promised a thorough investigation. But they couldn't find the culprits, wrote it off as a prank, and we had a perfect record.

Con, however, had other things to worry about besides getting arrested for Grand Theft, God. She hadn't heard from Lee Masters in nearly two weeks.

"One week, four days, he hasn't called."

"He will."

"He won't. He won't call. Ever."

"He really likes you, Con."

"I blew it. I should have stayed a virgin. He thinks I'm a slut."

"If he only likes you when you're a virgin, then you don't want him. He's a crud."

"I do," Con said, "I want him. Even if he's a crud. Even if he's a murderer. Even if he's"—she threw her hands into the air—"a *Nazi war criminal*."

"Con, you're getting carried away."

"O.K., scratch the war criminal."

"Maybe he's real busy, with finals or something."

"No wonder he doesn't call. He thinks if he makes love to me he's got to bring along a combat surgical team."

"Oh, Con."

"You think it doesn't cramp your love life, having three medics and a nurse standing at the foot of the bed with fifty units of plasma?"

For a minute I thought if Lee Masters didn't call, then I'd be sure Con would go to New York with me and we'd do all the things we'd dreamed about. But Con's round face was so miserable that I immediately took back the thought.

When the three o'clock bell rang, Con and I walked out of school together. Sean met us at the end of the front walk.

"I can't walk home today," he said. "I've got to go to the dentist."

"O.K. I'll see you later," I said.

He took both my hands in his and just looked at me. "I wish I didn't have to go to the dentist."

"Me too."

We just stood there a minute, gazing into each other's eyes, and then he leaned over and kissed me, as if he were going off to D day, not to the dentist. I watched him as he trotted off in the direction of downtown Crystal Springs, and I guess what I was feeling as I watched that familiar lope must have leaked out of my heart and into my eyes.

Con looked at me. "Shit," she said, "you're in love with him!"

"Yeah, I guess I am."

"Is he still going to be a priest?"

I nodded. "Yeah. I guess so."

"We should just become nuns," Con said. "Just be fucking *nuns* and not have to worry about this shit."

The thought of Con as a nun made me laugh. "Where'd you put your lovers, Sister Constance?"

"Who the hell knows? In the chapel, maybe. Let them pray while they wait. Want to get a soda at People's? Why the hell should I diet?"

"You're on," I said.

TWELVE

St. Leon Redux

I looked at St. Theresa wistfully. I'd grown accustomed to her face—the sour-ball expression, the eyes cast to the ceiling—and to her borrowed body in girdle and bra.

"I wonder if I should take her?" I said. "The new staff is never going to keep her up there. A bunch of nerds. Not like us."

We were saying farewell to the *Messenger* room. We had packed boxes of our old stories, our memos, our blasphemous sayings about the saints, and were moving out. The new staff had been selected, and the last issue of the *Messenger* would be in their hands, not ours. I picked up a copy of the lead editorial for the next issue. It was about how Catholic girls should be more devoted to Mary and pray for the conversion of Russia.

"Look at this garbage," I said. "Tripe!"

The glory days were over; gone, like snow upon the desert's dusty face, as Omar put it. The new editors were docile, well behaved, nice. The nuns were certainly breathing a sigh of relief to see us go; we fought about everything—the rotten food in the lunchroom, the rotten books in the library, the speakers at assemblies, the ban on sleeveless dresses. Maybe part of it was just your standard adolescent rebellion, but I learned a valuable lesson from being part of the *Messenger*—that people in power, no matter how well intentioned, no matter how much they believed themselves to be the guardians of your best interests, could do arbitrary, unjust, and simply stupid things. "Who shall guard the guardians?" asked the Roman poet Juvenal, and Con and Mollie and I answered, with an arrogance uncharacteristic of nice Catholic young ladies, "We will!"

I took the Little Flower down from the wall. I simply couldn't bear to think of her crumpled up and unceremoniously dumped in a trash can; she'd been the witness to the plots, the plans, the tragedies, and the triumphs. She'd been there in the days that would pass into legend, witnessed the greatness, the glory of the Greatest *Messenger* Staff in History. The Little Flower, bra and all, was truly our patron saint.

"I'll take her and put her in my room in college," I said to Con. "Unless you want her. 'Course, if we get to room together, we could share her."

Con looked up at me as if she hadn't heard. Her eyes still looked a little bleary; she hadn't gotten back from Annapolis until after 2:00 A.M. Lee, it turned out, had been on a training cruise for two weeks, and that's why he hadn't called her. He had written her a letter, but the postman delivered it next door by mistake, and the neighbors were away.

As soon as he got back, he ran for a phone, so Con's Annapolis shuttle was back in business. While he was away, Con and I had both gotten our acceptances to Maryland, on the same day.

"*Diamondback*, here we come!" I crowed.

"The greatest!" Con whooped. "The greatest *Diamondback* staff ever. We'll be *immortal!*" But now Con's eyes were glazed.

"Con," I said, "I asked if you wanted the Little Flower."

"What?" she said. "I'm sorry, Peg."

"Never mind, I'll take her. Hey, I wonder how early we

have to let them know at Maryland that we want to room together. We could get assigned to room with some real jerks instead of with each other."

"Well. . . "

"We shouldn't put that off. You know how schools are; they screw things up so easy."

"Peggy," Con said very seriously, "close the door."

I did, and looked at her, curiously. She reached down the front of her uniform dress and pulled out something that was hanging by a gold chain around her neck. I stared at it, flabbergasted. It was a small miniature of the Naval Academy ring, and in the center of it sparkled a lone, gorgeous diamond.

"A miniature," I said. "You have a miniature!"

"Lee gave it to me Saturday," Con said.

"But that means, that means—"

"Yeah. I'm engaged."

I tried to grasp the enormity of it. "You're going to marry him! Lee Masters!"

"Yeah, I guess I am."

"Con," I said, "I can't believe it. You're engaged! And you'll be getting married one of these days."

"June twenty-second," she said.

My jaw dropped. "June twenty-second! But, Con, that's so soon!"

"Yeah, it is. But Lee wants us to get married right after he graduates, so we can go to his first post together."

"His first post? But what about college? What about Maryland?"

"Well, if he gets Patuxent—he's put in for it—then I could still go to Maryland."

"But you—I mean, we can't room together."

"Not unless you're up for another ménage à trois," she said with a grin.

"Yeah," I said, "I guess that would make it a little

tough to study." I sat down, trying to let the whole thing sink in. "You're getting married!"

"In the chapel at the Naval Academy," she said.

"Con, you'll be the first girl in the class to get married. Trish Kennedy's wedding isn't until June thirtieth."

I thought of how, in September, Con used to make fun of the two girls who were getting married in June, who were planning their weddings down to the last detail, and who wore their engagement rings on chains around their necks. The nuns wouldn't allow Immaculate Heart girls to be officially engaged before graduation, or to wear their diamonds. Con declared that being a June bride, walking down the aisle in a long white dress, was disgustingly bourgeois. She was going to be married, she said, in a red, low-cut cocktail dress in an *intime* little ceremony at the St. Regis, and no damn finger sandwiches and little cookies. It was going to be Dom Perignon and pâté, and people were going to drink the champagne out of dancing slippers and get so drunk they'd throw chairs out the windows. Somehow, I couldn't see Lee Masters tossing an armchair out of the seventeenth floor of the St. Regis.

Con slipped the miniature back down inside her dress. "Peg," she said, would you be my maid of honor? I'd really like you to."

"Of course I would, Con. I'd be very happy to. Thank you for asking me."

I stood up and walked to the window. I could see that the new spring grass had by now completely replaced the blackened, burned area of the field we'd set aflame with Mother Marie. Just a few days ago, it seemed, there was no grass there. Things happened so quickly when you were almost grown up. Somehow, I'd always counted on Con being there, at least at Maryland. Her certainty about us, about how good we were, was one of the things that would make my dreams happen. Now, I'd have to do it all alone. I turned around to face her.

"Maybe *you* ought to take the Little Flower, Con."

She shook her head. "Can you see some admiral's face if he got a load of old Theresa with her boobs hanging out? He'd croak."

"You could keep her out of sight."

"No, Lee would think it was vulgar." She was quiet for a minute and then added, "He thinks a lot of things are vulgar."

"Well, I'll keep her safe."

Later that day, I told Sean about Con's engagement and her upcoming marriage.

"Con getting married? Gee!"

"Yeah, I sure didn't expect that."

"But wasn't she already accepted at Maryland?"

"Yeah, she was. We were going to room together."

"I thought so."

"Now I'll be the only kid from Immaculate Heart who's going to Maryland," I said. We were walking home from school, slowly. "I won't know anybody."

"You'll make friends."

"I guess so. But I don't make friends real easy, Sean. I wish. . . "

"What?"

"I guess I wish Con wasn't getting married so soon. I mean, things just seem to be happening so fast."

"I know," he said quietly.

"I wish I could go back and start the year all over again. I remember, freshman year seemed to drag on forever, and this year—it's almost gone."

"Yeah, it is."

I stopped walking, suddenly. "Everybody leaves me," I said. "My father and now Con, and then you—" I felt the tears starting in my eyes.

"Oh Peggy!" Sean said, and he put his arms around me and I just wanted to bawl, right there, like I did when I was a little kid and something hurt. But I didn't. If I was going

209

to be a grown-up, I couldn't go around blubbering every time something hurt. Besides, I hated people who wallowed in self-pity. Things changed, nothing was forever. You had to learn that to grow up. But it sure was hard sometimes.

So I just sniffled a little and said, "Don't mind me. Just a little graduation blues."

"Peggy—" Sean said, and I could see the pain in his green eyes. Another minute and he'd be putting iodine on me.

I tried to smile. "I'm O.K., Sean, really I am. Actually, it'll be a lot of fun meeting new people. I'll have new friends, we'll have lots of good times. I'm really looking forward to it," I said cheerfully. If I kept blathering on, maybe I could actually convince myself.

But I didn't have a lot of time to brood about my problems, because a new one cropped up the next day that put everything else on the back burner. Con walked up to me right before the history final, looking totally drained of color.

"You got your period? You look rotten."

"I should only have my period. I should only have the *stigmata!*"

"Oh my God, Con, you're pregnant!"

"Peggy, I am not pregnant. I have heard of birth control, you know. What do you think I am, Catholic?"

"Then what's up?"

"This," she said, and she handed me a copy of the *Catholic Herald.* There it was, under a big black headline— ST. LEON OF SKORYTT—A MAN FOR OUR TIMES. The blurb that introduced the story gave full credit and thanks to the source of the story—the *Marian Messenger* at Immaculate Heart High School.

"Oh *shit!*"

"What a time for this to happen. A couple of weeks, and they couldn't lay a glove on us."

210

"Hey, Con, maybe our luck will hold. Maybe no one will notice."

"Are you kidding? Everyone reads the *Catholic Herald*—even those guys at Catholic University who specialize in saints. There's obscure saints that even *God* doesn't know about, but those guys do."

Two days went by, then three, then four, and at first we held our breath, and then began to relax a little bit. We were the Greatest *Messenger* Staff in history. Nothing could go wrong for us.

But on a Thursday afternoon, in the middle of the Religion final, the P.A. system squawked on, and Sister Robert Mary's voice coughed out, "Will Miss Peggy Ann Morrison and Miss Constance Marie Wepplener please come to the office *immediately!*" I knew we were in deep shit. When Sister Robert Mary used your middle name, it was nothing but trouble.

I looked at Con and she looked at me. We got up and walked out of the room together.

"This is it," I said. "Curtains."

"I wonder if we'll be expelled?" Con said.

I saw my whole future shattering in front of me. I would be drummed out of high school and probably drummed out of journalism. The *New York Herald Tribune* would never hire anybody who'd invented a saint. I wouldn't get into college, and I'd probably start to drink. I'd age thirty years in five, and I'd end up wandering the streets of Washington with all my belongings in a shopping bag, begging. My former classmates would pass by me on the street and when I asked them for a dime, they'd kick me away:

"Please, just a dime for a glass of muscatel so I can get through the day."

"You're a disgrace to Immaculate Heart. To all the girls Forever Brave and True. To the Blessed Mother. To the *uniform!*"

211

"Please, a piece of gum, an old Tootsie Roll, anything, for old time's sake!"

"And to think, once *you* were the managing editor of the Greatest *Messenger* in History!"

My stomach started to quiver. I felt the tears welling up. I gritted my teeth. *I am not going to cry!* I told myself. They could put me up against the wall and shoot me, but they weren't going to get one lousy tear.

"We'll probably get excommunicated," I said. "They'll tack our names on the doors of churches all over the world. 'Peggy Ann Morrison and Constance Marie Wepplener are cast into the outer darkness.' They'll deny us the sacraments and we won't graduate and people will shun us."

"They can't do that," Con said.

"Why not?"

"Because we are under the *personal* protection of the Little Flower. And the Maidenform Bra Company."

I looked at her. "I Dreamed I Was Excommunicated in My Maidenform Bra?"

"That's the spirit," she said. "We may go down, Peggy, but we go down with class."

I had to grin at that, and the grin was still on my face as we walked into Sister Robert Mary's office. It faded, fast. Waiting for us there were my mother, her face pale and tense, and Sean, and Dr. McCaffrey, and Brother Martin from Sacred Heart, and the principal. (Con's mother had been called, we later learned, but had said she was too ill to come. "Yeah," Con said, "how was I going to introduce her with all the crud on her face? This is my mother, Joe Louis?")

The whole group looked as if they'd all been invited to a wake. My stomach started to quiver again. But I glanced at Con, who had her head up and was looking nonchalant, as if she'd just dropped in for a chat. You had to say one thing for Con. She had *style*.

Sister Robert Mary held up a copy of the *Catholic Herald*

and said, "It has come to my attention that the story reprinted here from the *Messenger* is a fake. A complete fabrication. Is this true?"

"Yes, Sister, it is," I said. Con nodded. I looked over at Sean. I knew why he was here. He'd passed a copy of the *Messenger* story to the editor of the *Sacred Heart Beacon* suggesting that the *Beacon* run it. The editor did.

"So stories that appeared in the *Beacon* and the *Messenger* were untrue," the principal said.

"Yes," Con said.

"Sean isn't to blame for any of this," I said to Brother Martin, a thin, reedy man with bug eyes and a reputation for an ill temper. "He didn't have anything to do with this."

Brother Martin looked at Sean. "Is this true?"

"Yes, Brother. I mean, I didn't make up the story."

"When it came out in the *Messenger*, Sean didn't know it was a fake," I said. I had chosen my words carefully. I was telling the truth. Sean didn't know about St. Leon until three days after it ran.

"Is this right, Sean?" asked his father.

"Yes, sir."

Dr. McCaffrey gave a little sigh of relief, and then he gave me a look that said if he had his way, I'd be an instant martyr. I wondered whether he'd boil me in oil or turn me on the rack until I looked like a licorice stick. Then he turned to Sean and said, "I'm very glad to know you weren't involved in this willful, this *malicious* deception."

Brother Martin said, "Sean, I'm sorry to have included you in this. It seems you were just another victim. Dr. McCaffrey, I'm sorry to have wasted your time."

"Sean's going to be a priest, you know," Dr. McCaffrey said. I saw Sean wince.

"Yes, we're very proud of Sean," Brother Martin said, his bug eyes showing a hint of human kindness.

Sean looked at me and I jerked my head toward the door, trying not to be too conspicuous. *Go. Get the hell out.*

You're in the clear! Getting excommunicated could put a small dent in his plans for the priesthood.

But Sean didn't move, and those cool green eyes were opaque. "Brother," he said, "it's true that I didn't know about it at first, but I knew St. Leon was a fake when I gave the story to the *Beacon*."

Oh Sean, I thought, *that damned conscience*! But I was proud of him, too, even though it was a dumb-ass thing to do. Sean never was one to duck and run.

"Sean!" his father groaned. "You didn't!"

The kindness in Brother Martin's eyes went out like a light. It was replaced, I thought, by simple blood-lust. I hoped the rack was safely put away in mothballs, because I could see Brother Martin smiling as he turned, and turned, and turned—there we'd be, Sean and Con and Mollie and me, hanging by our thumbs in the basement of the Vatican. The pope would walk by and say to Brother Martin, "These the four kids who canonized Leon Trotsky?"

Brother Martin would nod, and smile his cruel, Peter Lorre smile.

"Oh please, Your Holiness, we didn't mean to do any harm!" I'd cry out.

"They're just children, Brother Martin," the pope would say. "Don't you think we should show them mercy?"

Brother Martin would smile, and he'd raise his thumb toward the ceiling, higher, higher—and then he'd turn it over and plunge it toward his toes.

The pope would look, and then he'd shrug and walk away saying, "That's how the cookie crumbles, kids."

Sister Robert Mary sighed. "Just what on earth got into you girls?"

"We just wanted to liven up Saints Corner," I said. "It was pretty boring."

"Boring!" croaked Brother Martin. "Are you saying *saints* are boring?"

214

"*Very* boring," Con said, "after you've heard their stories 5,000 times." Her level gaze met that of Brother Martin, and she didn't flinch.

"So you made up a saint," said Sister Robert Mary.

"Right," I said. "It was just a joke."

Brother Martin practically foamed at the mouth. "A joke! Inventing a saint is a *joke*!" I didn't guess Brother Martin had a real big sense of humor.

"You just made up the story? Out of whole cloth?" The principal asked.

I swallowed hard and said, "Not exactly."

"What do you mean, Peggy?"

"Skorytt is a proper name, scrambled up."

"A name?"

"Yes, Sister."

"What name?" I saw Sean blanch.

"Trotsky."

Dr. McCaffrey's mouth gaped open in astonishment. "Trotsky! St. Leon is Leon *Trotsky*?"

"More or less."

Sister Robert Mary turned away. I had the sudden wild notion that she was hiding a grin, but when she turned back her face was somber.

"The speeches, where—"

"*The Communist Manifesto*," I said.

Dr. McCaffrey glared at his son. "Sean, you knew this?"

"Yes, sir."

"And you weren't horrified?"

"No, sir. I thought it was pretty funny."

"It was parody," said Con. "An ancient art form."

"It was a gag," I said. "But we shouldn't have printed it."

Sister Robert Mary looked at me. "You realize that you violated your trust, Peggy. The readers expect everything that appears in the *Messenger* to be true."

215

"Yes, Sister, I know."

"And you have embarrassed not only our school, but Sacred Heart and the *Catholic Herald* as well."

Con nodded. "We didn't figure it would go this far."

Brother Martin was standing in the corner, his bug eyes bugging even further. He was getting real worked up, I thought. I expected to see his eyes just pop right out of their sockets and go *sprong*! across the room.

"Immediate expulsion!" he thundered. "We must demand immediate expulsion of anyone involved in this!"

I saw Dr. McCaffrey go pale. I had a suspicion he wasn't thinking of Sean, but of how it was going to look for the Catholic Layman of the Year when his son got kicked out of Sacred Heart for making a saint out of Leon Trotsky. My mother looked as if she were about to cry.

"Expulsion!" thundered Brother Martin. Con and Sean and I looked at each other. (Mollie, the lucky dog, was home with the flu. Maybe they'd just excommunicate her by mail.) This was it, the worst thing that could happen. We were all going to get kicked out of school. Our lives were ruined. They might as well just shoot us now and get it over with.

"Perhaps we'd better discuss this," said Sister Robert Mary.

A ray of hope. Maybe they weren't going to pull the switch. *"Jesus Mary and Joseph,"* I prayed.

"I see no other choice," said Brother Martin.

"It is possible," said the principal, "that if we expel these students greater harm might be done."

"I don't understand," said the brother.

"As it stands, the *Catholic Herald* is simply going to run a correction saying that the St. Leon story was a very tasteless joke thought up by some high school students. But if we expel these students, the entire story would come out. Wouldn't the *Washington Post* just love a story about a group of high school students who sainted Leon Trotsky?

Catholic students. Think what a scandal that would cause, Brother."

"Yes, I hadn't thought of that, Sister."

"It could be most embarrassing, not only to our schools, but also to the whole archdiocese."

"Yes, that's true. But they cannot go unpunished."

Now, I thought, he's going to bring out the rack.

But Sister Robert Mary said, "Brother, these students are all graduating with honors. Peggy Morrison was going to deliver the second valedictory. I believe Sean McCaffrey was to write the student invocation. I suggest we strip them of all graduation honors and simply let them graduate, unheralded, with the rest of the class."

I breathed a long, slow sigh of relief and looked at Sister Robert Mary with gratitude. This was a classy lady. Of course, it meant that I wouldn't get to deliver my fiery tirade on abuses of censorship, and Angela Pignatelli would give some wimpy talk about the Blessed Mother, but at least I wouldn't have to be a bag lady.

"I hope," she said, looking at us sternly, "that you have all learned a good lesson from this incident."

We all nodded, somberly. I wondered if it would be in bad form to grovel in front of her and kiss the hem of her habit. My mother still looked as if she were going to cry— from relief. Brother Martin looked like a barracuda whose prey had just escaped. I wondered what they'd do if they knew that it was us who kidnapped Christ and nearly burned the school down. One thing was for sure. I wasn't going to tell them.

Dr. McCaffrey gave me a withering stare and then he looked at Sean. "I'll see *you* at home, young man," he said.

Sean and Con and I walked out of the office, weak in the knees, but glad we had got out with our skins.

"I'm sorry, Sean," I said. I knew he had been working for weeks on the invocation.

"That's O.K.," he said.

Con flung her arms towards the sky. I'll wear Maiden-form bras for the rest of my *life!*" she cried.

"She almost got thrown of school and she's thinking about underwear?" Sean said.

"You know Con, she's such a fashion plate," I said.

"I will never understand women," he said.

I was sure Sean was going to get absolutely murdered by his father, but he only got grounded for three days. Dr. McCaffrey was so relieved that Sean hadn't been kicked out of school that he tempered his justice with mercy. He didn't even say Sean couldn't go to the big graduation party, which the seniors at Sacred Heart and Immaculate Heart were giving. Every year, the two senior classes rented a cabin in Sligo Creek Park and had a big blowout, complete with hot dogs, a graduation cake, and beer. It was a tradition that everybody came in costume, so I decided to be a jungle explorer and wore a khaki shirt, khaki bermudas, and Sean's father's pith helmet. Sean didn't tell me what he was going as, so when I arrived at the back door of his house I was ready to be surprised. He came down the stairs wearing a long white shirt over jeans, a hatchet at his belt, a red bandanna around his forehead, and a very peculiar contraption suspended over his head made of a coat hanger covered with gold foil. I knew what it was supposed to be right away—a halo.

Just then Dr. McCaffrey came into the room, threw me a perfunctory grunt, and looked at Sean.

"What on earth are you supposed to be?" he asked.

"Johnny Appleseed," Sean said.

"Johnny Appleseed?"

"Yeah, see my hatchet? It's for chopping away the brush so I can plant seeds."

"But what's that thing on your head?"

"Oh, I'm a very modern Johnny Appleseed. It's a radio transmitter. I'm in constant radio contact with the department of agriculture, so they can tell me where to plant the trees."

"Oh," said Dr. McCaffrey. "That's nice. Very wholesome. That's a good idea, Sean."

"Thanks, Pop."

"You're rotten," I told him as we walked out the door. "But sometimes, Sean, I think you're father isn't too swift."

"Well, I couldn't tell him I was going as St. Leon Trotsky, could I?"

The party was in full swing when we got to the cabin in the park. There was a fire roaring in the big stone fireplace, and kids were roasting hot dogs and guzzling beer and talking about their plans for next year. The beer was really flowing—a lot of the seniors had reached eighteen and could drink legally, and the rest of us just did what we always did, drank it anyhow. Con was there—without a date, of course—in a black dress and heels and lots of mascara. "Mata Hari," she explained. Mollie was Pocahontas, with a feather in her hair, and Davy was James Dean in *Rebel Without a Cause*, wearing black pants and a leather jacket—which he wore a lot anyhow. I hadn't seen much of Davy lately. Mollie said he was in a rotten mood, because of graduation.

"Hey Davy," I said. "Do they have it worked out? Are you graduating?"

"Yeah, they're changing a couple of *F*'s to *D*'s to get me out. They sure as hell don't want me back again next year."

"What are you going to do this summer, Davy?" Sean asked.

"Bum around for a while. I don't know yet. Go up to Pittsburgh a little later on, maybe."

Mollie had a math scholarship to Penn, and during the summer she had a job at her uncle's store in Pittsburgh. Davy already looked a little bit lost. I wondered if Mollie didn't mean a lot more to him than he ever let on.

Con came over and dragged me to the fire to roast a hot dog with her, and we ate hot dogs until we were stuffed, and then we had a piece of the special cake that had a big red heart on it and said, "Congrats, Hearters!"

219

The kids started to break up in little groups—the jocks in one corner, the drama kids in another—talking, drinking, and in some cases, necking. We were all feeling nostalgic. We even sang the Immaculate Heart school song, which we all loathed:

> Immaculate Heart
> Immaculate Heart
> Girls forever brave and true
> We'll follow Mary our Mother
> Always loyal to you.

Con and Sean and I settled in one corner of the room, sitting very close together.

"Hey," Sean said, "remember our manage à trois. We never did get to finish it."

"*Ménage*," Con said. "And we didn't finish it because you nearly drowned yourself in the goddamned creek."

"I'll never forget you lying on your bed in my panties and moaning that you were going to die," I said.

"Actually, Sean," Con said, "you look real cute in panties."

"Almost as cute as you look in a bra," I added.

"Too bad Mr. Kasten wasn't there," Sean said. "He would have had an orgasm for sure."

"Ain't that the truth," I said. We were already talking about high school as if it were in the past. As if we were old grads come back for reunion and reminiscing.

"Come on, let's ménage, for old time's sakes," Con said, and she leaned over and kissed Sean. He laughed and kissed her back. The three of us just sat there, kissing, not really with passion, but because it felt so good to be together, feeling the warmth of the fire and the sweetness of nostalgia. While Con and Sean were kissing, I looked up and saw Mollie, sitting and talking with a group of kids, and Davy standing by the fire—looking out of place and alone, like a Martian, I thought.

220

Sean kissed my ear and growled and I giggled and took another swig of beer. Things were getting fuzzy around the edges. I was pleasantly high, but I'd have to watch it, because I usually went right from high to throw up, and I was having too much fun to barf and ruin it all.

I noticed that Con was kissing Sean very enthusiastically and I said, "Hey, you're not supposed to kiss like that; you're practically a married woman!" She giggled and said, "I'm practicing," and went right on kissing Sean.

I took another sip of beer and glanced around again. Davy was standing, now, by the table where the food was spread out. He looked very strange, intent, and there was something about his face that made me go rigid with alarm. I knew something was about to happen. I saw Davy reach out his hand and pick up the knife we used to cut the cake.

He's going to slash his wrists again! I thought. But I was wrong. Davy took the knife, looked at it, and plunged it right into his chest with a swift, decisive motion. Then he got a quizzical look on his face and began to crumple, slowly—it seemed he was falling in slow motion to the ground.

I realized that no one else had seen it but me and I tried to scramble to my feet. Sean grabbed my wrist and pulled me back, saying, "Your turn," and started to kiss me. But I said, "Sean, no, it's Davy!"

He looked up and then he said, "Oh my God!" and we both ran to Davy, who was lying on his back, the knife protruding from his chest, and his blood already soaking the front of his shirt. Some of the kids thought it was a gag, and started to laugh, "Hey, that's a gas!" but Sean yelled, "Somebody go get the rescue squad. Fast!"

One of the seniors who had a car ran out to the parking lot. I grabbed a dish towel from the table and tried to press it against the spot in Davy's chest that the blood was coming from. Mollie was suddenly kneeling beside me, her gray eyes wide with disbelief.

"They've got to hurry," Sean said. "We need help."

Davy's eyes were looking up at us, his gaze moving around. He focused first on Mollie, and then his eyes went to Sean.

"Oh my God—" he said.

"You'll be O.K., Davy," I said. "Help is on the way."

"Oh my God—" he said again.

And then Sean took his hand and said, "Oh my God, I am heartily sorry for having offended thee—"

And Davy nodded.

"I detest all my sins because I dread the loss of heaven and the pains of hell—" Davy's hand tightened on Sean's as Sean said the Act of Contrition. And as I watched him, I thought that if God had really called Sean He had made a good choice, because people in trouble just turned to him instinctively. It was as if they sensed a power there, to help and to heal.

Time seemed to have stopped, everything was frozen. It seemed to me, later, that I knelt there for hours and hours, hearing Sean's steady voice reciting the prayer, and Davy's eyes riveted on Sean's face. But it must have been only a matter of seconds; then there was a strange gurgling sound that came from Davy's chest—later I learned that blood was flooding his lungs, that he was literally drowning in his own blood. Mollie drew in her breath with a ragged, terrible sigh, and Davy's eyes were suddenly blank and staring. His eyes were open but there was nothing—no one—behind them. I knew he was gone.

Sean knew it too. He reached over and closed Davy's eyes and said, "Lord, have mercy on him. Grant him peace, grant him peace, grant him eternal peace."

I was worried afterward that I hadn't done things right, that if I had just been able to press in the right place I could have stopped Davy's bleeding. But one of the doctors in the emergency room told me that nothing would have saved Davy, not even a surgical team standing right beside him. The wound was mortal; this time, he meant it to be.

Sean was shaken to the depths over Davy's suicide. He agonized over it, ran it through his mind over and over again.

"He called me a couple of times to go to the movies, and I said I was busy with finals. I turned away from him, when I could have helped. What kind of a person am I?"

"Sean, Davy didn't kill himself because you didn't go to the movies. It wouldn't have made any difference. How could you know?"

"I could have helped."

"You said it yourself, Sean, there wasn't anyplace where he belonged. He couldn't do anything about it."

"I think I could have helped."

"You helped him, Sean. At the end, you knew what he wanted and nobody else did. He wanted to die, Sean, and you helped him die in peace."

He shook his head. "I *could* have helped him, I know it."

There was no arguing with him. There would never be any lost causes for Sean. He would always believe that if he could just try harder, if he could just *be* better, he could change things. He'd break his heart over battles that couldn't be won, people who couldn't be helped. I'd already started to learn that, sometimes, you had to cut your losses. You had to know when to walk away.

Sean never would. Maybe that was why I loved him.

THIRTEEN

Childhood's End

S ean went into one of his moody spells after Davy died. I
knew enough not to bug him when he got like that. He
was all wrapped up inside his own head, trying to think
things out, sifting. I was used to Sean's moodiness, but this
was a little different. There was something that hadn't been
there before: a sadness in those green eyes that was too old
for a boy of eighteen. No, not a boy, a man. I thought I
knew what I saw in his eyes—the shadow of mortality.
Davy was the first person our age Sean ever knew who'd
died. He'd been holding Davy's hand when the spirit just
slid out of the flesh. In one instant he'd been holding the
hand of his friend, and in the next, he was gripping a
corpse. And if he was going to be a priest, he'd have to
stare into the face of death again and again.

He'd be called in, often, to make the sign of the Cross
in oil on the foreheads of people who were about to shuffle
off the mortal coil. In catechism class, the nuns had always
told us that if you died in the state of grace you'd have a
happy death. I always pictured myself, in bed, smiling a
little wanly, sort of like I had gas, and then drifting off happily to heaven while everybody waved, as if they were
seeing me off for two weeks at Ocean City. But there wasn't
any joy in Davy's eyes that night, only pain and fear. I
wondered if Sean was realizing what being a priest would

really be like. He'd always thought it was going be to so glorious, saving souls for God. "I will make you fishers of men." But what was it he would draw up into his net— people's fears, people's sins, people's dying?

I was waiting for Sean in his living room one Saturday—he was walking in the park—when Dr. McCaffrey came up to me and said, "Peggy, is Sean all right?"

I looked at him. I was surprised that he had noticed, being so busy with tits and rubbers and all.

"Yeah, he's O.K. It's just that Davy was his friend."

"I know. But Sean seems to be so quiet. So down. He . . . you don't think that he . . ."

"Sean? You mean you think that Sean might kill himself?"

"Well, I've just read that sometimes suicides, well, teenagers sometimes—" he let the sentence hang in the air. I stared at him, astonished. He really was worried about Sean. And then I saw him, really *saw* him. You know how it is when you're around somebody a lot, you look at them but you don't really see. I was startled at how old he looked. The wavy gray hair was thinning on top and the lines under his eyes were more deeply etched than I had thought. He didn't look at all like The Nemesis of Smut. He looked like a worried, aging man. He seemed vulnerable.

Life was really weird. For so long, grown-ups were so big, so powerful; and then all of a sudden one day you looked at them and they weren't like grown-ups any more. You saw them plain and clear, and they were just ordinary. And that made you feel sad, somehow.

I said to him, "You know Sean. He's always been moody."

"I know, Peg, but—well, you're sure?"

"I'm sure. He's O.K."

When Sean got back I told him his father was worried about him and he gave a short laugh. It wasn't like his explosion when he thought something was really hilarious, or

225

the gleeful cackle he'd let out when something struck him as absurd. It was a hard, brittle sound. I looked at him sharply.

"Yeah," he said, "he doesn't want the future Father McCaffrey snuffing himself. How do you give a dead person to God? 'Here, Lord, take my son, he's only decomposed a little bit around the edges.'"

"Sean!"

He repented instantly. "I didn't mean that," he said. But I knew he did. Now and then he let a little corner of the bitterness show. I found myself taking Dr. McCaffrey's side, which was strange, considering the way he felt about me.

"He really is worried, Sean."

"No he isn't."

"He is too. Go talk to him. Don't be a jerk, Sean."

We walked into the living room together. Sean's father was standing by the fireplace, the inevitable Scotch in his hand. His face brightened when Sean came in.

"Sean! Oh, Sean. Well, how are you, son?"

"Fine, Pop."

Dr. McCaffrey put down his Scotch and walked over to Sean. He was about to put his arm around Sean's shoulder in his fake hearty way, but thought better of it. He just stood there, awkwardly, looking at Sean expectantly. He was nervous, I realized. Here was a guy who taught Fundamentals of Communication—who drew little boxes showing how people encoded and decoded messages—and he didn't know how to talk to his own son. Maybe because he hadn't really done it in so long.

"I'm sorry about Davy," Dr. McCaffrey said.

"Yeah," Sean said. Sean could be real stubborn, sometimes, and proud. He wasn't going to give his father the benefit of the doubt.

"How could a boy that young, with everything to live for, do that?" Dr. McCaffrey asked. He seemed genuinely mystified.

"He was unhappy," Sean answered.

"But he had everything ahead of him."

"No he didn't," Sean said, quietly. "Davy didn't have anything ahead of him."

"Do you really think that's true?"

"For Davy it was true."

I thought I saw Dr. McCaffrey shiver just a bit, as if somebody had walked across his grave. He said, "Not like you, Sean. You have so much ahead of you. Why, there's the seminary, and ordination. . ."

Sean frowned. Dr. McCaffrey, with his unerring talent for saying the wrong thing at the wrong time, had done it again. I looked at Sean. His green eyes were like shuttered gates; no way was he going to let his father in. And Dr. McCaffrey was stumbling around, trying to reach out, and doing it all wrong. I wanted to yell at him, "Tell him you care about him, not the guy in the black suit. *Tell* him!"

"And we'll be so proud of you, your mother and I, we're always talking about what it'll be like, your ordination—"

I saw Sean's spine stiffen. His eyes now were tight little chips of green ice. Dr. McCaffrey could feel the freeze as well as I could. For the first time I could remember, he was at a loss for words. But he was trying. At least he was trying. Maybe Davy's suicide had done it; maybe that made Dr. McCaffrey understand how lucky he was to have a son like Sean, a lovely, loving young man. Who was alive, and not lying forever still under the earth.

"Sean—"

Sean walked a few steps away from his father, and turned to the window. His head was up, his shoulders unnaturally erect. After all these years I could read his body like a book. He stood that way when his pride was hurt, like the time I beat him thirteen–zip in a game of horse and he said it didn't bother him but I knew better.

Dr. McCaffrey took a tentative step toward his son. Sean turned around to look at him. I saw Sean waver. One thing about Sean, he didn't stay mad too long, especially where his father was concerned. How he could love the Nemesis of Smut so much I couldn't figure, but he did. "It's going to be O.K.," I thought.

And Dr. McCaffrey, seeing the thaw, rushed in where angels fear to tread.

"Bill and you, you're my boys!" he said.

Sean stepped backward and his eyes iced up again. Always second string.

I thought, at that moment, that I could actually see the crevice split the floor between them, stretching far down into an infinity that was cold and dark, and I sensed the chasm growing wider as they stood and looked at each other, the father on one side of the yawning gap and the son on the other. Dr. McCaffrey might not have been real swift, but he recognized his mistake. It was too late. He tried to step forward again, but something in Sean's eyes stopped him. His shoulders sagged and he retreated.

Usually I just felt like shaking Dr. McCaffrey; right now I wanted to brain both of them. They just stood there, in painful silence, watching each other across the distance that would grow wider and wider over the years. Someday, I thought, they'd have to scream to be heard and finally they wouldn't be able to hear each other at all. But what the one wanted to say and the other wanted to hear was so simple, so absurdly simple: "I love you."

"Well," Dr. McCaffrey said. "Well." His eyes implored Sean's for an instant, but Sean just stood preternaturally still. Dr. McCaffrey turned to walk out of the room and Sean moved forward on the balls of his feet. I thought for an instant he was going to go after his father, but he didn't. He turned and walked out the back door instead, leaving me standing alone in the living room. I just stood there, staring at the furniture.

I had always thought that every part of life was pretty much the same as any other part; that it was a moving band, and while you couldn't live anything over again ("The moving finger writes," Omar said.), you always had time to make things right. But that wasn't true. There were moments in life when doors opened—when you had a chance to say or do something—and if you didn't do it the doors closed and the chance was lost beyond recall. That scared me, because of the way I kept things tucked inside of me, never wanting to show it when I was hurting. And I was stubborn, too, and proud, more than Sean, even. I wondered if, someday, a door would open for me and I'd see it, but somehow I'd mess it up, like Sean and his father just did. I'd hold my tongue and the door would close, and I'd never say it: "I love you."

But I didn't have too long to brood about it, because the next day Con drafted me to go on an important errand. I agreed, but I was a little shocked at the size of the box I had to lug to the car.

"Con, two *gross* of condoms? How the hell will you ever use all these?"

"Go thru 'em in a week," she grinned.

Con had Lee's card to use the commissary at Bethesda Naval Hospital, and she was in charge of getting the rubbers, because everything was a lot cheaper there. The only problem was you had to buy in bulk.

We lugged the carton of condoms to the black Ford. "If I drop these, it's goodbye tootsies," I said. "How do I explain to Dr. Parkinson that I broke my foot when a ton of Trojans fell on them?"

Con and I had driven out to Bethesda in the Ford, laughing, giggling, singing, and feeling newly grown up. We were now bona fide high school graduates. Con was getting married in two days, and going out to get the rubbers (Sister Justinian would have *croaked*) was the most sophisticated thing we'd ever done.

"Just think, Con, two days and it's O.K. to screw."

"Yeah, that'll really be weird. Just for old time's sake, now and then I'll scream, 'I am a child of Mary!'"

"Are you scared, Con? I mean, this is *life!*"

"I know," she said. "And I'd never get divorced—unless he was a real *rat* or something. And then I couldn't get married ever again."

"You could have lovers."

"Yeah, but it's not the same. This is *forever*."

The word was so awesome that we just sat there for a minute, letting it hang in the air between us like a visitation from the Holy Spirit.

"You'll write me. Promise."

Lee hadn't gotten Patuxent; he had been assigned to Great Lakes Naval Training Station, and Con and Lee were off to Michigan right after the wedding. Con had her traveling outfit all picked out—a blue suit with a red blouse, and a little blue pillbox hat with a veil to match.

"I'll write, Peggy, I promise. Hey Peg, you'll never guess who's getting married right before me and Lee."

"Who?"

"Dolly."

"You're kidding! (Dolly's image was stamped forever on my mind the way I had first seen her, bra on and pubic hair hanging out.) Is she marrying the guy she was with that night, what's his name?"

"No, another one."

"Another one? Con, she must have screwed half the fleet."

"Just about. But you should see her carrying on now. She's doing the whole demure virgin bit."

"Dolly?"

"Yeah. She even said to me with a straight face that she was going to give her unsullied body to her husband on her wedding night."

"Con, bodies don't *come* any more sullied than Dolly's."

230

"She blanked it all out. I think she's convinced herself she's actually the Virgin Mary."

I had this sudden image of Dolly, clad in a blue mantle and a bra, her pubic hair flashing, appearing to a couple of Portuguese children and saying, "Russia must be converted." They sure wouldn't put that on a Holy Card.

I had gone shopping with Con to pick out the dress I would wear as Con's maid of honor. We picked a blue one, since Con said that was my color, and she wanted one that wasn't too "bridey." We found a dress in Promtime, and it had a neckline that would never have gotten the approval of Father Clement Kliblicki, and a full skirt. We bought a cartwheel hat to match the dress, and I had shoes dyed to match. The morning of the wedding I got up and put on my makeup, then I slipped into my dress and put on the hat, and I looked into the mirror. I was astonished to find a lovely young woman staring back at me. Could that be me? That—woman? What had happened to the kid who always used to be there?

My mother came in and smiled at me.

"Peg," she said. "You're grown up. How did it happen so fast?"

"I don't know," I said.

She looked at me, quietly, and then a frown crossed her face. I noticed that there were shadows around her eyes that hadn't been there before.

"Peg, whatever you do, finish your education. Learn to do something. Don't ever—don't ever let life hit you like a truck."

I nodded. It wasn't until years later, of course, that I realized what she had done. She moved in to take over Dad's business; she paid the bills; she kept the house repaired; kept our lives rolling on pretty much as they had before—like a bus that had stopped, but had then resumed its appointed course. She never let me know that we had been at the edge of an abyss, that she had thrown a safety net across it and we hadn't fallen in.

"If your father hadn't had the business," she said, "if he'd just been working for a salary someplace—I don't know what I would have done." She shook her head. "And I never thought about it. I never worried. Learn to take care of yourself, Peg."

"I will, Mom."

"I'm very proud of you, Peg," she said. "I hope you know that."

Sean came to pick me up and he took both my hands in his and he looked me up and down. "Peggy," he said, "you're beautiful!" You look so beautiful!" He looked pretty good himself, I thought, all dressed up in a blue suit and tie, and when we walked out the door together, I imagined it wasn't just my old house, but the St. Regis, and people on the sidewalk were stopping to stare at us, we were such a glamorous couple.

"That's Peg Morrison, the Pulitzer Prize winner," they'd say.

"Who's that with her?"

"That's her lover, Sean McCaffrey, the Hero-Priest of the Amazon."

"They let priests *do* that?"

"Not usually, but he saved so many souls that they gave him celibacy leave."

We drove down to Annapolis in the Caddy, and Sean went to take a seat in the chapel and I went back to the dressing room to help Con get ready. I promised her I'd do it; she said no way was she going to let her mother back there. I said that was kind of mean, but she stuck to her guns. She was alone, sitting at a vanity, when I came in. She was wearing a long-line bra and a girdle, and her stockings and shoes. She gave a low wolf whistle when I came in and said, "Oh Peg, you look fan*tas*tic! Hey, this bra pulls in my waist, but it pushes everything out down below. Do my hips look eight miles wide?" She took a bite of a half-eaten Mars bar that was lying on the vanity. "I just had to have something in my stomach so I wouldn't throw up."

"You've got a full skirt, so nobody's even going to notice your hips."

"*I* know they're there. They keep sending me little messages: 'Hello, it's your hips. One more bite of that candy bar and we're going to bust this girdle wide open.' " She peered into the mirror. "Oh shit, I got a zit. My wedding day and God sends me a zit."

"It's hardly noticeable. Besides, I don't think God sent it."

"Yes He did. Probably because we kidnapped Him and rolled Him up like a rug. 'Take that, Constance Marie Wepplener. Shazam, a zit!' "

"Well, it's no problem."

"So you say. If Lee sees it, he'll stop the ceremony and he'll say, 'Everyone go home. I'm not marrying anyone with a zit!' And then I'll have to become a fucking nun. Come on help me into the damn dress."

I went to get the dress out of the plastic bag, but Con said, "Wait, I have something for you," and she fished around in her pocketbook a minute, and pulled out a large black notebook and handed it to me.

"Your journal. Con, it's your journal!"

"Yeah," she said. "It is."

"But don't you want it?"

"I want you to have it, Peggy. It's yours. You keep it."

"But Con—"

"You keep it, Peggy. You're the one—I just want you to have it."

"We were the greatest, Con. There'll never be another bunch like us."

"There never will be," she said. "We're immortal! And maybe someday you can use it. To write something about us. So people will remember."

"I will," I said. "I promise."

We just stood and looked at each other, and then Con said, "Omigod, the dress!"

I helped Con slip it on over her head, and I zipped it up. Then I helped her put on her veil, adjusting it so that it sat the right way on her head, not tilted or anything.

"How do I look?" she asked.

"You look beautiful, Con."

And she did look beautiful, swathed in yards and yards of white lace, her curls held stiff in place by frozen droplets of hair spray. But as I looked at her, she seemed—smaller, diminished somehow by the dress. It was as if all her fire had been dampened by the lace, simply extinguished by acres of frilly bridal fabric, as if it were some kind of chemical foam. The whole outfit, it seemed to me, conspired to restrain her—the dress, the girdle, the veil, even the hairspray; it was all holding her in *place*—woman's place, I thought suddenly. She didn't look like a comet that would blaze across the sky. She looked like every ordinary girl whose picture appeared in the bridal section of the Washington *Post*.

Con, *my* Con, who taught me about being beautiful and damned and burning the candle at both ends and tasting the well of life, was going to be a Navy wife. She was going to pour tea for admirals' ladies and play bridge on long, dull afternoons and traipse around the country, from one Navy base to another, for the rest of her life.

Suddenly I felt betrayed, deserted, and I had to look away. She must have known what I was thinking because she said, "I can go to college, Peg, wherever Lee is stationed. I'll take courses. Why, all the traveling I'll do, the experiences I'll have—it'll be perfect for a writer."

But her eyes were uncertain, hesitant. The old sureness was gone. And for the first time, instead of me wanting her approval, she wanted mine; wanted it desperately.

"You bet your ass you'll be a writer," I said. "The best."

She nodded, grimly. "I love him, Peg. I really do."

"I know."

"He loves me. I didn't. . ." She paused. "I didn't think anybody ever really would."

I had to turn away again, because I suddenly felt as though I was going to cry. Was this the price you had to pay for someone to love you? To give up your dreams? I didn't want the new *loved* Con. I wanted the old unloved one, who could swear like a trooper and blaspheme the biggest saint in heaven and who could make me feel special. I wondered if I would ever find her again.

Then Con's father came in to take her arm, and the organ began to play. I walked out in front of Con, moving slowly down the aisle. I saw Con's mother seated in a pew, the last faint tinges of a bruise hardly visible on her cheek beneath the heavy powder. But what really struck me were the rows and rows of white uniforms, waves of them. It made me realize that this was Lee's world she was entering, a sea of maleness. I wondered if Con would simply disappear into it, like Jonah being swallowed up by the whale.

I snuck a glance back at Con as I turned the corner in front of the altar, and she had a tight, scared smile on her face. I wondered if she was thinking the same thing I was, if she had an idea for the first time of what she was up against. Rebelling against the system at Immaculate Heart wasn't so very hard, after all. You could burn pictures of Mother Marie Claire and swipe Christ and get a boy into the Big Sex Talk, but how did you fight the U.S. Navy? Especially when the next promotion depended on your being nice to the captain's wife? Navy wives were supposed to be like nice Catholic girls—polite, docile, better seen than heard. Suddenly, I felt the entire weight of the chain of command—hundreds and hundreds of those white uniforms. They seemed to reach up to the stars, pressing down on Con. And she seemed so frail, standing there by the altar in her white dress. She had never seemed that way before.

Oh Con, don't let them do it to you, I thought. *Fight them! Fight them!*

The old Con could have done it, could have beaten them all. But the new Con, standing quietly beside Lee, looking up at his handsome, bland, unremarkable face—about her I wasn't sure.

The ceremony was lovely, and when it ended, Lee took Con's arm, guided her firmly under the arch of swords, and people threw rice. I didn't get to see much of her at the reception—finger sandwiches, little cookies and domestic champagne—before she disappeared to get into her going-away outfit, and then she and Lee waved to everybody, and suddenly she was gone.

I was quiet on the long drive home, lost in my thoughts, and Sean was too. I looked over at him, thinking how much I loved his face in profile, its finely chiseled features, the eyelashes that were almost like a girl's. He was leaving on the 8:45 train tomorrow morning. The future wasn't the future anymore. It was now. The horses had run their course.

"Well," Sean said. "She's married. Con's married."

"Yeah, she is."

"It was a nice wedding."

"If you like weddings."

"Don't you like them? Weddings?"

"I'm not getting married. I'll be too busy covering wars."

"Oh."

I don't want to marry anyone but you, I thought, *and you're going to be a stinking priest*. But I said, "You all packed?"

"Yeah."

"Train leaves early."

"Yeah, it does."

We rode in silence for a while. I thought about Con, in her white dress, about how much I owed her, and I thought about me. I wasn't going to be a nice, polite little Catholic girl, ever again.

"Sean," I said, "tonight we're Doing It."

"We are?"

"Yes."

"Well—"

"What's the matter, you think it's a sin?"

"No," he said. "Not with us."

"Then what's the matter?"

"Well, it's just—"

"I knew it. You're chickening out."

"No I'm not."

"Just like you always used to do. You said you'd sneak into the movies with me and you never did. We were going to run away to Florida, remember, and I even packed my suitcase and you chickened out."

"You had twelve Tootsie Rolls and your bathing suit. And you were eight years old. How far did you think you'd get?"

"It's the principle of the thing. You always chicken out. Chicken! Chicken! Chicken!"

"Peggy—"

"You don't want my body, fine. I'll go sell it on the street. 'Step right up folks, one gen-yoo-ine Catholic virgin—don't let the brown oxfords turn you off, she'll untie 'em—'"

"Peggy, stop that!"

"Why should I?"

"Jeez, you are in some mood today."

"Why shouldn't I be? My best friend is going off to fucking Michigan and my other best friend just rejected me. If the End of the World was tonight, that would be the *good* part of my day."

"I'm not rejecting you."

"It certainly sounds like it."

"It's just that, Peggy, I've never really done it before and I don't know if I'll get it right."

"That didn't seem to bother you the night you practically raped me in the back seat."

"I did not practically rape you. Besides, you didn't seem to object too much."

"Oh, right, I'm just a slut. You're like every other guy, you want a girl to make out with you, and when she does, you think she's some kind of a tramp. Jesus, Sean!"

"Peggy, I never thought that! I swear to God I never did!"

"Let's just drop the whole subject, O.K.?"

"You *know* I never thought that. You're just trying to pick a fight with me, just like you always used to do. You always did, you know."

"Sean," I said with great, offended dignity, "I do not wish to discuss it."

We drove in silence, Sean scowling and me trying to get the look on my face of a haughty queen far above the common herd. When we reached the entrance of the street where we lived, I said to Sean, "Just drop me at my house, please." But he pulled the Caddy up in front of his house instead.

"Very well, I'll walk. I *know* the way."

"Peggy—"

"Goodnight, Sean." I tried to get out of the car but he grabbed me and pulled me to him and started kissing me. I pretended to be mad about it, but I couldn't pretend for very long. Then he took my hand and guided me out of the car.

"Where are we going?"

"My bedroom."

"Where's your parents?"

"Out with the archbishop. They said they'd be home late."

I walked with him into his bedroom, and I looked around; it was all so familiar. I wondered how many hours I'd spent playing in this room when we were kids. We used to line our fuzzy animals up against the bed and have make-believe banquets, with plates and silverware and pea-

238

nut butter. Two of those old animals were still sitting on Sean's bookshelf: Fuzzy and Teddy, their button eyes still bright and their red lips smiling. Were we going to Do It in front of Fuzzy and Teddy? I wondered what they'd think.

"Look, Fuzzy, it's our old friends! Hi there, little Sean! Hi there, little Peggy. Oh, Fuzzy, isn't it good to see them?"

"Sure is, Teddy."

"Want to play banquet, Sean, Peggy? We'll have lots of peanut butter. Sean? Peggy? What are you doing? What are you doing? Oh My God, Fuzzy, they're screwing! Little Sean and little Peggy are screwing! Oh, I can't watch!"

"I can, Teddy. Our own porno flick. It's a lot neater than those stupid banquets."

"Fuzzy, I always suspected you had a filthy mind."

We got undressed and climbed into bed, and it was wonderful to be naked in a real bed with Sean. If we were married, I thought, we could do this every day, sleep together in a bed with no one to tell us what we shouldn't do. I loved the feel of him against me under the crispness of the sheets, loved the way he tasted, the way he smelled, the way he looked. We just kissed for a long, long time, and then we kissed and touched and then we just touched and I lost count of how many times I'd been on the roller coaster. And Sean was moaning a lot—he was a big moaner, Sean was.

Finally he said, "Peggy, I want to do it now," and I said yes and he reached up on the window sill and got the condom. (He'd had it for two weeks, he admitted later, in case he turned into a raging animal.) He slid it on and the next thing I knew, zip, he was inside me, no pain, no mess. People said some girls stretched their hymens playing sports. Did that mean I'd lost my virginity to a jump shot? What a downer that would be.

"Oh My!" Sean said. "Oh. Oh. OH!"

It felt really nice with him inside me; I felt I'd just like to stay that way for a couple of weeks— of course, it might

239

be hard to do a lot of things that way, like go to the movies or pee. I could feel Sean's weight on me, the sweet burden of his body, and then he started to move, slowly at first and then faster and then he said, "Peggy, I can't—I can't—I have to—Oh! Oh! Ohhhhhhhhhh!"

And his whole body shook and then he collapsed on top of me, still breathing very hard. I reached up and wiped a bead of sweat from his forehead, thinking this is how a woman feels with the man she loves: pleased and proud.

"Peggy," he said, "you didn't, you didn't—"

"Oh Sean, it was really nice, it really was!"

"Nice!" he wailed. "I wanted it to be wonderful!"

"Was it wonderful for you, Sean?"

"Oh yes. Oh yes, it was!"

I twirled a lock of his hair around my finger. "I'm glad."

"But you didn't, you didn't—"

"Yes I did, lots of times."

"But that was before. I was too fast. I knew I'd mess it up."

"You didn't, Sean, honest you didn't!"

"I did. Oh Peggy, I'm sorry!"

"Sean, I really loved it, really I did!"

"Yeah, but—"

And all of a sudden there was a sound. A door opening. "Sean? Are you in there?"

And there was a click and the room was suddenly flooded with light, as if it were God, looking on the void and proclaiming, "Let there be light!" Unfortunately, it was not God. It was Dr. Liam McCaffrey. There, in the doorway, stood the Nemesis of Smut, in the flesh. He was staring at us, and the look on his face was familiar. I recognized it from the pup tent.

Oh no, I thought, *not again!*

"Oh My GOD!" he said.

Same old dialogue.

240

When the light flicked on it hit Sean like a bolt of light-ening and he leapt upright with a yelp, turning to face his father. It was an instant replay of thirteen years ago; there he was again, without his pants on.

"*What* is going on here!" Dr. McCaffrey demanded.

I made a grab for the covers and pulled them up so high they covered my nose. Sean stood there, staring at his father, open-mouthed. His father's gaze traveled down to Sean's crotch; the rubber dangled there, forlornly, the little nest of white liquid settled in the tip.

"Oh Sean," his father groaned, looking at the condom as if he were staring at the face of Lucifer himself. "Sean, a–a—*rubber!*"

Sean grabbed a pillow with one hand and put it in front of his crotch. "Hi, Pop!" he said.

It was a gallant effort at nonchalance, but that is hard to achieve when you are standing there naked with a rub-ber dangling from your prick and a pillow in front of your crotch. That took a little more savoir faire than Sean was able to drum up at the moment.

Dr. McCaffrey looked at me the way Jehovah looked at Cain. "That girl. What has she done to you? That harlot!"

"Pop, don't say that!"

"Mary *Magdalen*. Harlot."

"Pop, don't talk like that to Peggy," Sean said, an edge to his voice.

"A bad seed. I knew it that day when she ravished you in the tent. Bad seed. Whore of Babylon!"

"I didn't ravish him," I said. "You can't ravish someone when you're five."

"Harlot!" he shrieked. "Whore of Babylon!"

"Pop! Stop it!" Sean said.

But Dr. McCaffrey was warming to his topic. He was working up to the same pitch of frenzy he reached half an hour after the rubber chicken in some Knights of Columbus hall when he was decrying dirty movies. "Whore! A clean Catholic boy and you despoil him! Whore of Babylon!"

"Pop," Sean said, "Get out of my room."

"Don't you talk like that to me, young man!"

"Shut up and get out of my room!" Sean said. I'd never heard him talk like that to his father before. Dr. McCaffrey blinked.

"Sean—"

"Get out of my room. Now!"

"Sean, don't you threaten me!"

"Get out of here, Pop, or I swear—" Sean took a step toward his father. Dr. McCaffrey beat a hasty retreat back to the hall. "Sean, you have to get up so *early*," he said plaintively. Sean closed the door in his face.

Sean and I got dressed, quickly, and I wondered if some evil witch had been hovering over my cradle at birth. Some girls got fairy godmothers; I got a semicrazed professional Catholic layman. Anytime I ever tried to make love to someone, he'd suddenly appear. There we'd be, my lover and I smooching away, and we'd see a puff of smoke and there would be Dr. McCaffrey, screaming, "Whore of Babylon!"

"Who the hell is that?" my lover would ask.

"Oh don't mind him."

"*Harlot!*"

"Who is he, anyhow?"

"My next door neighbor, the Nemesis of Smut."

"Mary *Magdalen!*"

"Does he always do this?"

"Yeah, usually. Just ignore him. Kiss me!"

"*Bad seed! Whore!*"

"Uh, Peg—"

"Yes?"

"I think I have to go now."

"But we haven't even done anything!"

"*Whore of Babylon!*"

"Listen, Peg, it's been swell, but don't call me; I'll call you."

I struggled back into my taffeta dress and Sean zipped me up, and then he picked the car keys off the dresser and we went out the back door. We drove down to the park and Sean pulled me close and stroked my hair.

"Oh Peggy, I'm so sorry. I wanted it to be wonderful for you! I wanted it to be something you'd remember!"

"Sean, I said, "I think I'll remember it."

"Don't pay any attention to my father. He didn't mean all those things he said."

"Yeah, he did. It's O.K. But one thing."

"What?"

"Who is the whore of Babylon?"

"Beats me. Maybe it's Jane Russell."

And then I started to crack up, and he did too, and we laughed and laughed, nearly until we cried, and then we just sat together quietly, not saying anything. Time passed, and we sat there, listening to our heartbeats, just clinging together like two shipwrecked sailors holding onto a spar. Sean touched my hair, and my face, as if he was trying to commit them to memory, so he would never forget them.

"I love you, Peggy," he said. "I love you so much."

"I love you, Sean."

He was quiet for a moment. Then he said, "Oh, I do love you. And I love God too. I thought—I thought I had things figured out. Oh Peggy, I don't know what to *do!*"

"I know," I said.

"How can I leave you? How could I be a priest, and never, never—" He let the words hang in the air. "Oh shit!" he said.

We sat there, holding each other, and I wanted to say to him, "Sean, you forget about the priesthood and I'll forget about the Pulitzer Prize and we'll just run off together and love each other because I love you with all my heart, all of me, and all we'll ever need is each other. Don't go, Sean. Don't go."

But I didn't say it.

For all the power of the force drawing us together, there was another pulling us apart. Like a pair of migratory birds, we were feeling within our breasts a signal, an urging, telling us that there were places we must go, things we must do, and we had to answer that call, not knowing where it would take us, or why. Sean had to find out for himself if it really was God calling him, flowing through his bones that golden morning; or if it was another voice, or simply the echo of a body exulting in being alive and young on a morning in spring. And I had to find out what I could do, what I could be.

But I wondered, as I sat there holding him, why Sean couldn't have God *and* me. Why did he have to choose? If giving up the kind of love we had made priests special to God, it took them away, far away, from the rest of us, who weren't special at all. But maybe one day, I thought, Sean would find out that God didn't want him. No, that was wrong. Maybe he'd find out that *he* didn't want God—not in that special, splendid, isolated way. And maybe then, he would find his way back to me. I had the feeling I'd be there. Not in Crystal Springs. But someplace.

I kissed him goodbye on the train platform in Crystal Springs the next morning. Dr. McCaffrrey and his wife stood at the far end of the platform, pretending I didn't exist. Who wants to say good morning to the Whore of Babylon?

"They let me write once a week," he said. "I'll write every single week, I promise."

"I'll write too. And listen, if the food is rotten and they show dumb movies, will you come home?"

"If you need me, Peg. I'll come. If you ever need me, I'll come. Even if I'm a million miles away."

"I know."

"I love you."

"I love you, Sean. I always will."

"Oh Peggy—" he said, and he couldn't say anymore. There was a mist over his cool green eyes. He picked up his bag, and he got on board the train, and when he found his seat he leaned out the window to wave to me. He kept waving as the train pulled away. I watched the train as it moved out of the station, slowly at first, and then faster, then getting smaller and smaller as it moved off into the distance, carrying Sean McCaffrey off to God.

I didn't cry. I had discovered that some things just hurt too deeply for tears. I walked home slowly from the train station; it was a good three miles, but I wanted time to think, to put the pieces of my life together. I walked, not really seeing the landscape, and suddenly I realized I was in front of Immaculate Heart High School. But a very strange thing had happened to it. It had grown very small. Four years ago, when I walked into that building as a freshman, it seemed so huge it nearly blotted out the sun. Had it shrunk? Or had I grown taller?

I didn't know it then, but in saying goodbye to Immaculate Heart, I was saying goodbye to a world that in a few short years would simply cease to exist. I would not have believed it then, because that world seemed timeless, stretched out beneath the sun as eternally as the Eternal City itself. But the Church we knew—Sean and Con and Mollie and I—was the last gasp of another age, the remnants of an immigrant religion of mysteries and miracles, saints and visions. It would be swept away by winds that had already begun to stir.

The building was deserted now, and the senior class had scattered. Mollie had left for Pittsburgh two days ago, and right now Con would probably be unpacking her things in a little apartment at the Great Lakes Naval Training Station. And we'd never have a garret to bring our lovers to. Oh Con, don't lose your dreams. Burn the candle at both ends. Be *immortal*, Con.

I thought of Davy, who had never lived to grow up at all. I guessed he had never wanted to; he was quiet, now, in the earth. The pain of living was already too much for him at seventeen. And, of course, I thought of Sean.

I pictured him in the little room I'd seen in a photograph of the seminary, a small, bare room with a crucifix on the wall. I saw him there, trying to be *good*, trying to forge the iron of his soul in the fires of the priesthood. Would he find peace and joy there? Sean, be happy. Whatever you do, wherever you go, be happy. Be happy, my love.

I walked on, and Immaculate Heart vanished in the distance behind me. I was going off to a world that was bigger and colder; one that didn't care at all about St. Theresa, the Little Flower, or the miracle of Fatima, or Mother Marie Claire, or Saints Corner, or Marylike dresses. I wondered if I could survive out there. Dear God, did I have the brains, the strength, the will to make it out there? Was I good enough? Was I?

There was nothing to do but find out.